JOHN SCHREINER'S

OKANAGAN

WINE TOUR GUIDE

JOHN SCHREINER'S

OKANAGAN

WINE TOUR GUIDE

THE WINERIES OF BRITISH COLUMBIA'S INTERIOR

—————————— 5TH EDITION ——————————

whitecap

Copyright © 2006, 2007, 2010, 2012
    and 2014 by John Schreiner
Whitecap Books

First edition published 2006
Second edition 2007
Third edition 2010
Fourth edition 2012
Fifth edition 2014

EDITED BY Jesse Marchand and Patrick
    Geraghty
DESIGNED BY Stacey Noyes / LuzForm
    Designs
TYPESET BY Andrew Bagatella
PROOFREAD BY Kaitlyn Till
MAP BY Eric Leinberger
PHOTOGRAPHY BY John Schreiner unless
    otherwise noted

Printed in Canada

LIBRARY AND ARCHIVES CANADA CATALOGUING IN PUBLICATION

Schreiner, John, 1936–, author
    John Schreiner's Okanagan wine tour
guide: the wineries of British Columbia's
interior. -- Fifth edition.

ISBN 978-1-77050-230-7 (bound)

    1. Wineries--British Columbia--
Okanagan Valley (Region)--Guidebooks.
2. Wine and wine making--British
Columbia--Okanagan Valley (Region). 3.
Vintners--British Columbia--Okanagan
Valley (Region). 4. Okanagan Valley (B.C.
: Region)--Tours. I. Title.

TP559.C3S35 2014   663'.20097115
    C2013-908279-4

The publisher acknowledges the financial
support of the Canada Council for the
Arts and the Government of Canada
through the Canada Book Fund (CBF).
Whitecap Books also acknowledges
the financial support of the Province
of British Columbia through the Book
Publishing Tax Credit.

Canada Council   Conseil des Arts
for the Arts   du Canada

BRITISH COLUMBIA
ARTS COUNCIL
Supported by the Province of British Columbia

14 15 16 17 18   5 4 3 2 1

To Marlene. Without her support,
I could not have written this and
14 other books.

CONTENTS

WHY I WROTE THIS BOOK

WHY DID I WRITE THIS BOOK? The answer is easy: I enjoy being around wine people, who are among the most colourful and creative people I know. I like what they produce, and derive added pleasure from the wines because I have come to know many producers intimately. I tell their stories in this book in the conviction that you will also get more from the wines if you know the backstories.

I began touring British Columbia's wine country about 40 years ago when only a half-dozen wineries were open. The quality of the wines then bore no resemblance to the impressive wines available today. But the optimism and the determination of that early generation of wine growers was enough to bring me back every year. There has been such an acceleration of new wineries that this book has 196 wineries and vineyards profiled, many which are less than 10 years old. Every year there are new wineries to visit and, or so it seems to me, there is always better wine to taste at the old favourites.

One anecdote illustrates how dramatically the wines have improved. Bradley Cooper, now the winemaker at Township 7 and at his own Black Cloud Winery, was a journalist when he made one of his first Okanagan wine tours in the early 1980s. He wanted to select a mixed case (12 bottles) of wines to take home, but found only 10 worth buying. Today, he says, he can fill a case with good wine at almost every winery. This is my experience as well. I travel to the Okanagan and

Similkameen several times a year to taste and stock up on those interesting, limited-production wines that do not always make it to local wine stores.

Equally appealing is the passion displayed by wine people. Donald and Elaine Triggs, who opened Culmina Family Estate Winery in 2013, are examples of this compulsive passion. Donald has been a Canadian wine executive since 1972 (except for a seven-year career detour with a British agricultural chemicals company). As chief executive, he built Vincor into the fifth largest wine company in the world until Vincor was taken over in 2006 by Constellation Brands, the world's largest wine company. At an age when most people retire, Donald and Elaine have ploughed their considerable life savings into a major new Okanagan winery. "Retirement to me is a nasty word because it implies stopping," Donald says. "I don't think life is about stopping. It is about continuing and doing what you love."

In the tasting rooms I have visited, everyone is having fun. At the Krāzē Legz Vineyard and Winery in Kaleden, Sue and Gerry Thygesen work hard to imbue visitors with the easygoing atmosphere of a 1920s speakeasy, even wearing period dress and filling the wine shop with the jazz and honky-tonk music of that era. Rustico Farm Winery proprietor Bruce Fuller, decked out in a 10-gallon hat, serves wine informally in tumblers while pinning sheriff badges on visitors who are sworn in as wine deputies. At Van Westen Vineyards, the wines taste even better because of the informal warmth that Rob Van Westen brings to a tasting room that consists of a couple of barrels in an old apple packing house. At Ruby Blues Winery, the effervescent Prudence Mahrer waives the tasting fee for anyone who is smiling. And if they are not smiling when they walk into the wine shop, they certainly are by the time they leave.

The Okanagan and Similkameen valleys are among the world's most scenic wine regions, although this is not always appreciated. Summerland-born Tony Holler, a pharmaceutical entrepreneur who became one of the owners of Poplar Grove Winery, recounts being on a business trip in California in 2004 that included a day in the Napa Valley. He was awestruck by the vineyards and winery architecture until his wife, Barbara, interjected, saying "Tony, wake up, the Okanagan Valley is far more beautiful than this valley . . . and it's got a big lake." Deciding she was right, he bought his first vineyard property a few months later on the Naramata Bench and then built a home beside the lake.

Besides wine and scenery, the valleys are fascinating studies in geology, ecology and First Nations culture. I would refer students of geology to a book published in 2011 by the Okanagan Geology Committee, called *Okanagan Geology South: Geological Highlights of the South Okanagan Valley, British Columbia*. The Desert Centre near Osoyoos provides guided walks through Canada's only pocket desert. The self-guided tour at the Burrowing Owl Estate Winery includes information on the fragile environment of the South Okanagan. The excellent Nk'Mip Desert Cultural Centre next to the Nk'Mip Cellars winery interprets the history and culture of the First Nations. The tranquil gardens at the Pacific Agri-Food Research Centre near Summerland offer the perfect spot to relax between winery visits. The Kettle Valley Trail ascends from Penticton and leads along the upper border of the Naramata Bench, providing stunning vineyard panoramas. The Golden Mile Trail on the hills above the Tinhorn Creek winery offers breathtaking views of the South Okanagan.

This is the rich tapestry in which the wineries operate. I have never tired of exploring it. Neither will you.

GEOGRAPHY
FOR WINE TOURISTS

THE FOLLOWING IS A QUICK GUIDE TO WINE country geography, from the south to north, starting with the Similkameen Valley and proceeding to the Okanagan Valley, the Shuswap region and the Thompson River Valley. The list of wineries included in each region makes it easier to plan wine tours. The order assumes that you enter wine country at the south end, by way of the Crowsnest Highway (No. 3). Reverse the order if you enter wine country from the north, by way of the Trans-Canada and Highway 97. You can also start in Kelowna (getting there by car via the Coquihalla Highway or by air) and head north or south, depending on where your favourite wineries are located.

THE SIMILKAMEEN VALLEY
The Similkameen is a narrow valley, with steep, brooding mountains on both sides and a passive river (except during spring floods) winding along the valley bottom. There is very little rain or snow and the persistent wind adds to the desert-like dryness. With nearly 300 hectares (740 acres) of vineyard, the Similkameen is dwarfed as an appellation by the Okanagan, which is 20 times the size. Under irrigation, all but the late-ripening vinifera grapes grow here in a climate marked by 181 frost-free days, more than 2,000 hours of sunshine, blistering summer heat and occasional sharply cold winter days. There are numerous other farms in the valley, growing tree fruits, vegetables and grains. About half of the farms are organic, perhaps the highest concentration

of organic farms in British Columbia. In Keremeos (population 1,200), the excellent fruit stands at either end of town are crowded with buyers all season long.

The valley's vineyards and wineries are all between the Keremeos area and Richter Pass—the low mountain pass near the American border through which Highway 3 undulates on its way to Osoyoos. Grapes have grown here at least since the 1960s on well-drained sand and gravel soils. There is benchland on the east side of the valley, above the highway, where apple orchards have been gradually replaced with vineyards.

SIMILKAMEEN WINERIES

CERELIA VINEYARDS & ESTATE WINERY

CLOS DU SOLEIL WINERY

CORCELETTES ESTATE WINERY

CROWSNEST VINEYARDS

EAU VIVRE WINERY & VINEYARD

FORBIDDEN FRUIT WINERY

HERDER WINERY & VINEYARDS

HUGGING TREE WINERY

LITTLE FARM WINERY

OROFINO VINEYARDS

ROBIN RIDGE WINERY

RUSTIC ROOTS WINERY

SAGE BUSH WINERY

ST. LASZLO VINEYARDS ESTATE WINERY

SEVEN STONES WINERY

3 CRU WINES

VINEGLASS RENEWAL RESORT

OSOYOOS LAKE BENCH

The southernmost vineyards in the Okanagan grow on the Osoyoos Lake Bench. This is one of the narrowest points of the Okanagan Valley—Osoyoos, in fact, is a First Nations word meaning "narrows of the lake"— and one of the hottest. Osoyoos (population 5,000), the Spanish-themed lakeside town against the United States border, averages summertime temperatures that are three to five degrees higher than Penticton.

This is predominantly red wine country. The most extensive vineyards are those that Vincor International planted in 1998 and 1999 on the eastern and northeastern sides of Osoyoos Lake, on sandy slopes rising about 60 metres (197 feet) above the valley floor. These have been named Bull Pine, SunRock, Bear Cub, McIntyre and Whitetail, and are now showing up on Jackson-Triggs wine labels. Leading varieties are Merlot, Cabernet Sauvignon, Syrah, Pinot Noir and Canada's earliest successful Zinfandel block. Whites are also planted, notably Chardonnay, Sauvignon Blanc and Viognier. The bench on the western flank of the valley rises significantly higher and has a more complex mix of sand, clay and gravel. Reds also dominate plantings here. The Osoyoos Larose Vineyard high on the western slope grows only Bordeaux reds—Merlot, Cabernet Sauvignon, Cabernet Franc, Malbec and Petit Verdot. The large producers that get Osoyoos Lake Bench grapes include Jackson-Triggs, Mission Hill, CedarCreek, Osoyoos Larose, Inniskillin Okanagan and Nk'Mip Cellars.

WINERIES

ADEGA ON 45TH ESTATE WINERY

BLUE SKY ESTATE WINERY

LARIANA CELLARS

LASTELLA

MOON CURSER VINEYARDS

NK'MIP CELLARS

OSOYOOS LAROSE ESTATE
  WINERY

YOUNG & WYSE COLLECTION
  WINES

THE GOLDEN MILE

If you hike the hills on the west side of the Okanagan River south of Oliver, you can still find remains of 19th-century gold and silver mines. That is one reason for calling this stretch the Golden Mile. Today, however, the name refers to the salubrious conditions for growing grapes. In contrast to the deep sand of Black Sage Road, which you can see when you look across the valley, the soils here are well-drained clay and glacial gravel. Olivier Combret, whose family came here in 1992 after many generations as winemakers in France, is categorical: "The site cannot be questioned in terms of its capability of producing wines. It is always advantageous to be exposed to the sunrise side rather than to the sunset. In many varieties, this produces more flavours." Cool afternoon shadows fall over the vines while the east side of the valley continues to bake for several more hours. Consequently, wineries on the Golden Mile make fruity white wines as well as vibrant red wines with bright flavours.

You should hike the hills if you are reasonably fit and wearing good shoes. The 10-kilometre (six-mile) Golden Mile hiking trail extends along the flank of the mountains above the vineyards. One access point is at the north end, near the kiosk dedicated to Fairview, the long-vanished mining town. Another access point is at the uphill end of the Tinhorn Creek winery vineyard; trail maps are available in Tinhorn's wine shop. The trail provides spectacular views over the Okanagan Valley as well as access to the remains of the 19th-century gold and silver mines.

WINERIES

CASSINI CELLARS

CASTORO DE ORO ESTATE
   WINERY

C.C. JENTSCH CELLARS

CHECKMATE ARTISANAL WINERY

CULMINA FAMILY ESTATE WINERY

FAIRVIEW CELLARS

GEHRINGER BROTHERS ESTATE
   WINERY

GOLD HILL WINERY

HESTER CREEK ESTATE WINERY

INTERSECTION ESTATE WINERY

KISMET ESTATE WINERY

MAVERICK ESTATE WINERY
MONEY PIT WINERY
ORCHARD HILL ESTATE CIDERY
ROAD 13 VINEYARDS

RUSTICO FARM & CELLARS
TINHORN CREEK VINEYARDS
WILLOW HILL VINEYARDS

BLACK SAGE ROAD

This is the road to drive if you want to see acres and acres of vines, rising up to the low mountains on the east side of the valley. Black Sage Road also shows up on maps as 71st Street. It curls around the eastern side of Oliver (population 4,500), finally petering out at Constellation's Osoyoos Lake Bench vineyards. The views over the valley and also of vineyards crowding the road make this one of the Okanagan's most scenic drives.

Winemakers have discovered that these sandy vineyards, in sun from early morning until the end of the day, grow powerful red wines as well as full-flavoured whites. There are few places in British Columbia where vines grow in leaner soil. Most vineyards are on fine and very deep sand that was deposited a long time ago, when this was the beach of a vast inland lake. In its natural state, the arid earth hosts wiry grasses, tumbleweed, sage and Okanagan rattlesnakes. Irrigation is essential. "It's a really unique little area," Richard Cleave, a veteran vineyard manager, says of Black Sage. "We get very little rainfall, especially during the summer months when we get less than three inches on average. We have to use very, very few chemicals. We get very few bugs, so we use very few insecticides. It's just a unique area to grow grapes."

In the growing season, the large swing between hot days and cool nights produces grapes yielding wines with ripe fruit but bright acidity, an ideal combination. While only a handful of wineries are located on or near the road, many premium wineries in other regions use Black Sage grapes, among them Sumac Ridge, Tinhorn Creek and Mission Hill. Chaberton Estate Winery in the Fraser Valley and Muse Winery on Vancouver Island (among others) also buy Black Sage grapes.

WINERIES

BLACK HILLS ESTATE WINERY

BURROWING OWL ESTATE WINERY

CANA VINES WINERY

CHURCH & STATE WINES

COVERT FARMS FAMILY ESTATE

DESERT HILLS ESTATE WINERY

HIDDEN CHAPEL WINERY

INNISKILLIN OKANAGAN
   VINEYARDS

JACKSON-TRIGGS OKANAGAN
   ESTATE WINERY

LE VIEUX PIN

MONTAKARN ESTATE WINERY

OLIVER TWIST ESTATE WINERY

PLATINUM BENCH ESTATE
   WINERY

QUINTA FERREIRA ESTATE
   WINERY

SADDLE RIDGE VINEYARDS

RIVER STONE ESTATE WINERY

SILVER SAGE WINERY

SQUEEZED WINES

STONEBOAT VINEYARDS

TIME ESTATE WINERY

OKANAGAN FALLS

This compact vineyard region, with twisting back roads well worth exploring, includes landscapes of legendary beauty. A view of the vineyards at the Blue Mountain Vineyard & Cellars, where rows of vines undulate with perfect precision toward a hazy blue horizon, is widely reproduced in industry literature, websites and even screen savers. A hike to the top of Peach Cliff or a drive to the See Ya Later Ranch winery's heritage tasting room affords incomparable views of the region. A back road worth exploring leads east on McLean Creek Road, swinging around to emerge on Eastside Road, not far from Blasted Church Vineyards.

The Okanagan Falls soil types vary so dramatically that some vineyards grow fine Burgundy grapes; others succeed with Alsace whites and still others with Bordeaux varieties. This is a wine tourist's paradise, with every style of wine available, from sparkling wine to icewine. See Ya Later Ranch's Hawthorne Mountain vineyard boasts the highest elevation vineyard (536 metres or 1,760 feet) in the South Okanagan, with an unusual northeastern exposure. As a result, this vineyard is comparatively cool and produces some of the finest Gewürztraminer and Pinot Gris in the valley.

WINERIES

BC WINE STUDIO

BLUE MOUNTAIN VINEYARD
    & CELLARS

LIQUIDITY WINES

LUSITANO ESTATE WINERY

MEYER FAMILY VINEYARDS

NOBLE RIDGE VINEYARD & WINERY

SEE YA LATER RANCH AT
    HAWTHORNE MOUNTAIN
    VINEYARDS

STAG'S HOLLOW WINERY

SYNCHROMESH WINES

WILD GOOSE VINEYARDS
    & WINERY

SKAHA LAKE

Twisting but scenic, Eastside Road is the shortest route from Penticton to Okanagan Falls. It has recently been discovered by wine tourists, who usually drive the longer but faster Highway 97 between the two communities. Now that there are two wineries in picturesque Kaleden, wine tourists need to plan a circle route around Skaha Lake. Those preferring to linger—the scenery again is beautiful—may wish to seek out one of several bed and breakfast accommodations, such the secluded God's Mountain Estate.

Currently, several exceptional wineries overlook Eastside Road. The vineyards here all have good western exposure and benefit from the effect of the lake. Even though Skaha Lake is relatively shallow (maximum depth is 55 metres or 180 feet) and small, with only 30 kilometres (19 miles) of shoreline, it tempers the climate and extends the ripening season in late autumn.

In earlier times, one of Canada's larger peach orchards flourished on the bench of land between the lake and the cliffs to the east. Peaches are notoriously tender. It is an axiom that grapes will thrive wherever peaches grow. The constraint to this viticulture region is the narrowness of the arable bench, which backs against silt and clay cliffs. The Skaha Bluffs southeast of Penticton, which rise to 80 metres (272 feet), are popular with rock climbers. Painted Rock Estate Winery helped pay to pave the road to the parking lot used by the climbers.

WINERIES

BLACK DOG CELLARS

BLASTED CHURCH VINEYARDS

KRĀZĒ LEGZ VINEYARD
   & WINERY

LIXIÉRE ESTATE WINERY

PAINTED ROCK ESTATE WINERY

PENTÂGE WINERY

TOPSHELF WINERY

VINDICATION CELLARS

NARAMATA BENCH

The number of wineries, thanks to the superb growing conditions for grapes and the remarkable landscape, makes Naramata Road the hottest winery address in British Columbia. There are 37 producers in this region, with several more in development, up from 23 listed in the first edition of this book in 2007. Vineyards along the road have been selling for double the price of vineyards in, for example, California's long-established Mendocino County. Why? Well, first, there is not much land available. Second, it is easy for wine tourists to move from one superb winery to the next on what is the Okanagan's most concentrated route of fine wine.

Okanagan Lake tempers the climate and there are seldom vine-killing winter temperatures. The infrequency of late spring frosts and a very long autumn bring grapes to optimal ripeness. Merlots and other Bordeaux reds grow well here, along with elegant Pinot Noir, peppery Syrahs, full-flavoured Pinot Gris, Sauvignon Blanc, Riesling and Viognier. The bench on the eastern shore of the lake is a narrow strip of land that drops down from what's left of the Kettle Valley Railway (now a good walking and biking trail) to the rugged lakeshore bluffs. The vines are bathed in sun from mid-morning to the end of the day and the views from many tasting rooms take the breath away. Several wineries offer good bistro-style dining for those who wish to linger in this superb setting.

WINERIES

BELLA WINES

BENCH 1775 WINERY

BLACK CLOUD WINERY

BLACK WIDOW WINERY

D'ANGELO ESTATE WINERY

DAYDREAMER WINES

DEEP ROOTS VINEYARD

ELEPHANT ISLAND ORCHARD
   WINES

FOXTROT VINEYARDS

HILLSIDE ESTATE WINERY

HOWLING BLUFF ESTATE WINES

JOIEFARM

KANAZAWA WINES

KETTLE VALLEY WINERY

LA FRENZ WINERY

LAKE BREEZE VINEYARDS

LANG VINEYARDS

LAUGHING STOCK VINEYARDS

LOCK & WORTH WINERY

MARICHEL VINEYARD

MISCONDUCT WINE COMPANY

MOCOJO WINERY

MONSTER VINEYARDS

MORAINE VINEYARDS

NICHOL VINEYARD

PERSEUS WINERY

POPLAR GROVE WINERY

RED ROOSTER WINERY

RUBY BLUES WINERY

SERENDIPITY WINERY

TERRAVISTA VINEYARDS

THERAPY VINEYARDS

3 MILE ESTATE WINERY

TIGHTROPE WINERY

TOWNSHIP 7 VINEYARDS
   & WINERY

UPPER BENCH ESTATE WINERY

VAN WESTEN VINEYARDS

SUMMERLAND AND PEACHLAND

When developer John Moore Robinson founded Summerland in 1902, he advertised it as "Heaven on earth, with summer weather forever." That salubrious climate also accounts for Summerland's significant agricultural hinterland, seldom explored by visitors. Highway 97 sweeps by on the eastern side of Giant's Head. This stubby extinct volcano overshadows the quaint town (population 11,000) whose Tudor-style architecture is mirrored in the Sumac Ridge winery.

For many years, Sumac Ridge was the community's only winery. Recently, numerous new wineries have opened, mostly on the western side of Giant's Head, where there are good southeastern-facing slopes for grapes. The bucolic countryside, with twisting valleys extending deep into the mountains, is worth exploring (you might even find the buffalo farm). Between Summerland and Peachland, most of the vineyards cling to steep slopes running down toward Okanagan Lake, and are usually not visible from the highway. The exception is Greata Ranch, whose majestic spread of vines and red-roofed winery occupy a postcard-perfect plateau just below the highway. There are also vineyards on the hillsides above Peachland (population 5,000) awaiting discovery by wine tourists who venture off the beaten path.

What most of the vineyards in this area have in common is cool-climate grape-growing conditions. Expect to find good Pinot Noir, Chardonnay, Pinot Gris, Pinot Blanc and Gewürztraminer.

WINERIES

- BARTIER BROTHERS
- BONITAS WINERY
- DIRTY LAUNDRY VINEYARD
- 8TH GENERATION VINEYARD
- FIRST ESTATE WINERY
- GREATA RANCH ESTATE WINERY
- HAINLE VINEYARDS & DEEP
   CREEK WINE ESTATE
- HEAVEN'S GATE ESTATE WINERY
- OKANAGAN CRUSH PAD WINERY
- SAGE HILLS ESTATE VINEYARD
   & WINERY

- SAXON ESTATE WINERY
- SILKSCARF WINERY
- SLEEPING GIANT FRUIT WINERY
- SONORAN ESTATE WINERY
- SUMAC RIDGE ESTATE WINERY
- SUMMERGATE WINERY
- SUMMERLAND HERITAGE CIDER
   COMPANY
- THORNHAVEN ESTATES WINERY
- TH WINES

THE SLOPES OF MOUNT BOUCHERIE

Just a 20-minute drive south of Kelowna's urban sprawl, the Mount Boucherie wine region's best vineyards continue to hold off the pressure of land developers. Although many of the wineries here also have vineyards in the South Okanagan or the Similkameen, they husband these precious slopes. Bathed by the reflected light from Okanagan Lake, Mount Boucherie vineyards are well suited to delicate premium varieties like Pinot Noir and Riesling. Quails' Gate, which practises some of the best viticulture in the valley, even succeeds with Merlot, Cabernet Sauvignon and, remarkably, a small block of Syrah near the lake.

The Stewart family, owners of Quails' Gate, have grown grapes here since the mid-1950s, having begun planting even before the floating bridge was built across the lake at Kelowna in 1958, replacing ferries and rail barges. The most mature vines at Quails' Gate include a block of Maréchal Foch planted in 1969.

Such old blocks are the exception; most vineyards on these slopes have been replanted since 1990 with premium varieties. Some of the steeper slopes have been given over to palatial homes, whose owners are drawn by stunning views over the lake. Arguably, the best lake view from any of the wineries belongs to the Mission Hill winery, perched on the brow of the mountain, some 130 metres (426 feet) above the surface of the lake.

WINERIES

BEAUMONT FAMILY ESTATE
  WINERY
BLACK SWIFT VINEYARDS
KALALA ORGANIC ESTATE
  WINERY
LITTLE STRAW VINEYARDS
MISSION HILL FAMILY ESTATE
  WINERY

MT. BOUCHERIE ESTATE
  WINERY
NICHE WINE COMPANY
QUAILS' GATE ESTATE WINERY
ROLLINGDALE WINERY
VOLCANIC HILLS ESTATE
  WINERY

THE VINEYARDS OF KELOWNA AND LAKE COUNTRY

This is a region for history lovers. The Okanagan's first vines were planted in what is now East Kelowna, at an Oblate mission founded in 1859 by a French priest named Charles Pandosy. The restored mission buildings, now a heritage site on Kelowna's Benvoulin Road, are worth a visit even though there was never a commercial vineyard (no vines remain today). Wine grapes have been cultivated on the nearby southwest-facing slopes since at least 1928.

Compared to the South Okanagan, the Kelowna area has cool growing conditions favourable to such white varieties as Riesling and Pinot Gris and reds such as Pinot Noir. Tantalus Vineyards and St. Hubertus have Riesling vines that were planted in the late 1970s; these now produce remarkably intense wines.

Another piece of history is the old Calona Vineyards winery, which sprawls untidily across three hectares (seven acres) near downtown Kelowna. This is British Columbia's oldest continually operating winery (established in 1932). Those who venture beyond the Calona wine shop may find a small collection of artifacts—like a 1930s Champagne bottler—and photographs from the era of early Okanagan wine production. Another essential stop in the area is the British Columbia Wine Museum on Ellis Street in downtown Kelowna.

The Lake Country vineyards, which date from the 1970s, are about half an hour's drive north of Kelowna on the eastern shore of Okanagan Lake. The restaurants at the Summerhill Pyramid and Gray Monk wineries offer captivating views over the lake while CedarCreek's restaurant offers a vineyard view.

WINERIES

ANCIENT HILL ESTATE WINERY

ARROWLEAF CELLARS

BOUNTY CELLARS

CALONA VINEYARDS

CAMELOT VINEYARDS ESTATE
    WINERY

CEDARCREEK ESTATE WINERY

DOUBLE CROSS CIDERY

EAST KELOWNA CIDER COMPANY

EX NIHILO VINEYARDS

50TH PARALLEL ESTATE

GRAY MONK ESTATE WINERY

HOUSE OF ROSE WINERY

INTRIGUE WINES

MEADOW VISTA ARTISAN FARM
    WINERY

NAGGING DOUBT WINES

THE ORPHAN GRAPE

PELLER ESTATES WINERY

SANDHILL WINES

ST. HUBERTUS ESTATE WINERY

SCORCHED EARTH WINERY

SPERLING VINEYARDS

SPIERHEAD WINERY

SUMMERHILL PYRAMID WINERY

TANTALUS VINEYARDS

THE VIBRANT VINE / OKANAGAN
    VILLA ESTATE WINERY

THE VIEW WINERY

VERNON AND SALMON ARM

While this region is almost two hours north of the Okanagan wine trail, its position astride the Trans-Canada Highway helps attract visitors. The wine touring signs that have gone up beside highways in recent years direct a burgeoning number of visitors to these northern wineries.

Grape growing this far north succeeds only where microclimates are unusually favourable or wine growers are unusually determined. In Vernon, vineyards are planted on steep slopes whose southern pitch creates even more frost-free days than Black Sage Road. The northern arms of Okanagan Lake also help to moderate the climate. Closer to Salmon Arm, the vineyard at the Larch Hills Winery, with the highest elevation (700 metres or 2,300 feet) of any British Columbia vineyard, grows grapes on a steep, south-facing slope but, without a lake anywhere near it, only the earliest-ripening grape varieties succeed. Winters are chill at this elevation, but the heavy snowfall dumps an insulating blanket on the vines. There is enough precipitation in the Salmon Arm area that, generally, the vineyards are not irrigated. Several vineyards have been planted around the shores of Shuswap Lake. Nearly all northern wineries turn to Okanagan vineyards to source varieties, such as Merlot, that will not mature this far north.

WINERIES

BACCATA RIDGE WINERY

BX PRESS CIDERY & FARM

CELISTA ESTATE WINERY

EDGE OF THE EARTH VINEYARDS

LARCH HILLS WINERY

OVINO WINERY

PLANET BEE HONEY FARM
& MEADERY

RECLINE RIDGE VINEYARDS
& WINERY

SUNNYBRAE VINEYARDS
& WINERY

THE KOOTENAYS

The clue that grapes can be grown in the Kootenays is the name of a small town just east of Trail: Fruitvale. There is a considerable history of successful tree fruit production in the region, with a climate in which early to mid-season grape varieties will thrive. In the words of a provincial tourism brochure, "This is the warm side of the Rockies."

The word Kootenay has Aboriginal roots. In the language of the Ktunaxa First Nation, the word quthni means "to travel by water", a reference to the many rivers in the scenic region.

The region runs along Highway 3 from Grand Forks in the west to Creston in the east, and from the United States border north to about

Nelson. There are microclimates throughout where grapes and other fruits are grown. Additional wineries are under consideration for the region. There has been a small but promising vineyard trial at Grand Forks and a blueberry winery has opened in Castlegar.

WINERIES

BAILLIE-GROHMAN ESTATE
   WINERY
BRONZE WINES
COLUMBIA GARDENS VINEYARD &
   WINERY

HERON RIDGE ESTATES WINERY
SKIMMERHORN WINERY
   & VINEYARD
SOAHC ESTATE WINES
WYNNWOOD CELLARS

THOMPSON RIVER VALLEY

Planting wine grapes around Kamloops pushes the envelope, but that is not deterring those who believe they have special microclimates. In 2008, Kamloops businessman Ed Collett began developing a promising limestone slope about 16 kilometres (10 miles) east of Kamloops; in recent years, several northern wineries have purchased grapes from his vineyard. He built a winery two years after releasing several vintages made for him in a custom crush winery. In 2010, John and Debbie Woodward planted a vineyard north of Kamloops, on the banks of the North Thompson River. Both of these vineyards are largely planted with vinifera varieties. Which vinifera grape vines survive the occasionally hard winters of the interior remains to be determined.

A large planting of winter-hardy Minnesota hybrid varieties has begun on two other properties a little further east of Kamloops and on either side of the Thompson River. The varieties growing here were developed specifically by plant breeders in Wisconsin and Minnesota to survive hard winters. Most of the vineyards of Quebec are planted with these hybrids—perhaps they will determine the future of winemaking in the interior.

WINERIES

BONAPARTE BEND WINERY
HARPER'S TRAIL ESTATE WINERY
LEFT FIELD CIDER COMPANY

MONTE CREEK RANCH ESTATE
   WINERY
PRIVATO VINEYARD & WINERY

THE
WINERIES

ADEGA ON 45TH ESTATE WINERY

Ringing the church bells to communicate important village events was an art that Alex Nunes learned one summer in his native Portugal. He was 13 and home from a stint in the seminary. Although he emigrated to Canada two years later, the memory of the two big bells in that village church inspired Alex to add a bell tower to the winery's facade when it was built in 2011. There is, however, no bell in the tower, at least for now. "It is just for show," Alex says. "It is either buy one, or go back to my hometown and steal one at midnight," he says joking.

The winery, whose warm butterscotch tones fit with the desert landscape of Osoyoos, was designed by Alex and his brother-in-law, Fred Farinha, who own the winery with their wives, Maria and Pamala. The winery sits high on the vineyard's west-facing slope. The tasting room windows offer a grand view over the town and the lake. The 557-square-metre (6,000-square-foot) winery has thick concrete walls and a naturally-cooled cellar, for 400 barrels buried against the hillside. The interior's public areas acquired the instant patina of age by having walls finished with Italian clay and tiles on the floor.

The winery's European ambiance reflects the proprietors' Portuguese heritage (*adega* is Portuguese for "cellar"). Alex was born in Portugal in 1950 while Fred was born in Penticton in 1966. Their families were among the many Portuguese immigrants who came to Osoyoos at that time as tree fruit growers. Both Alex and Fred operated orchards until about 2005 when vanishing returns from tree fruits left them with a stark choice: sell the land or plant grapes. "We decided to keep the land and build a winery," Alex says.

They planted three vineyards totalling 15.4 hectares (38 acres), supporting 5,000 cases a year, with extra grapes for sale to other wineries. "Create our own future, you could call it," Alex says. Wine, after all, is in their blood. "We had wine on our tables and in our homes, always, since we were born," Alex remembers. "Your mom would ask

ALEX NUNES AND FRED FARINHA

to you go to the tavern in the village to get a litre of wine. It did not matter if you were five years old or ten years old. You would just go and get it." While they use a consulting winemaker, Alex and Fred, with years of experience as home winemakers, do almost everything themselves. "We are hands-on," Fred says. "We are in the field and we are also in here."

They grow no Portuguese grape varieties because they doubt the vines could survive Okanagan winters. But that has not stopped them from making Portuguese-inspired wines. Merlot stands in for Touriga Nacional to make a port-style wine.

OPENED 2011

7311 45th Street
Osoyoos, BC V0H 1V6

T 250.495.6243

W www.adegaon45.com

WHEN TO VISIT
Open daily 10 am – 5 pm May to October, and by appointment.

MY PICKS

The whites are all refreshingly fruity, including Chardonnay, Pinot Gris, Viognier and a blend called Felicidad. The reds—Merlot, Cabernet Franc, Malbec and a Bordeaux blend called Quarteto Tinto—are bold and robust. Manuel is a Merlot deliberately made in a lighter Pinot Noir style with the addition of 25 percent Viognier.

ANCIENT HILL ESTATE WINERY

This splendid Robert Mackenzie–designed winery overlooking Kelowna International Airport returns viticulture to where it began in the North Okanagan, when the Rittich brothers planted grapes near here in 1930. Natives of Hungary, Eugene and Virgil Rittich concluded that vinifera grapes could be grown successfully and wrote a book (British Columba's first wine book) on how to grow grapes and make wine. Severe winters that occurred periodically doomed those pioneering trials in the Ellison district, as it was known.

The modern-day pioneers are Richard and Jitske Kamphuys (rhymes with "compass"), who came from Holland in 1992 and bought an apple orchard. Richard, who was born in 1963, completed an advanced economics degree at the historic Erasmus University in Amsterdam before deciding he wanted a rural lifestyle for himself and his family.

He considered growing grapes as soon as he and Jitske, a former doctor's assistant, bought the orchard but was put off by general pessimism at that time about the future of British Columbia's wineries. The previous owners, encouraged by the Rittich trials, planted grapes on the hillside in 1944, but abandoned the vineyard when the hard 1949–50 winter killed many of the vines and even some apple trees. About 40 of those ancient vines, probably Okanagan Riesling, still survive.

Richard and Jitske replaced the orchard in 2005 with 27,000 vines over about six hectares (15 acres). They have chosen mid-season ripening varieties: Pinot Gris, Gewürztraminer, Lemberger, Zweigelt and Pinot Noir. The biggest block, more than a quarter of the vineyard, is Baco Noir, a red French hybrid that is notably winter hardy. "I should have had more Baco Noir and less Zweigelt," Richard says. He has begun to plant Baco Noir among the Zweigelt vines, easing into a vineyard transition.

"That hybrid seems suited to this area," he believes. "It came through in a lesser year as well as in a good year." To make the point, he pours a glass of Baco Noir from 2010, a cool year. The wine is full-bodied with rich flavours of plum and chocolate. The visitors to Ancient Hills's baronial tasting room almost always favour Baco Noir.

MY PICKS

The Pinot Gris, the Gewürztraminer and the rosé all show excellent cool-climate aromatics. Lazerus is an easy-drinking medium-bodied blend of Zweigelt, Lemberger, Pinot Noir and Baco Noir. The winery's best seller is the Baco Noir.

OPENED 2011

4918 Anderson Road
Kelowna, BC V1X 7V7
T 250.491.2766
W www.ancienthillwinery.com

WHEN TO VISIT
Open daily 10:30 am – 5:30 pm
April to October, and by appointment.

PICNIC AREA

JITSKE AND RICHARD KAMPHUYS

ARROWLEAF CELLARS

To begin its second decade, Arrowleaf Cellars has opened a tasting room and barrel cellar in a 465-square-metre (5,000-square-foot) building designed by Robert Mackenzie, one of the Okanagan's top winery architects. The new tasting room is four times the size of the previous one, indicating how popular this friendly winery is with wine tourists.

Named for the Okanagan's familiar springtime flower, Arrowleaf Cellars came about because Joe Zuppiger's five children did not care for milking cows. Once dairy farmers near Zurich in Switzerland, the Zuppigers moved to an Alberta dairy farm in 1986. When it became clear that his children wanted to do something else, Joe bought this 6.5-hectare (16-acre) North Okanagan vineyard in 1997. A born farmer, Joe had also grown fruit in Switzerland.

After the Zuppigers sold grapes for several years, son Manuel, born in 1976, enrolled in Switzerland's top wine school. He graduated in 2001 and showed such promise that he landed a practicum with Grant Burge, a leading Australian winemaker, before returning to Arrowleaf.

Just over half of Arrowleaf's production, currently about 9,000 cases, is white wine. The Arrowleaf vineyard was first planted in 1986 exclusively with white varietals, including the prized Alsace clone of Gewürztraminer, along with Bacchus, Pinot Gris and Vidal. Since taking over the property, Joe has added Merlot and Zweigelt and arranged long-term contracts with nearby vineyards for Pinot Noir and Riesling.

The winery nestles on a plateau at the edge of the vineyard, with an excellent view from the winery's picnic benches of Okanagan Lake to the west. Even more appealing than the view is the value. The unpretentious Zuppiger family charges reasonable prices for wines that could sell for more.

MY PICKS

The excellent reserve wines are released under the Solstice label. They include Gewürztraminer, Pinot Gris, Pinot Noir and a premium red blend called Solstice Reserve. The mid-tier range of varietal wines, including the best Bacchus in the Okanagan, is very reliable and good value. Even the winery's three entry-level wines, called First Crush, have won an enviable number of awards.

OPENED 2003

1574 Camp Road
Lake Country, BC V4V 1K1
T 250.766.2992
W www.arrowleafcellars.com

WHEN TO VISIT
Open daily 10:30 am – 5:30 pm
May to October; 10 am – 6 pm
July to August; and Friday to
Sunday 11 am – 5 pm April,
November and December.

PICNIC AREA

JOE AND MARGRIT ZUPPIGER

BACCATA RIDGE WINERY

Sheldon Moore is the author of *Remember Zen: Awaken the Buddha-Nature Within*. The Buddhist principles he absorbed while working in the Far East now guide him in the organic vineyard and in the winery. "Zen is my approach to winemaking," he says. "I try to be natural. I tell the pickers when they come here not to come in a bad mood and spoil the mood in the vineyard. You have to do things simply and enjoy what you are doing."

Born in 1964, Moore grew up on a farm near Fort St. John in northern British Columbia. However, he started his career in Calgary as an engineer and then transferred to Australia where a girlfriend from an Italian family fired his early interest in wine. He spent about 15 years in Australia and Southeast Asia, ultimately ending up in a senior position with Cisco Systems, a global technology company. The job involved an enormous amount of travelling. "It was a great lifestyle but when you do it for 15 years, that is a long time to live in airplanes," he says.

He returned to Canada in 2001 and, with a winery in mind, bought a 65-hectare (160-acre) farm on a slope overlooking the Shuswap River, just north of Enderby. The botanical name of the farm's yew trees, *taxus baccata*, prompted the winery name. Moore based himself in the Shuswap wine region, rather than the Okanagan, because he prefers the greener vegetation of the north.

On the best slopes of his farm, he has planted four hectares (10 acres) of vineyard, only a fraction of the potential vineyard land available to him. Believing that northern vineyards should focus on cool-climate varieties, Moore selected Ortega, Siegerrebe, Gewürztraminer, Oraniensteiner, Gamay, Pinot Noir, Zweigelt and Maréchal Foch. They have flourished on his site, which is frost-free late into the season.

He would like to plant more Siegerrebe because he admires this aromatic white. Only voracious wasps, which sucked the juice from 20 percent of his crop in 2013, are deterring him. He eschews the chemical sprays he could use. "If you read the warnings," Sheldon says about one chemical, "you are not supposed to walk into the vineyard for two weeks after you spray it. The pickers are usually picking the grapes two weeks after spraying. They would absorb it through the skin. So I grow my grapes naturally. There are no pesticides or fungicides used."

MY PICKS

Sheldon likes to make blends and it shows in the appeal of Northern Expressions White and Northern Expressions Red. As well, the medium-bodied Maréchal Foch has appealing cherry flavours.

OPENED 2012

68 McManus Road
Grindrod, BC V0E 1Y0

T   250.838.0512

W   www.baccataridgewinery.ca

WHEN TO VISIT
Open daily 11 am – 6 pm April to October.

SHELDON MOORE

BAILLIE-GROHMAN ESTATE WINERY

Over years of vacationing here, Calgarians Bob Johnson and Petra Flaa developed such affection for the Creston Valley that they bought a cherry orchard, only to discover how hard it is for weekend farmers to sell cherries. They had a better idea when they saw former fruit growers Al and Marleen Hoag build the Skimmerhorn Winery, Creston's first winery. A case of wine has a longer shelf life than a case of fresh cherries. In 2006 Bob and Petra bought a property right next door to Skimmerhorn, planted vines and, in 2009, built a spacious winery to process their first vintage.

A former technology manager, Petra now runs the 5.8-hectare (14½-acre) vineyard with skills acquired from University of Washington correspondence courses and Al Hoag's counsel. Pinot Noir comprises two-fifths of the vines. The rest of the vineyard is planted with Pinot Gris, Chardonnay, Sauvignon Blanc and Schönburger, along with 250 Kerner plants for icewine.

Born in 1958 in Red Deer, Bob is a reservoir engineer with Sproule Associates, a consulting firm he joined in 1984. Long interested in wine—he and Petra have been members of Opimian—Bob made wine at home for a number of years and then became a serious collector. But he has neither the time nor the desire to become a professional winemaker; he is more interested in marketing the 3,000 to 5,000 cases that the winery eventually plans to produce.

When the winery advertised for a winemaker, no experienced Canadians applied. "We had some very junior applications but we weren't willing to bet the farm on someone who had a little bit of education and no experience," Petra says. Like Skimmerhorn, this winery turned to New Zealand, recruiting Dan Barker, the owner and winemaker of the Moana Park Winery in Hawkes Bay. Full of youthful energy (he was New Zealand's Young Winemaker of the Year in 2003), Dan

BOB JOHNSON

PETRA FLAA

now spends the southern hemisphere's off-season making wine in the northern hemisphere.

Bob and Petra's winery is named for a Kootenay area pioneer, William Baillie-Grohman. He came in 1882 with Teddy Roosevelt to hunt trophy mountain goats. Impressed with the area's farmland, he organized a British syndicate to divert the Kootenay River and settle colonists on the drained land. The scheme ultimately failed when a lawyer made off with investment funds but Baillie-Grohman's colourful story lives on.

OPENED 2010

1140 27th Avenue South
Creston, BC V0B 1G1

T 250.428.8768

W www.bailliegrohman.com

WHEN TO VISIT
Open Wednesday to Sunday
11 am – 5 pm mid-June to early
September and weekends
mid-May to mid-June.

PICNIC AREA

MY PICKS

Dan Barker is a very good winemaker and it shows in the excellent wines, including Gewürztraminer, Pinot Gris, Chardonnay and two Pinot Noirs.

BARTIER BROTHERS

The first two wines released by Bartier Brothers were The Cowboy, a white, and The Goal, a red. Michael and Don Bartier, who were born in Kelowna, recall Okanagan history with those labels. The Cowboy was inspired by the rodeo career of the late Kenny MacLean of Okanagan Falls, the World Rodeo Champion in 1962. The Goal recalls the 1955 World Hockey Champions, the Penticton Vees.

Today, the brothers have begun to make their own Okanagan history with this winery. Launched initially under the Okanagan Crush Pad umbrella, Bartier Brothers is positioned to put its own roots down on a vineyard on Black Sage Road. "The wines are the culmination of my career, the sum of everything I have learned," Michael says.

The brothers are sons of an accountant. Don took up that profession in Calgary in 1978, where he pursued an oil industry career. Influenced by Michael's passion, he planted the Lone Pine Vineyard, a small block of Gewürztraminer in Summerland, several years before the brothers collaborated on their initial vintage in 2010.

Michael, who was born in 1967, obtained a degree in recreational administration at the University of Victoria in 1990. "I wasn't interested in the recreational field," he admitted later. "By the time I realized that, I was too far along in my degree to stop those studies." After graduating, he spent five years selling wine.

Michael returned to the Okanagan in 1995 and briefly considered becoming a rock climbing guide until taking a job at Hawthorne Mountain Vineyards (now See Ya Later Ranch). He was quickly promoted to assistant winemaker. He began taking winemaking courses and, in 1998, did a vintage at the Thomas Hardy Winery in Australia. Since 2002, he has honed his craft at Stag's Hollow, Township 7, Road 13 and, finally, at Okanagan Crush Pad with multiple client wineries.

MICHAEL BARTIER

By the 2012 vintage, Bartier Brothers was producing more than 2,000 cases, with most of the fruit from Cerqueira Vineyard, which the brothers have under contract. This six-hectare (15-acre) Black Sage Road vineyard with unique mineral content, is planted with Sémillon, Chardonnay, Syrah and the Bordeaux varietals, giving Michael many options to demonstrate what he has learned in 20 years.

MY PICKS

Everything—notably the Gewürztraminer, Merlot, Syrah and The Goal.

OPENED 2011

Okanagan Crush Pad
16576 Fosbery Road
Summerland. BC V0H 1Z0

T   250.809.9711

W www.bartierbros.com

WHEN TO VISIT

Open daily 10:30 am – 5:30 pm June to September: select weekends in the shoulder season: and by appointment.

BC WINE STUDIO

"Do you know what a cicerone is?" Mark Simpson asks rhetorically. Few would recognize that this is the title for a certified beer server; Mark almost certainly is the Okanagan's only winemaker who has passed the day-long beer exam. "My universe revolves around beer, wine and food," he says.

Born in England in 1960, Mark launched his career in 1982 with Molson brewery (now Molson Coors) after earning a microbiology degree at the University of British Columbia. In 1992 he became the brewmaster for the Granville Island Brewing Company in Vancouver. He came to winemaking in 2001 as research director for RJ Spagnols Wine and Beer Making Products which had just been acquired by Vincor International. "I got to buy grapes and juice from all over the world for the wine kits," he says. "And I was part of the Vincor wine-making team and got to hang out with the Vincor winemakers."

In 2007, Mark set up a food and beverage consultancy called Artisan Food and Beverage Group. To raise his profile with the clients for whom he was making wine, he created his own wine label under Artisan called Siren's Call. "It is like buying a billboard," he says. For another of his clients, a technology company, he created the label include() wine.

One of his clients was Stephen Carter, a young Vancouver business-man who wanted to develop a winery. In 2012, Mark and Stephen teamed up to buy a 2.6-hectare (6½-acre) Okanagan Falls vineyard that now is the base for BC Wine Studio. Here Mark makes his own wines and does custom winemaking. What he calls "studio winemaking" provides the challenge and the variety that his questing nature requires.

The wine shop is nestled at the bottom of steep vine-clad slopes planted in 1988 by former owner Jack Braun. Mark and Stephen have taken over a remarkable varietal portfolio from Siegerrebe to Cabernet

Sauvignon. As well, they buy grapes from select vineyards in the Okanagan and the Similkameen.

MY PICKS

Siren's Call Harmonious is the flagship red blend. Also, look for Siren's Call Viognier and Siren's Call Syrah. Other interesting brands from this winery are include() wine, Noble Beast and Phasion.

OPENED 2013

2434 Oliver Ranch Road
Okanagan Falls, BC V0H 1R2
T   250.460.2495
W www.bcwinestudio.ca
     www.artisangroup.ca
     www.includewine.com

WHEN TO VISIT
Thursday to Sunday noon – 5 pm
May to mid-October, and by
appointment.

MARK SIMPSON

BEAUMONT FAMILY ESTATE WINERY

You may wonder why there is a musical staff on the Beaumont labels and a guitar in the tasting room. Long before Alex Lubchynski grew grapes for a living, he played and sang with weekend bands in Alberta, one of which was called The Twilighters. An excellent singer and guitar player, Alex often turns Beaumont's tasting room into a lively hootenanny, especially when other musicians drop in.

Both Alex and Louise, his wife, were born in Alberta and were farmers there before coming to the Okanagan in 1990 to build houses. Louise's hometown of Beaumont inspired this winery's name. The couple decided to return to farming in 1995 when they bought an orchard in the Lakeview Heights district near West Kelowna, and promptly replanted it with vines. They now operate three vineyards totalling 14.5 hectares (36 acres) in what is largely a residential neighbourhood.

The vineyards all are organic. "We did not want the kids to be near the chemicals," Louise explains. Scott, their son, has joined the family on the farm. Alana, his sister and now the winemaker, learned how to drive the tractor by the time she was eight. "I have always done work in the vineyard," Alana says. She began studying business at Okanagan College until a winemaker suggested she should study wine. She switched to the college's wine-making courses and her parents, who had been selling all their grapes, developed the family winery. Alana added to her practical skills by doing vintages at two other Okanagan wineries, two vintages in Australia and one in New Zealand. In the spring of 2011, she spent two months travelling in the wine regions of Europe, from Portugal to Champagne.

The Lubchynskis still sell most of their grapes, but only after Alana gets to choose select lots of grapes for her wines. The winery makes between 1,500 and 2,000 cases a year. Alex is not rushing to be larger. He also keeps all his options open. In the spring of 2013, he briefly

LOUISE AND ALEX LUBCHYNSKI

listed the winery just to see how many interested buyers there were. "This is a money-making facility," he says.

MY PICKS

The attractions here, besides Alex's fine voice, include the rosé wines, the Pinot Gris, Pinot Blanc, Gewürztraminer, Gamay, Pinot Noir and Heritage (a blend of Pinot Noir and Gamay). All are moderately priced and organically grown.

OPENED 2008

2775 Boucherie Road
Kelowna, BC V4T 2G4

T 250.769.1222

W www.beaumontwines.ca

WHEN TO VISIT
Open daily 10 am – 6 pm May to October.

BELLA WINES

Bella Wines is the Okanagan's only winery that exclusively makes sparkling wine. "A lot of regions in BC are absolutely perfect for making bubbles," says winemaker and co-owner Jay Drysdale, whose enthusiasm for sparkling wine is close to obsessive. The passion is shared by his partner, Wendy Rose, whose Californian father imported Champagne for the family's personal consumption. "When Jay first told me that he wanted his own brand of sparkling wine, I laughed," Wendy recalls. "I said, 'Dude, I have been drinking Alain Vesselle Champagne every day for the last 30 years'."

Together, they launched Bella (named for Jay's dog) in 2012 with just 245 cases of two wines, one from Gamay and the other from Chardonnay. As planned, they doubled production to release 600 cases in 2013. After making initial vintages at the Okanagan Crush Pad, Jay and Wendy established their own winery near Naramata in time for the 2014 vintage. They also planted 1.6 hectares (four acres) of Gamay and Chardonnay vines. "I have always had a big soft spot for Gamay," Jay says. "I joke that Gamay makes the best Pinot Noir in BC."

Born in Kamloops in 1972, Jay learned wine while paying his way through college by cooking in Vancouver restaurants. There was a career detour to Calgary where, among other ventures, he developed a chain of spas. But after taking a sommelier course, he began working in wine stores. He moved to the Okanagan in 2004, first to run an Oliver restaurant and wine store and then in 2008 to work with the British Columbia Wine Institute.

In 2010 Jay took a sales position with the Enotecca group of wineries. "That's when I fell in love with winemaking," he says. With coaching from Le Vieux Pin's winemaker Severine Pinte, he began making wine for personal consumption while enrolling in Washington State University's winemaking program.

"I got hooked in the winemaking, and I knew I wanted to do my own thing," Jay says. "Then I met Wendy, who shares the passion I have for bubbles." She is a financial consultant for technology start-ups. Her father was a businessman whose hobby was wine. "My Dad was in technology," Wendy says, "and I went into technology, but he was never prouder than when I called and said, 'Guess what I am doing? We have our own bubbles house now'."

Their target is to take Bella's production to 3,000 cases a year, all of it bottle-fermented and hand-riddled sparkling wine.

MY PICKS

Everything. The two Chardonnay sparklers are crisply dry while the rose-coloured Gamay adds notes of strawberry to its dry finish.

OPENED 2012

4320 Gulch Road
Naramata, BC V0H 1N0

T   778.996.1829

W www.bellawines.ca

WHEN TO VISIT
Open daily 10 am – 5 pm during summer, and by appointment.

JAY DRYSDALE AND WENDY ROSE

BENCH 1775 WINERY

By naming this winery for its street address, partners Jim Stewart and Val Tait wanted to recognize the Naramata Bench roots of both predecessor wineries—Paradise Ranch Wines and Soaring Eagle Winery.

Paradise Ranch, which makes only icewine and late-harvest wine, was named after the beautiful secluded 261-hectare (646-acre) one-time ranch at the north end of the Bench, backing against the cliffs of Okanagan Mountain Park. It has been a vineyard since 1981. Jeff Harries, a Penticton physician who owned it, partnered with Vancouver lawyer Jim Stewart to make icewine. When Jeff sold the vineyard in 2002 to Mission Hill, Jim kept the Paradise Ranch name, contracting with various wineries for icewine production. He settled again on Naramata Bench in 2011 by buying Soaring Eagle, a four-year-old table wine producer that was caught up in the bankruptcy of the Holman Lang Group.

To give the winery a fresh start, Jim changed the name to Bench 1775. In 2013, he brought viticulturist Val Tait into partnership as the winery's general manager. Born in 1964, she has an undergraduate degree in biochemistry and a master's in integrated pest management. She started working at the Summerland research station on plant viruses and then developed her independent consulting business with grape growers in the early 1990s as new vineyards were being planted. "I was lucky to get in on the industry when it was starting to grow," says Val.

At Bench 1775, she reorganized the ramshackle winery and quickly upgraded viticulture. "We have to be impeccable in the vineyard," she vows. "It's such a beautiful site and it has such great potential." The 7.5-hectare (18½-acre) vineyard's remarkable features include a lengthy private beach on Okanagan Lake. "There are very few wineries in the world that are on the water," Val says. "It is like we are working on a vacation site." Indeed, one of the member privileges of the Bench 1775 wine club is access to the beach.

JIM STEWART

VAL TAIT

In 2014, both Bench 1775 and Paradise Ranch were acquired by an immigrant business couple from Vancouver who have chosen to remain silent investors. Val Tait continues to manage the winery.

OPENED 1998
(AS PARADISE RANCH WINES)

1775 Naramata Road
Naramata, BC V2A 8T8

T 250.490.4965

W www.bench1775.com

WHEN TO VISIT
Open daily 11 am – 5 pm.

MY PICKS

Sauvignon Blanc and Chill (a white blend) are crisp and refreshing. The current reds are soft and juicy. Look for the bigger, longer-lived reds, notably Cabernet Franc, that the winery is adding to the portfolio. The Paradise Ranch icewines and late-harvest wines are excellent.

BLACK CLOUD WINERY

This winery results from the stubborn determination of winemaker Bradley Cooper and his wife and partner, Audralee Daum, to make great Pinot Noir on a shoestring. "It's becoming clear that the regulations for operating and licensing a winery favour those with substantial financial clout and basically keep people of modest means from playing any significant role," Brad complained in a 2011 blog post. To be licensed independently, Black Cloud would be required to tie up several hundred thousand dollars in a small vineyard and a separate winery. With limited resources, Brad and Audralee operate Black Cloud under the license of Township 7 Vineyards & Winery, where Brad has been winemaker since 2005.

This is a common arrangement in the Okanagan for ambitious but impecunious winemakers, at least at wineries that do not prohibit freelancing by their winemakers. Township 7 owner Mike Raffan, not one to stifle winemakers, has allowed Brad to consult to other wineries as well. Black Cloud was born when one of Brad's clients, who later went bankrupt, compensated him with 80 cases of Pinot Noir that he had made in 2006. Audralee was unimpressed. "She said, 'Great, just as things get going, another black cloud comes over,'" Brad remembers. The winery's name was born and they began hand selling the wine.

Born in New Westminster in 1958, Brad is a journalism graduate from Langara College. After several years as a writer and photographer with community newspapers, he switched to restaurant jobs where he became wine savvy. In 1997 Brad started working in the wine shop at Hawthorne Mountain Vineyard, then became a cellar technician and took Okanagan College's first winery assistant course. He honed his skills by working the 1999 vintage at Vidal Estate in New Zealand and the 2000 icewine harvest at Stonechurch in Ontario. In 2002, he left Hawthorne Mountain for the winemaking team at Mt. Baker Vineyards in Washington State. He returned to the Okanagan to join Stag's Hollow Winery in 2003 and then Township 7 in 2005.

Black Cloud specializes in Pinot Noir, sourcing grapes from vineyards on the Naramata Bench and Okanagan Falls. Audralee, a children's counsellor who has also worked in various Okanagan wine shops, markets the wines, with free shipment of as little as one bottle serving as an inducement. A growing list of private wine stores and restaurants in British Columbia also stock the wines.

MY PICKS

The well-made Pinot Noirs are released in two tiers: Altostratus at about $35 a bottle and Fleuvage at about $25. Some of the wines are also released in magnums.

OPENED 2009

1450 McMillan Avenue
Penticton, BC V2A 8T4

T 250.490.7314
   250.488.2181

W www.blackcloud.ca

WHEN TO VISIT
No tasting room; sales by appointment.

BRADLEY COOPER

BLACK DOG CELLARS

David Rendina, who bought this vineyard in 2010, is a Winston Churchill buff, which inspired the Black Dog name. Churchill suffered throughout his life from clinical depression, which he called his "Black Dog." Kate Durisek, his daughter, explains: "For us, it is a bit of a metaphor for overcoming obstacles in life." Mastering cider and wine making is the challenge that Kate and Niklas, her husband, have taken on since leaving jobs in Vancouver and moving to the Okanagan in 2012.

They became interested in wine and cider at about the same time that David bought this four-hectare (10-acre) vineyard across the road from Blasted Church Winery. The vines—mainly Pinot Blanc and Pinot Noir—are close to 30 years old and most of the production is sold to Gray Monk Estate Winery. The vineyard allowed David, who is an environmental engineer, to climb on a tractor and pursue his interest in farming.

"With my family getting this property up here, Nik and I felt we wanted to get out of working in a corporate environment and get back to an entrepreneurial lifestyle," Kate says. Born in Vancouver, she started her career in culinary arts (Chef Karen Barnaby was a mentor), moving on to restaurant industry consulting and food products development. She also spent five years as a business strategy advisor at BC Hydro. Nik, who was born in New Hampshire in 1979 (his mother is Canadian), moved to Vancouver in 2005 to become general manager of a wholesale distribution company.

A rising interest in cider led Nik and Kate to study cider making at Washington State University. After they moved to the Okanagan, Nik, who already has a biology degree, took the Okanagan College enology course. The couple worked with several consultants on the initial vintages at Black Dog Cellars and are now taking over production.

With Gray Monk buying most of their grapes, Black Dog Cellars

KATE AND NIKLAS DURISEK

is primarily making a dry apple cider. They also believe there is more room for a start-up producer in cider than in wine. "I am fairly familiar with the restaurant industry in Vancouver and I know there is an appetite for cider," Kate says. However, they also have plans to make a sparkling rosé with some of their vineyard's Pinot Noir.

MY PICKS

The debut product, Howling Moon Okanagan Original Craft Cider, is crisp and refreshing.

PROPOSED OPENING 2014

385 Matheson Road
Okanagan Falls, BC V0H 1R5

T   250.497.5991

W www.facebook.com/blackdog
    cellarswine

WHEN TO VISIT
No tasting room.

BLACK HILLS ESTATE WINERY

No Okanagan red wine is more eagerly awaited than Nota Bene, the Bordeaux blend made by Black Hills in every vintage since 1999. Even with producing about 4,000 cases a year (and capped at that), most of the wine, now selling at over $50 a bottle, is snapped up days after release.

The key to Nota Bene is its anchoring Cabernet Sauvignon (in most vintages), almost a third of the vineyard and half the blend. The winery grows four clones of this variety—sparingly, at about two tons an acre—in a four-hectare (10½-acre) block in its sun-bathed Black Sage Road vineyard. Winemaker Graham Pierce picks and ferments the clones separately, combining them later with the Merlot and Cabernet Franc in each vintage's final blend. It is a remarkably consistent and terroir-driven wine.

The vineyard was planted in 1996 by the founders of Black Hills, Senka and Bob Tennant and Susan and Peter McCarrell, two business couples from Vancouver. When the McCarrells retired in 2007, Black Hills was acquired by Vinequest Wine Partners, a group of 265 investors including Glenn Fawcett, now the winery's president, and Victoria-born Hollywood actor Jason Priestley. They expanded Black Hills by upgrading what was already a new winery, buying the neighbouring vineyard and opening the Wine Experience Centre, a million-dollar showcase for the wines in a vineyard setting. The Wine Ambassadors at Black Hills ensure a memorable experience.

The focused portfolio includes three whites—Alibi, a blend of Sauvignon Blanc and Sémillon, a Viognier and a Chardonnay—and three reds, led by Nota Bene. Black Hills was the first winery in Canada to plant Carmenère, a rich and peppery red almost extinct in its native Bordeaux terroir but flourishing in Chile. About a hectare (2½ acres) is growing here, including a block where the variety was grafted onto Chardonnay vines because of the demand for Carmenère. In the 2009

GRAHAM PIERCE

vintage, the winery added Syrah, following in 2010 with Viognier.

In 2011, the winery added a second label called Cellar Hand, to house the wines that remain after the final blends are made each vintage. Second label wines from a good producer are always great value—as the great Bordeaux châteaux have shown with their second labels.

MY PICKS

You should join the winery's Cellar Club to get in line for these wines. Everything made here is good, including the Cellar Hand range. Nota Bene is a collectible wine capable of aging. At a vertical Nota Bene tasting hosted in 2013 by a collector, the 1999 Nota Bene—the first vintage—emerged as the favourite wine of the evening.

OPENED 2001

4318 Black Sage Road
Oliver, BC V0H 1T1

T 250-498-6606 (Wine
   Experience Centre)
   250.498.0666 (office)

W www.blackhillswinery.com

WHEN TO VISIT
Wine Experience Centre (4190
Black Sage Road): open daily
10 am – 6 pm May to October,
offering choices of hosted
tastings.

FOOD SERVICE
Joy Road Vineyard
Kitchen

BLACK SWIFT VINEYARDS

This is the second winery to be assembled by Terrabella Wineries, the winery holding company run by Rob Ingram, a Summerland chartered accountant. Terrabella purchased Penticton-based Perseus Winery in 2011, and two years later the vineyard for Black Swift was acquired. What both wineries have in common are high traffic locations.

Naming the winery involved navigating a thicket of trademarks. Rob's original choice was Helios, the mythological Greek god who drove the sun across the sky every day. It was a good metaphor for a vineyard bathed daily by the sun, except that it was tied up by someone else's trademark. After canvassing a number of other names, Rob settled on another high flier: Black Swift, a bird that breeds in British Columbia's mountains and is hard to see because it flies so high.

The 7.2-hectare (18-acre) Black Swift vineyard property is on Boucherie Road, just north of Quails' Gate and Mission Hill wineries. The winery counts on capturing drive-by wine tourists on the heavily-travelled Boucherie Road. "I was told Mission Hill is pulling in 130,000 visitors a year," Rob says. "Most of those people also visit Quails' Gate. If we can get 10 percent of that . . . " The spacious wine shop, with space for what Rob calls "a working man's bistro" is scheduled to open in the spring of 2014.

The vineyard was purchased from Horst and Ilse Mueller, a retirement age couple who had grown grapes there for about 20 years. The vineyard has 2.4 hectares (six acres) each of Pinot Noir and Pinot Blanc and 1.2 hectares (three acres) of Gamay Noir. Black Swift is launching with Pinot Noir and Chardonnay, made under the Perseus license.

The initial vintages for Black Swift have been made at the Okanagan Crush Pad winery. With ambitious plans for this winery, Rob is considering building a production facility as large as 1,394 square metres (15,000 square feet). This is planned for the southeast corner of

MATT DUMAYNE

the vineyard, keeping truck traffic and crush activity well away from the wine shop.

PROPOSED OPENING 2014

3189 Boucherie Road
West Kelowna. BC V1Z 2H1

MY PICKS

No wines available for tasting at press time.

BLACK WIDOW WINERY

In the summer of 2000, while looking for a getaway cottage with a few vines, Dick and Shona Lancaster saw this property on Naramata Road. At three hectares (seven acres), it was bigger than what they were looking for but, with producing vines and a panoramic view of Naramata Bench and the lake, it was too good to turn down. "Classic upselling," Dick says of the realtor. "And as soon as we got a vineyard, the goal was to set up a winery."

Born in Toronto in 1953, Dick grew up in Montreal and picked up an interest in wine from his father, Graham, then Air Canada's food services manager. Dick began making wine from wild grapes while still in high school. A three-month tour of European wine regions in 1976 sealed that interest. In Vancouver, where he and Shona lived from 1970 until moving to the Okanagan a few years ago, Dick was an award-winning home winemaker for more than 25 years.

You could call Dick a polymath, given all the skills he has acquired. Starting in biology, he earned a master's degree. Disillusioned by the lack of well-paying jobs, he took a real estate course, then sold cars and became district manager for a leasing company. Then he got a master's degree in business administration and finally qualified as an accountant. From 1992 until 2008, he was a vice-president with Imasco Minerals, western Canada's largest stucco manufacturer. Naturally, Black Widow's gravity-flow winery, which he designed, is finished in tawny-hued stucco. "How can I not use stucco?" he laughs.

The vineyard already had Gewürztraminer, Pinot Gris and Schönburger when the Lancasters bought it. In 2001, they added Merlot and a bit of Cabernet Sauvignon, selling grapes until launching Black Widow in 2006. "We like wines that have some real flavour and character to them, and that comes from really ripe grapes," Dick says.

The winery is named after the indigenous desert-dwelling spider that

DICK LANCASTER

is, fortunately, so shy it is seldom seen. The insect should be avoided because the bite (only the female's bite) is highly venomous.

MY PICKS

Everything. The winery's signature red is Hourglass, a bold Merlot-Cabernet blend. The Gewürztraminer and the Pinot Gris, both finishing dry, are packed with flavour. Oasis is a lovely aromatic blend of Schönburger, Gewürztraminer and Muscat. The winery's delicious dessert wines include a delightful Dessert Schönburger, a fortified Schönburger called Mirage and a port-style Merlot called Vintage One.

OPENED 2006

1630 Naramata Road
Penticton, BC V2A 8T7

T 250.487.2347

W www.blackwidowwinery.com

WHEN TO VISIT
Open daily 11 am – 5 pm July to September, and noon – 5 pm May, June and early October. Check website for occasional variances.

FOOD SERVICE
Hourglass Patio offers wine and cheese.

ACCOMMODATION
Two bed and breakfast units available primarily to Black Widow Wine Club members, previous guests or by referral.

BLASTED CHURCH VINEYARDS

The most original event at the Okanagan's fall wine festival is the free-spirited "Midnight Service" at Blasted Church. A professional gospel choir fills the cellars with spirited hymns while guests wash down southern soul food with the winery's best wines. The entire portfolio at Blasted Church reflects an irreverent take on worship, from the label caricature of a preacher to premium wines called Cross to Bear, Holy Moly, Nothing Sacred and OMG, the elegant sparkling wine.

This reflects the hand of Vancouver marketing consultant Bernie Hadley-Beauregard, who was hired in 2002 to rebrand Prpich Hills when the winery was purchased by Chris and Evelyn Campbell. Many of the labels that his firm generated for Blasted Church have won design awards and have been exhibited at the San Francisco Museum of Modern Art. That is significant international recognition for an Okanagan winery.

The Blasted Church name comes from how movers took apart a church in 1929 when relocating it to Okanagan Falls from the abandoned mining town of Fairview; they loosened the nails in the heavy timbers with a small dynamite charge. The church still serves a congregation in Okanagan Falls. That story provides a narrative for many of the labels.

Blasted Church now produces more than 25,000 cases a year from its 17-hectare (42-acre) vineyard (and with some purchased grapes). The winery has had a succession of veteran winemakers. The winemaker since 2011 is Penticton-born Mark Wendenburg, an expert in sparkling wine from his previous 18-year career at Sumac Ridge. The winery's portfolio of powerful reds and crisp whites also benefits from the expertise in the vineyard of Morton Serbon, a New Zealand born and trained viticulturist, who has been at Blasted Church for several vintages. On its website, the winery says he is "worth his weight in gold."

EVELYN AND CHRIS CAMPBELL

MY PICKS

I like all of the wines here, including the best-selling aromatic white blend, Hatfield's Fuse, and the finessed unoaked Chardonnay. The Merlot is excellent. The reserve reds are outstanding, especially Holy Moly, a Malbec Syrah blend. OMG is an outstanding sparkling wine.

OPENED 2000
(AS PRPICH HILLS)

378 Parsons Road
Okanagan Falls, BC V0H 1R5
T   250.497.1125
    1.8.SPELLBOUND (toll free)
W www.blastedchurch.com

WHEN TO VISIT
Open daily 10 am - 5 pm May to October, and by appointment.

MARK WENDENBURG

BLUE MOUNTAIN VINEYARD & CELLARS

The term "estate winery" is used rather casually in the Okanagan. Strictly speaking, it should apply only to wineries self-sufficient from their own vineyards. Blue Mountain is a true estate winery by that definition but has never used the term. Ian and Jane Mavety have been growing grapes on this picturesque Okanagan Falls property since buying the land in 1971. Their intimate understanding of the terroir here allowed them to produce top-quality wines that earned Blue Mountain a cult following almost as soon as the winery opened. Blue Mountain marched to its own drummer from the outset by making dry French-style wines—the kind the Mavety family liked to drink—when most other Okanagan wineries were making off-dry German-style whites.

The winery is steeped in French tradition that began when Ian and Jane travelled through France in the 1980s, doing the research that would eventually support their decision to plant Burgundy and Alsace varietals. Also, Rafael Brisebois, the consulting winemaker who helped make the initial vintages, had grown up in Alsace and worked for Piper-Heidsieck in Reims. Champagne became the template for Blue Mountain's sparkling wines and remained so when Ian and Jane's son, Matt, began to take over the cellar in 1997 with winemaking learned at Lincoln University in New Zealand. Matt's palate and style are influenced, however, by what he has learned during his own trips to France. Since 2001, in a quest for ever more complex wines, he has fermented an increasing percentage of the red wines with wild yeasts.

Wild yeast is but one trick in the Blue Mountain tool box for making complex wine from a single estate. The flagship variety is Pinot Noir. At least five clones grow here, with multiple plantings of each on the various soils and aspects of the 32-hectare (79-acre) vineyard. This ensures that Matt has a broad palette of flavours with which to blend wines that are rich and complex.

Blue Mountain's annual production, about 16,000 cases, is disciplined.

IAN MAVETY

MATT MAVETY

About a quarter comprises Champagne-method sparkling wines. The portfolio is completed with two reds (Pinot Noir and Gamay) and four whites (Chardonnay, Pinot Gris, Pinot Blanc and, since 2010, Sauvignon Blanc). The reserve tier wines once had striped labels and the others had cream labels.

Prior to 2010, the Blue Mountain tasting room was open primarily by appointment. The family, after all, had its hands full looking after 150,000 vines and handling all the regulatory and customer paperwork that goes with a winery. However, a summer-long tasting season was established after Matt's sister, Christie, brought her marketing skills to this family-operated estate winery.

OPENED 1992

2385 Allendale Road
Okanagan Falls, BC V0H 1R2

T 250.497.8244

W www.bluemountainwinery.com

WHEN TO VISIT
Open daily 11 am – 5 pm
May to early October, and by
appointment.

MY PICKS
Everything, including remarkable late-disgorged sparkling wines.

BLUE SKY ESTATE WINERY

Some wineries have hired big city consultants to create a name. Harpreet Toor is not one to complicate such decisions, let alone farm them out. He and Navpreet, his wife, discussed potential names while seated outside their home, surrounded by vineyards. It was one of those bright clear South Okanagan days. The brilliant sky inspired the name. "As a small farmer, we don't have much money to spend on consultants," he explains.

Born in India in 1969, he spent nine months on a local police force before he and his parents immigrated to the Okanagan in 1998. Typically hard-working immigrants, they accumulated the down payment by 2002 to buy an orchard just outside Osoyoos. Harpreet soon discovered that "our fruit industry can't compete with the U.S." In 2004, he replaced the trees with 4.2 hectares (10½ acres) of vines that flourish on an ideal southeastern slope dropping toward Osoyoos Lake. He planted just four varieties: Cabernet Sauvignon, Cabernet Franc, Syrah and Viognier. Next door, his brother, Bhola, planted a similar sized vineyard but put it up for sale in 2013.

While waiting for his vineyard to produce grapes, Harpreet earned a living by operating several service stations. He currently operates two Centex franchises in southern British Columbia. "That's why we are surviving," he says. "Otherwise, we might be bankrupt."

The lot of an independent grape grower is tough. Harpreet has had wineries offer the going average price for his varieties but, when harvest approaches, finding a pretext to cut the price or even refuse the grapes. "What are we going to do?" he says. "We can't take these grapes and sell them on the fresh market." In 2011, he took his fate in his own hands, got a winery license and, with the help of a consultant, began to make wine. "The middlemen selling wine are making better money than farmers," he concludes. He continues to offer some of his well-grown grapes to wineries while building the winery and the tasting room to support independent sales. The plan is to open the wine shop with at least four varietals, supplemented perhaps with Merlot, Chardonnay and Pinot Gris from purchased fruit.

MY PICKS

No wines available for tasting at press time.

PROPOSED OPENING 2014

11631 87th Street
Osoyoos. BC V0H 1V2
T 250.495.6692

HARPREET TOOR

BONAMICI CELLARS

Philip Soo and Mario Rodi are old friends with shared passions for wine. Mario, who was born in 1957 in northern Ontario, was just 12 when he started helping his immigrant Italian father crush grapes for the family's wine. Philip was born in Vancouver in 1969, the son of immigrants from Hong Kong who were just discovering what little wine culture there was in Canada at the time. "We had family celebrations but they never encouraged kids to drink," Philip remembers. Nonetheless, he recalls, "I was 12 or 13 when my first sip of alcohol, Baby Duck, was at a Christmas party."

It seems that was enough to get Philip interested. After getting degrees in microbiology and food engineering, he was offered jobs at a pharmaceutical firm and a company that produced gourmet salads but, having been a good amateur beer maker while in college, he took a job with a manufacturer of beer kits "because it was in line with my hobby." Subsequently, Andrew Peller Ltd. bought this company along with a wine kit company. Philip was then promoted to Peller's winery in Port Moody in 2000. When the winery closed five years later, he moved to the Okanagan to become a winemaking consultant.

Mario spent about 20 years in food and soft drinks sales before joining Peller in 1995 as the general manager of Winexpert, as the kit company was called. He and Philip, who reported to him, became close friends. Mario left Peller in 2009. Deciding to stay in the wine business, he proposed Bonamici to Philip. "He is a great winemaker," Mario says. "I focused on the sales and marketing for my entire career. I thought this might be an opportunity for us to get together and build something great."

Taking advantage of a great vintage in 2012, they bought grapes from Philip's favourite growers and contracted space in an existing winery to make about 1,000 cases of wine. Two wines were released initially,

PHILIP SOO AND MARIO RODI

a red blend and a white blend, and these will be joined 2014 by a big red and another white. Bonamici will operate as a "virtual" winery for several years but, when the brand is established, the partners will build their winery.

"We have a three year plan" Philip said in 2013. "This is our first year of it. If everything goes well, it could accelerate to two years. But our plan is to have our own facility in three to five years."

SALES BEGAN 2013

4828 Highway 97
Oliver, BC V0H 1T0
T 604.868.2356
W www.bonamicicellars.com

WHEN TO VISIT
No tasting room.

MY PICKS

The winery debuted with two 90-point wines, a white blend of Sauvignon Blanc and Viognier and a red blend of Merlot and Cabernet Franc.

BONAPARTE BEND WINERY

This winery takes its name from a nearby river that French fur traders named for Napoleon Bonaparte. The property it occupies is Bonaparte Ranch, established in 1862 and owned since 1993 by JoAnn Armstrong and her husband, Gary, a veterinarian. The fruit winery was conceived by JoAnn, an entrepreneurial accountant who put together a business plan that called for the construction of a handsome winery building.

"I have cattle barns down here," she says of Bonaparte Ranch, which grows most of the fruit for her wines. "I could have started the winery in a barn but I didn't think that was the right facility. It was not the image I wanted to portray right off the bat. We decided we were going to do it the right way, right from the start." The winery's tasting room is combined with a well-stocked gift shop and casual restaurant.

When it came to winemaking, the Armstrongs discovered that they were on their own. Okanagan consultants were not interested in an ongoing relationship that involved long drives. So the Armstrongs mastered winemaking, with JoAnn poring over winemaking texts and Gary dipping into his veterinarian's knowledge of chemistry. Son-in-law Casey McDonald has since also acquired winemaking skills.

"We were advised to make smaller batches, test batches," JoAnn says. She does not know whether it was courage or foolhardiness, but they plunged ahead with commercial lots, often as large as 1,400 litres (300 gallons) at a time. "I really wanted to get started," she says. "We had the building. We had the investment. People in the area were asking us what was going on. If we had taken the time to do a bunch of test batches, that would have put us behind another six or seven months. I thought if I was going through the effort, I wanted to be able to have a product for sale. I wanted to get started right away."

Bonaparte Bend, which now makes about 1,200 cases of wine annually from 12 varieties of fruit, was one of the earliest fruit wineries

JOANN ARMSTRONG

in British Columbia. Since this winery opened, fruit wineries have burgeoned, both here and across Canada. Spotting the rising popularity of ciders, the winery has now installed equipment to produce hard apple cider and other carbonated beverages.

MY PICKS

I liked the crisply fresh apple wine and the tangy rhubarb wine, which vies with gooseberry wine in popularity. The intensely-flavoured boysenberry wine is reminiscent of Gamay. The off-dry raspberry wine has flavours very true to the fresh berries.

OPENED 1999

2520 Highway 97 North
Cache Creek, BC V0K 1H0

T 250.457.6667 (active mid-April to mid-October)

W www.bbwinery.com

WHEN TO VISIT
Open Monday to Saturday 10 am – 5 pm (closing at 4 pm Sundays and holidays) May to September.

RESTAURANT
Bistro lunches 11 am – 3 pm.

BONITAS WINERY

As this book was being published, Lawrence Hopper and Diane Esslinger, his partner, had this winery for sale. The new owners, when confirmed, are expected to continue operating the winery, which has one of the Okanagan's most attractive settings.

The winery, just north of the Sumac Ridge winery, is not visible from the highway but perches at the end of winding McDougald Road, which drops sharply down toward the lake. Here, Lawrence built a gleaming white Mediterranean home in 1994 and wrapped a three-hectare (7½-acre) vineyard around it in 1999. The winery building echoes the design of his 465-square-metre (5000-square-foot) home. Postcards are made of vistas like this. "We have a pristine view," Lawrence says. The property has 300 metres (984 feet) fronting on the lake, nearly all in its natural state.

A lean, wiry amateur golfer with a driving range in his office, Lawrence was born in Cobden, Ontario, in 1954 and raised in Edmonton in a single-parent home, the oldest of nine children. His mother was a hairdresser—"and she taught us a good work ethic," Lawrence says. He started his career as a millwright in Fort McMurray then became a brewery salesman. He admits that beer was long his favourite beverage. Since coming to the Okanagan in 1986, he has juggled his career as an industrial lubricant salesman with his vineyard. Wines have been made for Bonitas by consultants, notably Bradley Cooper of Township 7.

Originally, Lawrence called the winery Hijas Bonitas," Spanish for beautiful daughters. It was meant as a compliment to his daughters, Chelsea and Tiera. However, customers had so much difficulty pronouncing the name that Lawrence simplified it to Bonitas.

LAWRENCE HOPPER AND DIANE ESSLINGER

MY PICKS

Start with off-dry Gewürztraminer, crisp Pinot Gris and buttery Chardonnay. The Pinot Noir shows the classic texture and strawberry notes of the variety.
Vino Tinto is a tasty, if eccentric, blend of Merlot, Pinot Noir and Syrah.

OPENED 2008

20623 McDougald Road
Summerland, BC V0H 1Z6
T 250.494.5208
W www.bonitaswinery.com

WHEN TO VISIT
Open daily 11 am – 5 pm April to October.

RESTAURANT
Bonitas Bistro
T 778.516.5596
Open for lunch seven days a week in summer.

BOUNTY CELLARS

It would not be unusual to enjoy a wine from Bounty Cellars without knowing it is, in fact, from this winery. While Bounty releases wines under its own label, many of its wines are made for clients under Bounty's "virtual winery" program. Those clients include growers who bring their own grapes to Bounty's winemakers and clients needing private label wines. "The Virtual Winery Program . . . lets you experience the benefits of owning a winery without purchasing land or equipment, growing and harvesting grapes, producing and bottling wine, or marketing and selling product," Bounty explains.

Perhaps its most prestigious client is Sparkling Hill Resort near Vernon, a luxurious $120 million development financed by Gernot Langes-Swarovski, the Austrian businessman who is also an owner of Swarovski Crystal. For the resort, Bounty has created a series of wines, some entirely from British Columbia grapes and some with Washington and California grapes. Bounty also designed striking labels—each with three sparkling crystals. The wines are sold in the resort but also retailed across western Canada, as a way of extending the resort's brand.

This nimble marketing, conceived by Bounty owners Ron Pennington and Wade Raines, sets the winery apart from its peers. Ron, who was born in Medicine Hat in 1962 and has a degree in chemistry, got his marketing acumen during a long career with Canada Safeway. He moved to the Okanagan in 2001 and set up his own marketing company in an industrial mall near the airport. When one of his winemaker clients suggested that Ron's sprawling building was big enough for a winery, the idea of Bounty was born.

The Virtual Winery is an extension of Bounty's original business of bottling private label wines for corporate and association clients. A typical land-based winery will have start-up costs of at least $3 million.

RON PENNINGTON (COURTESY OF BOUNTY CELLARS)

Ron calculates that Bounty can make 1,000 cases for about $125,000 (plus brand development costs).

Ron compares Bounty to a French *négociant*. In addition to making its own wine with purchased grapes, Bounty buys wine from other producers—both VQA wines and wine imported from the United States.

OPENED 2005

7 – 364 Lougheed Road
Kelowna. BC V1X 7R8

T   250.765.9200
    1.866.465.9463 (toll free)
W www.bountycellars.com

WHEN TO VISIT
Open Monday to Saturday 9 am – 5 pm.

MY PICKS

Bounty's VQA wines, available through the VQA wine stores, include Gewürztraminer, Pinot Blanc and Cabernet Sauvignon. The Bounty wines under the Crystal label include a fruity Gewürztraminer and an elegant Cabernet Sauvignon/Merlot.

BRONZE WINES

With this winery, Scot Stewart has achieved a number of firsts. It is the first of what Scot hopes will be a cluster of wineries in Grand Forks. It is believed to be the first producer in British Columbia with a dual winery and distillery license. And it is certainly the first producer to make cannabis-infused rye whisky.

Scot is something of a Renaissance man. Born in North Vancouver in 1967, he took up mead making in 1992, midway through a degree in philosophy at the University of Victoria. In 1996, two years after graduating, he accepted an offer from businessmen in Oregon to purchase Grendel Meadworks before it completed its licensing application in British Columbia. "It was a nice way to finish up university," Scot says with a chuckle.

His peripatetic career moved on to designing jewellery and then managing a family engraving company until it was sold in 2010. "I went back to doing what I love, which is making wine," says Scot, a veteran home winemaker. He was introduced to Grand Forks by his friend and now partner, Massimiliano Bottoni, who was taking over family property there. In 2011, the two developed a business plan for the winery and distillery, found some investors, and established Bronze Wines.

"There was nothing planted at the time," Scot says. "We have since planted vineyards, orchards, various berries and fruit and quite a bit of rhubarb, different things we need for our products." With grapes from their small vineyard and from three larger local vineyards, they have begun to make wines from varieties such as Gewürztraminer, Frontenac and Marquette. The latter are winter-hardy Minnesota hybrids. Their central ambition is to make a fortified Muscat modelled on similar Australian wines (with some advice from an Australian vintner). The still they built provides the fortifying spirit.

The spirits are being released under the True North Distilleries label. Green Hit, the cannabis-infused rye, was largely presold before release. They also plan to release Sunshine, a corn whiskey, several fruit brandies and a cannabis-infused Irish whiskey. "I am of Irish descent," Scot says. "My great-grandfather used to fancy a wee bit of the creature."

MY PICKS

No wines available for tasting at press time.

OPENED 2014

5450 Almond Gardens Road
Grand Forks, BC V0H 1H4

T   250.442.0676

W   www.bronzewines.com

WHEN TO VISIT
Open Tuesday to Thursday 10 am – 4 pm, and by appointment Friday to Monday.

BURROWING OWL ESTATE WINERY

If you are looking for winery founder Jim Wyse in summer, chances are he is around the property tending the 100 bluebird boxes or bat nursery boxes or is working to conserve the endangered burrowing owl. His dedication to the ecology has been the moral imperative here since 1993 when he began planting vines in this fragile environment. The underground barrel cellar is cooled naturally. A geothermal system, along with solar panels, heats and cools most of the winery complex. Even the lights are of a shielded design to reduce light pollution. "I am a bit of an astronomer," Jim says. "I love it up here when the stars are out."

The winery and its 55-hectare (136-acre) vineyard are on the northernmost tip of the Sonoran Desert. When Jim learned that the burrowing owl population had vanished, he put the winery's resources behind reintroducing the bird. The $2 fee for wine tastings—and the winery gets 100,000 visitors each year—supports the captive breeding program, which has begun to show success. With son Chris and daughter Kerri managing the winery, Jim now focuses largely on the conservation work.

Jim and his wife, Midge, began looking at vineyard properties when he was developing real estate in the Okanagan. The bench that Burrowing Owl now occupies had grown hybrid grapes for two decades until 1988 when, in a government-financed adjustment program, the vines were pulled out. After Jim bought the land, he replanted with premium European varieties. This sun-bathed sandy soil produces intensely flavoured red and white wines for which Burrowing Owl has gained a cult following since its first vintage in 1997.

Burrowing Owl makes about 30,000 cases a year. About a third is allocated for Internet sales, another third for wine stores and restaurants, and the final third for Burrowing Owl's wine shop. Older vintages no longer available anywhere else are still on the wine list of the

TOM DIBELLO

CHRIS WYSE

Sonora Room, one of the best winery restaurants in the Okanagan.

The recognizable style of Burrowing Owl's wines was set during the first seven vintages by Bill Dyer, a consulting winemaker from California. His style of rich reds has remained remarkably consistent even though subsequent winemakers trained mostly in Australia or South Africa. Of course, all have benefitted from the same well-managed vineyard. Tom DiBello, the current winemaker, is a University of California graduate who started his career at the legendary Stag's Leap Wine Cellars in 1983. Now a Canadian citizen, Tom came to the Okanagan in 2000, spending a decade as CedarCreek's winemaker.

OPENED 1998

500 Burrowing Owl Place
Oliver, BC V0H 1T1

T   250.498.0620
     1.877.498.0620 (toll free)
W www.bovwine.ca

WHEN TO VISIT
Open daily 10 am – 5 pm Easter
to October, and by appointment.

RESTAURANT
The Sonora Room (closed during
winter).

ACCOMMODATION
Guest House with 10 luxurious
rooms and one large suite.

MY PICKS

Everything, beginning with an iconic Meritage and a Syrah/Cabernet Sauvignon blend called Athene and a full suite of red varietals. The Pinot Gris, Chardonnay and Sauvignon Blanc are elegant and polished. An excellent port-style wine is Coruja (Portuguese for owl). Burrowing Owl's second label, Calliope, has a strong portfolio at value prices.

BX PRESS CIDERY & FARM

Born in 1976, David Dobernigg is a third generation Vernon apple grower. Grandfather Franz moved from Alberta in 1946 and bought an orchard. It expanded over the years and today has 12 hectares (30 acres) in Vernon's BX district. The district is named for the former 2,428-hectare (6,000-acre) ranch once operated by the owner of Barnard's Express & Stage Line. Once the largest stage line in North America, it closed after 50 years in 1920 when trucks and railroads took over. The name lives on in the district and now in a cidery.

Apples growers always need to add value to keep orchards viable. David and Melissa, his wife, settled on making cider while continuing to sell apples directly from their farm and to the industry packing house. They grafted nine cider apple varieties onto the trunks of 263 Golden Delicious trees (a variety on which they were losing money). The first small crop is expected in 2014, with full production the year after. Depending on cider sales, other trees in the orchard will be switched to cider varieties as well.

David and Melissa researched cider-making for three years, including making trial lots, before building the cidery in which their initial 10,000 litres were made in 2013. "We have both taken some courses from Peter Mitchell in Washington State on cider making," Melissa says, referring to the guru who has trained most of British Columbia's cider makers. "And I have taken the principal course on cider making." The first cider from BX Press is a dry carbonated cider packed in half-litre bottles and called The Prospector. The capacity of the cidery is about 50,000 litres a year. "We'll have to decide if we are happy at that volume," says Melissa, a mother of three. "We love the quiet country life."

Melissa grew up on a wheat farm in Saskatchewan and came to British Columbia to study business after her family moved there in

DAVID AND MELISSA DOBERNIGG

1998. Meeting David and moving to an orchard was pure serendipity. "We had a small orchard on one of our properties . . . gooseberry, sour plum, whatever you can grow in Saskatchewan," Melissa says. "I remember walking through there as a child and imagining that it was a real orchard. Who would have known then that I would have ended up here?"

MY PICKS

No ciders available for tasting at press time.

PROPOSED OPENING 2014

4667 East Vernon Road
Vernon. BC V1B 3H9
T 250.503.2163
W www.thebxpress.com

WHEN TO VISIT
Open Friday to Sunday 11 am – 5 pm June to September.

CALONA VINEYARDS

Sovereign Opal is the only wine grape developed at the Summerland Research Station that made it into commercial production. With a scant two-hectare toehold in John Casorso's Kelowna-area vineyard, the variety's existence seemed tenuous until recently. Now, new plantings in that vineyard have increased the area of Sovereign Opal to 3.6 hectares (nine acres) because the variety, a perfumed and spicy cross of Golden Muscat and Maréchal Foch, has found a growing following.

This has not been an overnight success. Calona's first Sovereign Opal was released in 1987. "It has taken years to figure it out," admits Howard Soon, the veteran in the team whose winemaking refinements account for Sovereign Opal's breakout popularity.

The Calona portfolio consists largely of aromatic whites made with a delicate touch by Sandy Leier. Born in 1978 and raised in Kelowna, she joined Howard's team in 2006 after getting a degree in chemistry, becoming the Calona winemaker in 2010. "I enjoy making aromatic whites," she says. "Sovereign Opal stands out among them. I prefer it to Gewürztraminer. Sovereign Opal is really different and people sometimes look for that. It is a nice wine to drink chilled on the patio in summer."

Given Calona's history, it seems right that this would be the winery championing the only commercial wine grape developed in the Okanagan. Calona is British Columbia's oldest continually operating winery. It was launched by Guiseppe Ghezzi, an Italian winemaker, backed by a group of Kelowna investors led by grocer Pasquale (Cap) Capozzi. The bland original name was Domestic Wines and By-Products. A province-wide competition in 1936 was won by a Fraser Valley resident who suggested Calona, claiming the prize of $20 and a case of wine. Since the Capozzi family sold in 1971, Calona has had several owners, with Andrew Peller Ltd. acquiring the winery in 2005.

Calona's buildings sprawl across the same acreage near downtown Kelowna that the winery has occupied since the 1940s. The patina of age and some of the tasting room artifacts recall the origins of Okanagan winemaking.

OPENED 1932

1125 Richter Street
Kelowna, BC V1Y 2K6

T 250.762.3332
   1.888.246.4472 (toll free)

W www.calonavineyards.ca

MY PICKS

WHEN TO VISIT
Open daily 9 am – 6 pm June to December; Monday to Saturday 9 am – 5 pm, and Sundays 9 am – 4 pm January to May.

Calona's Artist Series wines are among the Okanagan's best values in VQA wines, especially the unique Sovereign Opal, the Pinot Gris, the Pinot Blanc, the Gewürztraminer, the unoaked Chardonnay, the Pinot Noir and the Cabernet Merlot.

SANDY LEIER

CAMELOT VINEYARDS ESTATE WINERY

Since opening this winery, husband and wife Robert Young and Denise Brass, have added a unique wine country festival: the day-long Medieval Fair, celebrating European history and culture of the 11th to 16th Centuries. It is a colourful spectacle, including jousts by armour-clad individuals who belong to a Kelowna historical group called the Archduchy of Connacht.

Robert's father, R. J., who died in 1996, once named a family home Camelot; Robert and Denise honoured his memory by calling the winery Camelot and then added the touches from King Arthur's court that led to the annual fair. A sword embedded in a stone greets visitors. Inside the wine shop, there is a round table and replica suit of armour that Denise bought at auction for $650. "We had seen a genuine one from England," she says, a bit wistfully. "They were going for about five thousand pounds."

R. J. Young was ahead of his time when he planted a hectare (2½ acres) of Maréchal Foch vines on this property in 1974. Unable to get a winery contract, he soon pulled them out and planted apples. When Robert and Denise took over the farm, they continued to grow apples until 2006, when the price of apples was less than packing house handling charges. Vines replaced the orchard in the next year: 2.5 hectares (six acres) of Pinot Gris, Riesling, Gewürztraminer and Pinot Noir. The original plan was just to sell the grapes but, perhaps reflecting on R. J.'s experience, the couple chose to develop their own winery.

The venture is something of a retirement project, even if both are about 10 years from retiring. Robert, who was born in Quesnel, British Columbia, in 1961, and Denise, who was born in Britain, have been Air Canada flight attendants for about 20 years. They usually work together on the same international flights, on schedules that allow time to deal with the vineyard between flights.

ROBERT YOUNG AND DENISE BRASS

MY PICKS

Camelot offers excellent Pinot Gris, Chardonnay, Pinot Blanc, Riesling and Gewürztraminer, among its whites, and Merlot and Syrah, made from grapes grown in the South Okanagan.

OPENED 2009

3489 East Kelowna Road
Kelowna, BC V1W 4H1

T 250.862.8873

W www.camelotvineyards.ca

WHEN TO VISIT
Open weekends 11 am – 5 pm in April; daily 11 am – 5 pm May to October; Saturdays 11 am – 4 pm November to Christmas; and by appointment.

CANA VINES WINERY

If location is a key to success, Cana Vines Winery launched with an advantage. The winery, with its three hectares (7½ acres) of sunbathed vines, is beside the highway, just south of Vaseux Lake and north of McIntyre Bluff. Not many wineries enjoy as much drive-by traffic.

The vines were planted in 1997 by commercial fisherman Arnie Elgert. The varietal choices—Merlot, Pinot Noir, Pinot Gris, Riesling and Chardonnay—were made on the advice of his friend, Sandor Mayer, the winemaker at Inniskillin Okanagan. When Arnie bought the property in 1990, he just wanted to move his family to the Okanagan from Vancouver. "He was thinking of retiring from fishing," says Filipino-born Mindy, his wife, who had to learn to drive because they were miles from a community.

The family spent the better part of the decade picking rocks and deciding what to grow. Arnie rejected suggestions, such as growing ginseng, to join the Okanagan's burgeoning vineyard operators. Cana Vines was registered as the vineyard's name, inspired by a passage in the Bible about the first miracle attributed to Jesus—turning water into wine at a wedding at Cana.

Arnie was soon thinking about opening a winery. He sent Lisa, one of his daughters, to get a business degree at Trinity Western University with the object of having her run the business. Then in 2007, Arnie was stricken with cancer and died the next year. "We were so devastated," Mindy says. "We tried to get rid of the vineyard so we could forget everything and have a new start." However, they could not sell the vineyard because of an economic slump. As they continued to farm it and sell the grapes, Lisa and her mother decided to realize Arnie's dream. Lisa switched to Okanagan College for winemaking courses.

They arranged to have their initial 2011 vintage made at an existing winery. That gave them time to turn a three-car garage into a functional winery and to complete a tasting room and a picnic area with a fine view of vineyards and McIntyre Canyon to the south. And they have grafted some of their vines to additional varietals, giving them a bigger tool box for making blends.

MY PICKS

Cana Vines launched with a good Pinot Gris and a fine dry Merlot rosé, both from 2011, and a Pinot Noir rosé from 2012, with Merlot maturing in barrel.

OPENED 2013

129 Brauns Road
Oliver, BC V0H 1T2
T   778.439.3340
    250.498.0048
W www.canavineswinery.com

WHEN TO VISIT
Open Monday to Saturday
11 am – 5 pm May to October,
and by appointment.

LISA ELGERT

CASSINI CELLARS

This roadside winery's Tuscany-styled architecture has genuine roots. While Adrian Cassini, the owner, was born in Romania, his grandfather was Italian. Adrian's surname, in fact, was Capeneata. He changed it to Cassini after opening this winery.

His family in Romania had farmed grapes but Adrian credits his interest in wine to restaurant jobs he had both in Romania and in Canada (he came here at the age of 30). "I had a chance to discover the food that goes with the wine," he recalls. "I discovered the taste and the romance of the wine." When he moved to Vancouver, it was to sell and then manufacture and service equipment for fitness clubs. "I have that entrepreneur thing," he says. That led to making props for movie sets, then building houses. After an Okanagan vacation in about 2000, he wanted his own vineyard.

"I see myself in the vineyard," he says, waxing romantic during one interview. "I like the whole package. I like the Okanagan. I like the vineyards. I see myself walking the dog in that vineyard in a few years." Late in 2006, he purchased a lavender farm beside Highway 97, south of Oliver, now the site for his winery. After selling the lavender plants (another example of his entrepreneurism), he planted 2.2 hectares (5½ acres) of vines (Merlot, Cabernet Franc and Pinot Gris) in the spring of 2007. He secured consultant Philip Soo as his winemaker, to make wine with purchased grapes as well as those from for Cassini's modest vineyard.

Adrian applied his con brio style to the winery's design, notably the grand wine shop. Visitors discover a 10-metre (34-foot) bar long enough to accommodate 25 or so tasters. "I can put in another bar on wheels, depending on the need, so that people are not frustrated from waiting," he says. Large windows on each side of the tasting room afford views of the barrel room and part of the winery's production area so that visitors can, as Adrian puts it, "see the magic."

ADRIAN CASSINI

The magic is in the wines, invariably made in a style that is bold and generous; wines that are driven as much by Adrian's exuberant personality as by the terroir.

OPENED 2009

4828 Highway 97
Oliver, BC V0H 1T0

T 250.485.4370

W www.cassini.ca

WHEN TO VISIT
Open daily 10 am – 6 pm May to October.

MY PICKS

The Godfather is the winery's superb icon red, anchoring a family of powerful reds including Maximus, Nobilus Merlot, Malbec and Syrah. The Pinot Noir is elegant. The equally satisfying range of whites includes two Chardonnays, a Viognier, a Sauvignon Blanc and a delightful Pinot Gris called Mamma Mia.

CASTORO DE ORO ESTATE WINERY

Calgarians Bruno Kelle and Stella Schmidt changed the original tongue-twisting name of this winery to Golden Beaver after buying it in 2006. At the time, Australian wineries had popularized animal labels that became known as critter wines. It seemed that a Canadian winery should choose a beaver as its critter. As Bruno and Stella explained it, they have had to work like beavers to renovate the "fixer-upper" winery. The beaver's nickname was Goldie, of course.

The playful labels were effective in the wineshop. However, restaurateurs began asking for a "more serious" label. The challenge was "classing up" the beaver without dropping the animal from their labels. Using Google's translation function, Bruno discovered that castor is Latin for beaver; and the Latin word is the root for versions of beaver in other romance languages. Castoro de Oro was born. "It sounds Old World with a New World look," he explains. "We thought it would be a way to keep our story." Now, the beaver wears a top hat.

Bruno, a technical college graduate, grew up on a tobacco farm in Tillsonburg, Ontario. He helped his family diversify into culinary herbs and, after moving to Calgary in 1996 as a sales and marketing executive, even considered opening his own herb farm. Stella Schmidt, a bookkeeper, grew up in a family that trained dogs. She shares Bruno's passion for farming and that drew them to the lifestyle of Okanagan wine growers. Now, Bruno's son, Kurtis, who graduated from high school in 2012, has also become interested in winemaking.

The winery relies only on grapes from its 2.8-hectare (seven-acre) vineyard, planted in 1980 and 1981 and wedged between Highway 97 and the mountain to the west. The original owner planted more than a dozen varieties, including Merlot, Vidal, Pinot Noir, Pinot Blanc, Riesling, Gewürztraminer, Viognier and perhaps the Okanagan's only block of Siegfried Rebe, a German variety. Bruno, in fact, has so many varieties that he puts some into blends just so that the winery has a manageable portfolio.

STELLA SCHMIDT AND BRUNO KELLE

MY PICKS

Castoro de Oro has carved out a particular niche with tasty dessert wines called Vin de Curé. They are made by air-drying ripe grapes (Merlot and Vidal) to concentrate the flavours and the sugars. The winery makes a fine late-harvest from its planting of Siegfried Rebe.

OPENED 1995
(AS GERSIGHEL WINEBERG)

4004 Highway 97
Oliver, BC V0H 1T1

T 250.495.4991

W www.castorodeoro.com

WHEN TO VISIT
Open daily 10 am – 6 pm May to
mid-October; and noon – 5 pm
mid-October to April (closed
mid-December to mid-January).

C. C. JENTSCH CELLARS

On a Sunday afternoon in June, 2010, the Testalinden Creek mud-slide roared down the mountain, triggered when an old dam broke. It destroyed Chris and Betty Jentsch's home, and sent Betty and her daughter running for their lives. (Chris was not at home during the slide.) Thankfully, the slide missed the nearby Jentsch packing house, a modern building just beside the highway. This was a stroke of good fortune for Chris, who was able to repurpose the building and open it as a winery in 2013.

A self-described entrepreneur, Chris, who was born in Kelowna in 1963, is a third-generation Okanagan fruit grower. He became an independent apple grower in the 1980s, and built his first packing house in 1989 (an undertaking he was forced to repeat only a few years later, after a fire destroyed the packing house in 1991). When apple prices collapsed in the mid 1990s, he converted his orchards to cherries. "We were in a golden time for cherry exports, with a 63-cent Canadian dollar," Chris recalls. "Cherries were getting air freighted to Taiwan."

In 1999, Chris planted his first vineyard, 7.6 hectares (19 acres) on the Golden Mile, just south of the Tinhorn Creek winery. He sold it five years later to go to a much larger project—replacing his cherry trees with vines after overplanting led to a cherry surplus. "That was hard because we were ripping out highly productive cherry blocks that were picture perfect," Chris says.

In his usual style, Chris jumped in with both feet. Between 2005 and 2008, he planted 65,246 vines on a superb 19.4-hectare (48-acre) plateau on the Golden Mile. Once the vines produced, he sold grapes to several wineries, including Andrew Peller Ltd., until Peller's own vineyards were in full production. That led Chris to the final step of turning the packing house into a winery with a capacity of more than 10,000 cases.

CHRIS JENTSCH

The first C. C. Jentsch vintage was made in 2012 at Okanagan Crush Pad. Chris opened his winery with 300 cases of Viognier, 120 cases of Gewürztraminer, 550 cases of Syrah and about 900 cases of a Meritage blend called The Chase. He arranged to have Matt Dumayne, one the OCP winemakers, make the C. C. Jentsch wines in 2013.

OPENED 2013

4522 Highway 97
Oliver, BC V0H 1T1

T 778.439.2091
   250.498.7873 (for appointments)

W www.ccjentschcellars.com

WHEN TO VISIT
Open daily 10 am – 6 pm May to
October, and by appointment.

MY PICKS

C. C. Jentsch debuted with well-made and well-priced wines. In particular, The Chase at $20 is good value for a Meritage with all five Bordeaux reds in the blend. The Viognier is also very good.

CEDARCREEK ESTATE WINERY

This was a failing winery in 1986 when it was purchased by Okanagan-born Ross Fitzpatrick, a successful businessman and now a retired senator. A quarter century later, CedarCreek became one of the valley's best wineries, twice winning Canadian Winery of the Year awards. Early in 2014, the winery attracted a friendly purchase offer from Mission Hill proprietor Anthony von Mandl.

"CedarCreek was not up for sale," the senator says. "However, when approached by Anthony von Mandl, the Fitzpatricks saw another family with a shared vision for the Okanagan Valley who would continue their family legacy for generations to come. We have placed CedarCreek in very good hands."

While under new ownership, CedarCreek continues to operate independently, producing a portfolio crowned by its Platinum series of reserve quality wines. Darryl Brooker, the Australian winemaker who took over the cellars in 2010, crafts excellent vineyard-designated Pinot Noir, Riesling, Viognier and Pinot Gris, extending a range already including Chardonnay and Bordeaux varietals. The mature plantings in the CedarCreek vineyards at the winery and near Osoyoos complement Mission Hill's extensive holdings. The oldest Pinot Noir blocks at the winery, Block 2 and Block 4, are the length of a football field apart but Block 2 yields a bright, feminine wine while Block 4 yields a deep and powerful wine.

CedarCreek is one of a growing number of wineries operated by Von Mandl Family Estates. "Each winery operates independently, with separate staffing, management, and its own hallmark and identity," Anthony says. "The common purpose is to produce wines that can stand alongside the best in the world." CedarCreek's gleaming white Mediterranean architecture, its Vineyard Terrace Restaurant and its large tasting room continue to make this a favourite destination winery for tourists.

DARRYL BROOKER

Born in Canberra in 1973, Darryl came to the Okanagan after making wine in Australia, New Zealand and Ontario. With the confidence that comes with experience, he embraces both traditional and New World winemaking practices. He employs wild yeasts; he ferments some wines in concrete eggs. In 2013, CedarCreek became the first Okanagan winery to ferment some reds in a 400-litre clay amphora made in Italy. These practises all add to the texture and the complexity of the wines.

MY PICKS

Everything, including the aromatic Ehrenfelser which has a cult following; the German-style low alcohol Riesling; and especially the nuanced Pinot Noirs.

OPENED 1980
(AS UNIACKE)

5445 Lakeshore Road
Kelowna, BC V1W 4S5

T 250.764.8866
   1.800.730.9463 (toll free)

W www.cedarcreek.bc.ca

WHEN TO VISIT
Open daily 10 am – 7 pm May to October; and from 11 am – 5 pm November to April.

RESTAURANT
Vineyard Terrace
Open daily 11:30 – 3:30 mid-June to mid-September.

CELISTA ESTATE WINERY

Celista Estate Winery takes its name from the community on the north shore of Shuswap Lake. A scenic 30-kilometre drive from the Trans-Canada Highway, Celista is British Columbia's northernmost winery (until the 2015 opening of Northern Lights Estate Winery in Prince George).

The winery is the latest career for Jake Ootes (pronounced O-tis, like the elevator company) and Margaret Bailes-Ootes, his wife. Born in Holland in 1942, Jake came to Canada with his parents when he was eight and grew up in Renfrew, Ontario. After working as a journalist, he became a public information officer in Ottawa with the Department of Northern Affairs.

In 1967 he moved to Yellowknife as an executive assistant to Stuart Hodgson, the commissioner of the Northwest Territories. Three years later he took charge of public affairs and communications for the territorial government. In 1975 he bought a small newspaper in Fort Saskatchewan (near Edmonton), and built it into a trio of community papers that he sold eight years later to a large publisher. Returning to Yellowknife, he launched an in-flight airline magazine. "Then I decided I would go into politics," Jake says. He was elected to the territorial legislature in 1995, eventually becoming Minister of Education before retiring in 2003.

He and Margaret, the former owner of a Yellowknife art gallery, then moved to a 65-hectare (160-acre) farm at Celista that Margaret had acquired earlier. "This property was a bit of a wasteland," Jake remembers. "We thought we should plant grapes and get into wine." Beginning in 2002, he planted varieties already succeeding in other Shuswap vineyards, including Maréchal Foch, Ortega, Siegerrebe, Madeleine Sylvaner, Madeleine Angevine and Gewürztraminer. Needing another red variety, he added Gamay in a 2011 planting that has expanded the vineyard to three hectares (about seven acres). He

JAKE OOTES

has also purchased grapes from other vineyards in the region.

Jake relies on consultant Lee Holland (a winemaker at Dirty Laundry Vineyard). "I have never made wine," Jake says. "First things first—perfect the grapes." The compact winery is in a spacious former garage. The tasting room, which opened in July 2010 and which features two wood-panelled bars, is on the ground floor of their home, with breathtaking views over the bucolic countryside.

Celista's wine labels are memorable by having sketches of either Jake's bearded visage or Margaret in profile. "Are we enjoying it?" Jake says of the winery and vineyard. "Yes. We are working very, very hard but it is enjoyable and it is not stressful work."

OPENED 2010

2319 Beguelin Road
Celista, BC V0E 1M6

T 250.955.8600

W www.celistawine.com

WHEN TO VISIT
Open daily 10:30 am – 5:30 pm
mid-May to mid-October, and by
appointment.

PICNIC PATIO

MY PICKS

Riesling and two white blends—Celista Cuvée and Conundrum—showed the bracing fresh and crisp finish of the 2010 vintage, a classic cool-climate year. Marg's Rosé is a fine dry rosé while the Maréchal Foch is an easy-drinking red.

CERELIA VINEYARDS & ESTATE WINERY

Logger David Mutch, who grew up in the Similkameen Valley, is a farmer by avocation. For some years he and Peggy, his wife (a nurse), satisfied that avocation by growing hay until concluding that they could do far better with a vineyard. In 2005, they bought a derelict orchard near Cawston and began planting vines. Because they have full time jobs, they enlisted other family members to develop the winery.

David's daughter, Megan returned to the Similkameen Valley from Alberta with husband Corey Witter, an oil field worker, and their children. Megan, who was born in 1983, had worked as a pharmacy technician before becoming a full-time mother. When her family decided to open the winery, she took Okanagan College's winemaking course and, after mentoring with Orofino's John Weber, became Cerelia's winemaker. The winery currently makes between 500 and 1,000 cases a year.

When the winery was being launched, David's brother, Dennis, a retired businessman, and his wife, Roxanne, moved from Edmonton and also became involved in managing the winery. When the partnership dissolved in 2013, David and Peggy decided to reorganize the business and continue on their own.

Their 3.4-hectare (8½-acre) vineyard grows Gamay, Merlot, Pinot Gris, Chardonnay and Orange Muscat. In the 2013 vintage, the white varieties have been combined in a single blended wine. While most of the Merlot is aging in barrel, a portion was used for rosé, building on the success that Cerelia has previously enjoyed with rosé.

The wines are bottled with labels that show the vintage in Roman numerals. This evolves from the winery's name: Cerelia is the harvest festival for Ceres, a Roman goddess of agriculture.

MEGAN MUTCH

MY PICKS

The portfolio is undergoing a redevelopment. In the past, the whites were fresh and crisp, made in an uncomplicated fruit-forward style. The reds have included a Bordeaux blend, called Misceo, which won gold in one of the first competitions in which it was entered.

OPENED 2009

2235 Ferko Road
Cawston, BC V0X 1C2

T   250.499.8000

W www.cerelia.ca

WHEN TO VISIT
Friday to Monday 10 am – 5 pm
May to October, and by
appointment.

CHECKMATE ARTISANAL WINERY

A 1992 Chardonnay grown on this property put Mission Hill Family Estate Winery on the map after winning the first major international award for any British Columbia winery at a London wine competition. Two decades later, when the opportunity presented itself, Mission Hill proprietor Anthony von Mandl bought the property for CheckMate, a winery specializing in Chardonnay.

The original winery at this location was Domaine Combret (later renamed Antelope Ridge) and was operated by Robert and Olivier Combret. The Combrets, who immigrated to the Okanagan in 1992, had been wine growers in the south of France since 1638. With an eye for good terroir, they bought a premium hillside site. Olivier, who had just graduated from the Montpellier wine school, designed an innovative gravity-flow winery. His 1993 Chardonnay won the first medal for a Canadian wine at the Chardonnay du Monde competition in France.

The Combret vineyard adjoins the vineyard that grew the grapes for the Mission Hill Chardonnay wine. With the Combrets retiring from the wine business, Anthony bought both properties in 2012, combining them to give CheckMate about 12 hectares (30 acres) of vines. The history suggests this is a premier Chardonnay site.

The winery's gravity-flow design remains but the processing equipment has been replaced with the latest in winemaking technology. Philip McGahan, a young Australian who had been working with a top Pinot Noir producer in Sonoma, has been hired as CheckMate's winemaker and general manager.

Like CedarCreek, which Anthony bought in 2014, CheckMate operates independently from Mission Hill. "What this winery is going to be all about is making artisanal wines," Anthony says. "These wines are unfined. Everything is gravity fed. We are using a lot of wild yeasts. It will be unique in terms of wine styles, and a very limited number of wines will be produced there." In addition to Chardonnay, the winery expects to produce organic Merlot. Philip's experience with Pinot Noir has been harnessed for experimental wines with that variety.

Why CheckMate? "If you look at a chessboard, think of each of the individual squares being a block in a vineyard," Anthony explains. "It allows us to really dial in on specific blocks and make some very limited edition wines." Not having a tasting room emphasizes the exclusivity of the wines. "The winery is unlikely to be open to the public," Anthony says. "Because the general manager has a very small team, it is going to be hard to visit."

OPENED 2014

4799 Wild Rose Street
Oliver. BC V0H 1T0

WHEN TO VISIT
No public tasting room.

ANTHONY VON MANDL

MY PICKS

No wines were available for tasting at press time.

CHURCH & STATE WINES

While Church & State originated on Vancouver Island, it planted roots firmly in the Okanagan when it opened its Coyote Bowl winery in 2010. Crisply modern and gleaming with stainless steel and glass, this Robert Mackenzie–designed winery is set dramatically on the plateau, commanding a panoramic vista of vineyards and mountains. The real drama here is in the glass, with bold, ripe wines expressing the terroir of the South Okanagan.

The Brentwood Bay winery opened in 2002 as Victoria Estate, and was near failure two years later when it was purchased by Kim Pullen, a former tax lawyer with a knack for turning businesses around. The key to putting Church & State back on its feet was securing good Okanagan grapes through developing or leasing 44.5 hectares (110 acres) south of Oliver. At first, grapes were transported to Vancouver Island for processing until the winery moved production to a leased South Okanagan packing house, adding the Coyote Bowl facility for premium barrel-aged wines. Still open, the Brentwood Bay winery focuses on sparkling wines but also sells Church & State's Okanagan wines.

There is a clear style to the Church & State wines, the result of a meeting of minds between Kim and winemaker Jeff Del Nin, an Australian-trained Canadian who came to Church & State in 2008 from Burrowing Owl Winery. "We have a firm idea of what we want to make," Jeff says. "Our stylistic goal with reds is the 2006 Quintessential." He is referring to the flagship Bordeaux blend here. It is "beautiful, ripe, rich but soft and approachable, very friendly to people. They don't need to put it down for 10 years before it softens. That is what we are ultimately shooting for."

Church & State's objective is to produce 10,000 to 12,000 cases a year, 65 percent of it red wine. The red wine portfolio is built largely around the Bordeaux varieties that grow best in its South Okanagan vineyards. There are two blends, Quintessential and the Coyote Bowl

JEFF DEL NIN

Meritage, along with Merlot, Cabernet Franc and Cabernet Sauvignon. There is also a Syrah, a big red in the overall style of Church & State reds. The white wine portfolio is led by big whites—a Chardonnay made in the unabashed rich California style and a powerful Viognier—and a blend of three Rhône varieties, called TreBella. The common thread running through all the wines is how full they are on the palate. "I place a very high priority on the texture of the wines I make," Jeff says.

OPENED 2002
(AS VICTORIA ESTATE WINERY)

4516 Ryegrass Road
Oliver, BC V0H 1T1
T 250.498.2700
W www.churchandstatewines.com

WHEN TO VISIT
Open daily 11 am – 6 pm May
to October.

MY PICKS

The quality here is excellent, beginning with Quintessential. The premium tier is now labelled CBS for Coyote Bowl Series, followed by a Church & State tier. The value-priced tier is labelled Church Mouse. Perhaps the most sought-after white is the remarkable Gravelbourg Vineyard Chardonnay, made from mature vines farmed by grower Joseph Boutin.

CLOS DU SOLEIL WINERY

The world's best-known wine marathon is the Marathon du Médoc, a run that includes wine tasting stations. Perhaps it was competing there in 2002 with his wife, Bonnie Henry, that confirmed Spencer Massie's determination to open a winery four years later in the Similkameen Valley.

His interest in wine began long before that. Born in 1961 in the British Columbia coastal community of Alert Bay (his father was an air traffic controller), Spencer joined the Canadian navy in 1979 as an officer trainee. During a vacation five years later, he backpacked the French wine country. He was soon ordering wines for the ship's mess and leading on-board port tastings. He retired from the navy in 2000 as a lieutenant commander and, having acquired a master of business administration degree, set up a business incubator firm in Toronto. He moved that business to Vancouver in 2005 when Bonnie, a physician, took a senior medical post there.

Spencer and Bonnie enlisted three other couples as partners in the wine venture: Ottawa-based Gus Kramer, a former naval colleague, and Lisa Underhill; Peter and Andria Lee, a Vancouver business couple; and Calgarian oil executives Leslie LeQuelenec and his partner, Sue Lee. In 2013, Michael Clark, a former investment manager with winemaking training, joined to oversee winery and vineyard operations.

The Clos du Soleil vineyard is a four-hectare (10-acre) former orchard near Keremeos planted entirely with red and white Bordeaux varieties. "I love everything classic French," Spencer says. "My family roots go back to Normandy."

The wines, with an annual production of about 2,400 cases, reflect the French palates of the owners. The consulting winemaker is Kelowna-born Ann Sperling who, by coincidence, was a high school classmate there with Spencer. The wines are made primarily with grapes from the estate. When the winery can secure top-quality grapes

ANN SPERLING

SPENCER MASSIE

from other Similkameen growers, it releases these wines (currently a Pinot Blanc and a Merlot) under its Grower's Series label.

MY PICKS

Everything. Signature Red and its little brother, Célestiale, are fine Bordeaux reds. There are two interpretations of Sauvignon Blanc: Fumé Blanc is barrel-fermented and Capella is fermented in stainless steel. The Cabernet Sauvignon Rosé is outstanding.

OPENED 2008

2568 Upper Bench Road
Keremeos, BC V0X 1N4

T 250.499.2831
250.808.7744 (to book an appointment)

W www.closdusoleil.ca

WHEN TO VISIT
Open Thursday to Monday 10 am – 5 pm May to October, and by appointment.

COLUMBIA GARDENS VINEYARD & WINERY

In 2006 South African mining engineer Ben De Jager and his wife Tersia chose to emigrate to Canada. They never regretted the choice but, after living six years in Timmins and Flin Flon, they tired of cold winters and began looking at vineyards and wineries in British Columbia. Before taking up engineering, Ben, who was born in 1962, had studied at Marlow Agricultural College in South Africa where students managed the vineyard and made wine.

The founders of Columbia Gardens, the first winery in the Kootenays, had listed the winery for sale. When the De Jagers came across the listing, they visited the Columbia Valley and, as Tersia puts it, "fell in love with the area." They purchased the winery in August 2013. Because Ben is still commuting from a potash mine under development in Saskatchewan, they contracted Lawrence Wallace to make the 2013 vintage for them.

Lawrence, a veteran winemaker, is one of the former owners. He and the late Tom Bryden, his father-in-law, started planting grapes in the 1990s (the vineyard is now 4.8 hectares or 12 acres) on a family farm 16 kilometres (10 miles) down the Columbia River valley from Trail. The Bryden family had lived on this 20-hectare (50-acre) farm in the Columbia Valley since the 1930s, growing a range of products from vegetables to hay. They planted Maréchal Foch, Pinot Noir, Gewürztraminer, Auxerrois, Chardonnay and small blocks of Kerner, Siegerrebe, and Schönburger. Varieties not suitable for the Kootenays, like Merlot, were purchased from the Okanagan.

The De Jagers continue to produce what Tersia calls "the old favourites." They intend to expand production and sales, either by planting additional vineyard or by buying more grapes. Meanwhile, Tersia has renovated a house already on the property, turning it into a three-unit guest house with conference facilities. "We have lots of expansion in mind," she says.

TERSIA AND BEN DE JAGER (COURTESY OF COLUMBIA GARDENS)

The quiet charm of the Columbia Gardens wine shop continues to surprise first-time visitors, who do not expect a tasting room with sophisticated décor this far off the wine touring route. The shop is a comfortably appointed log house with a patio deck for wine tasting and picnic lunches in fine weather.

OPENED 2001

9340 Station Road
RR1, Site 11, Comp 61
Trail, BC V1R 4W6
T   250.367.7493
W www.cgwinery.com

WHEN TO VISIT
Open daily 11 am – 5 pm May to October, and by appointment.

PICNIC FACILITIES

MY PICKS

Maréchal Foch is the backbone for several wines here—the premium Maréchal Foch Private Reserve and Kootenay Red (a blend of several vintages of Foch). Garden Gold, Station White and Gewürztraminer are popular white wines. The Station Road Rosé, made from Pinot Noir, is refreshing. DeJager's Merlot, a new label, is made with Okanagan grapes.

CORCELETTES ESTATE WINERY

Chasselas vines dominate the one-hectare (2½-acre) vineyard at the winery, reflecting the Swiss heritage of Urs and Barbara Baessler and son Charlie, the winemaker. However, this family came to launch a winery in the Similkameen Valley by a circuitous route.

"It all started because my mom and dad on our place in Switzerland had the best bloodline in Simmental cattle," Urs says. A friendly big-boned man with a booming voice, Urs explains that his given name means bear; it fits him. Born in 1954, he was 17 when four Manitoba farmers bought six Simmental heifers from Domaine de Corcelettes, the Baessler family farm on Lake Neuchâtel. Urs accompanied the heifers to Canada, stayed the summer and decided he wanted to farm here. He spent several years travelling back and forth, learning how to farm in Canada while finishing compulsory military service in Switzerland. Staked by his grandfather with a down payment, Urs and Barbara bought a grain farm near Brandon and grew their first crop in 1978.

When wheat prices collapsed in the early 1990s, they diversified with a buffalo farm in Wyoming. Urs figures he was 10 years too early. There was little market for farmed buffalo among consumers who thought he was selling an endangered species. "I said let's quit this," he declared in frustration. "We did not like the winters either." He and Barbara moved to British Columbia in 2007, attracted by mountains reminding them of Switzerland, bought an organic garlic farm near Cawston and converted it to vines in 2010. "The goal always was to have some grapes," Urs says.

The goal became feasible after son Charlie, born in 1985, completed a degree in environmental engineering at the University of Lethbridge and came to visit his parents, taking a job as a vineyard worker. "Farming chose me," he says. In 2008, he joined Burrowing Owl Vineyards, eventually becoming one of the vineyard managers. The Baessler family decided that Charlie would be their winemaker, with

URS AND BARBARA BAESSLER AND SON, CHARLIE

Charlie learning under the tutelage of Bertus Albertyn, then Burrowing Owl's winemaker.

The winery, with a modest target of 1,500 cases by the fourth year, debuted with 112 cases of TriVium 2012, a white blend anchored by Chasselas, and 85 cases of Menhir 2011, a blend of Syrah and Cabernet Sauvignon. Menhir is the name for stone obelisks erected throughout Europe for ceremonial purposes by prehistoric peoples. A menhir stands on the Baessler family farm in Switzerland and Urs intends to erect a similar boulder at the winery.

OPENED 2013

295 Beecroft River Road
Cawston, BC V0X 1C1

T 250.408.8825

W www.corceletteswine.ca

WHEN TO VISIT
By appointment only.

MY PICKS

TriVium is a charming and refreshing blend of Chasselas, Pinot Gris and Gewürztraminer. Menhir is a generously full and satisfying red wine. Oracle is the winery's fruity Zweigelt rosé.

COVERT FARMS FAMILY ESTATE

The historic 243-hectare (600-acre) Covert Farms property north of Oliver achieved organic certification in 2010 and is believed to be the largest organic farm in the Okanagan. That includes the grapes on the winery's 12-hectare (30-acre) vineyard along with fruits, vegetables and more than 15 varieties of tomatoes.

No one can accuse Gene and Shelly Covert of monoculture farming, a criticism sometimes levelled at other grape growers. Farming is in Gene's blood. Born in 1971, he is the grandson of the farm's founder. He joined the family business after getting a degree in physical geography. Shelly, an Edmonton-born teacher, runs the farm's market selling organically grown produce directly to the public.

Covert Farms was founded in 1959 on the plateau just south of McIntyre Bluff by George Covert, a Californian who came to the Okanagan to grow tomatoes, onions, tree fruits and, ultimately, grapes. The vineyard was large enough in the early 1980s that a mechanical harvester was tested (with indifferent results, because the early harvesters mangled the vines). Except for six hectares (15 acres) of table grapes, vines were pulled out in 1988 to make way for new apple varieties.

In 2005, wine grapes returned. Gene's plantings included the five Bordeaux reds, Zinfandel, Syrah, Pinot Noir, Pinot Blanc, Sémillon, Sauvignon Blanc, Viognier and Roussanne. The severe early frost during the Canadian Thanksgiving weekend in 2009 killed a large block of vines that had been planted that spring; Gene put it down to the risks of farming and replanted. (Andrew Peller Ltd., with a larger vineyard on leased land at the farm, suffered similar damage, also replanted and installed 26 wind machines for frost protection.)

Because some of the farm's picturesque buildings could easily be turned into a winery, the partners launched quickly with purchased

GENE COVERT

grapes, making 500 cases of wine. In full production, the vineyard supports 5,000 cases a year.

The winery's appeal encompasses the farm's many other attractions, including farm festivals, guided tours and shopping at the farm market or picking your own produce. There is a hiking trail to the top of McIntyre Bluff. New since 2013 is a growing agricultural museum called the Covert Farms Agricultural Preservation Society.

OPENED 2006
(AS DUNHAM & FROESE)

300 Covert Place
Oliver, BC V0H 1T0

T 250.498.9463

W www.covertfarms.ca

WHEN TO VISIT
Open daily 11 am – 5 pm May to October, and by appointment.

MY PICKS

The top red and white blends are released under the Amicitia label, Latin for "friends." Notable as well is a blend of Cabernet Sauvignon, Zinfandel and Syrah called MDC, a tribute to Gene's late father, Michael. The winery also makes good Pinot Blanc, Pinot Noir and Merlot.

CROWSNEST VINEYARDS

Crowsnest Vineyards is a taste of Germany in the Similkameen. Here, you can wash down a plate of bratwurst or a huge Jaeger schnitzel with a glass of wine while chatting with a member of the Heinecke family, owners of the winery since 1998. Olaf Heinecke, the patriarch of the family, was born in Leipzig. After a career as a developer in Germany, he came to the Okanagan. Crowsnest was a struggling winery producing only 500 cases a year, almost all white, when Olaf bought it.

The entire family has been marshalled to turn it into the Similkameen's largest winery, now making 6,000 cases annually, almost half of it red. Sabine, Olaf's wife, keeps an eye on the restaurant, housed in the Landgasthof, the cozy inn that the winery added in 2005. Son Sascha, with a diploma in hotel management, presides over the tasting room with professional warmth. Clad in a white apron, he bakes about 500 loaves of remarkable bread daily in a wood-fired oven. Some visitors believe Crowsnest is worth a visit for the bread alone, never mind the wines.

Daughter Ann, who has a German winemaking diploma, makes the wines. The portfolio includes Merlot and Pinot Noir from the winery's own 5.5-hectare (13½-acre) vineyard. The most acclaimed whites are the Family Reserve Riesling and the unoaked Chardonnay Stahltank (the German word for the steel tanks in which the wine is aged before being bottled). Crowsnest has also released wines labelled Barcello Canyon, a name drawn from the nearby canyon that pierces the mountain range between the Similkameen and Okanagan valleys. The gravel road through the canyon is open in summer. The savvy locals advise driving it only with a sturdy vehicle—or with a rental car.

In 2013, the winery went on the market for $2.9 million. There are likely to be new owners during the life of this book.

I like the uncomplicated freshness of the Chardonnay and Riesling. Among the reds, my favourite is the Crowsnest Merlot.

OPENED 1995

2035 Surprise Drive
Cawston, BC V0X 1C0

T 250.499.5129

W www.crowsnestvineyards.com

WHEN TO VISIT
Open daily 10 am – 5 pm.

RESTAURANT
Bavarian cuisine, open daily
(except Tuesday) noon – 10 pm.

ACCOMMODATION
Country Inn with two large and
five medium-sized guestrooms.

SASCHA HEINECKE

CULMINA FAMILY ESTATE WINERY

The winery name is simply explained: it is the culmination of a career in wine for Donald and Elaine Triggs and their daughter, Sara. The parents spared no expense to create the South Okanagan's most ambitious winery at an age when others would retire. "Retirement to me is a nasty word because it implies stopping," says Donald, who was born in Manitoba in 1944. "I don't think life is about stopping. It is about continuing and doing what you love."

He began his career in 1972 with the winery arm of John Labatt Ltd., which he eventually left to run the North American operations of a British fertilizer company. But in 1989, when Labatt sold its wineries, Donald led the team buying them. This became Vincor, which had grown to become the world's 14th largest wine company by the time Constellation Brands (the largest) took over Vincor in 2006. After a brief year away from the industry, Don and Elaine bought what has become 22.6 hectares (56 acres) of densely planted vines on three mountainside benches on the Golden Mile.

They tapped the expertise of Alain Sutre, the same Bordeaux consultant they had worked with when Vincor (with a French partner) began the Osoyoos Larose vineyard and winery in 1999. Alain assured the Triggs family that they could produce even greater wines because the Okanagan terroir is much better understood. With that assurance, the Triggs have set out to raise the bar again, just as Vincor had done earlier with Osoyoos Larose. They even lured winemaker Pascal Madevon to Culmina from Osoyoos Larose.

The three vineyard benches, each with differing soils and elevations, provide winemaking options. Merlot, Cabernet Franc and Cabernet Sauvignon comprise the largest blocks, followed by Chardonnay, Riesling, Syrah, Malbec and Petit Verdot. The surprise is the Okanagan's first Grüner Veltliner, the Austrian white, planted on the highest elevation vineyard in the South Okanagan.

ELAINE AND DONALD TRIGGS

There are other surprises here. The gravity-flow winery's floor is a checkerboard of black and white Italian tiles under French chandeliers. The antique tasting room table came from the barn of Doukhobor leader Peter Verigin. The winery keeps visitor groups small but offers in-depth personal vineyard tours. There is no better place to view the Okanagan Valley than from Culmina vineyards, with a glass of wine in hand.

OPENED 2013

4790 Wild Rose Street
Oliver, BC V0H 1T0

T   250.498.0789

W www.culmina.ca

WHEN TO VISIT
Open daily 10 am – 5 pm May to October for tastings, tours and sales; Monday to Friday 10 am – 4 pm November to April for sales.

MY PICKS

Hypothesis is the winery's elegant red Bordeaux blend. The Burgundian-styled Chardonnay is called Dilemma because the Triggs family debated whether to keep the old Chardonnay vines that came with the property or to replace them with better clones. In the end, the old vines were removed.

D'ANGELO ESTATE WINERY

This winery has one of the most strategic locations on the Naramata Bench. Guests staying at the bed and breakfast units here find themselves within walking distance of half a dozen wineries, and they can take a break from wine touring by hiking the scenic Kettle Valley Trail, which swings just past the winery.

Sal D'Angelo, who runs a winery (also called D'Angelo) near Windsor in Ontario, which opened in 1989, has been attracted to the Naramata Bench since he started vacationing here in the early 1990s. He has a rare condition of the nervous system called Guillan-Barre syndrome which is far less trying in the dry Okanagan than in humid southern Ontario. Not that he has ever let the condition hold him back: during one four-hour medical treatment some years ago, he landed a $1,100 wine order from the doctor.

Born in Italy in 1953, Sal grew up in Canada in an immigrant home where his family made wine each fall. "I grew up with the smell of fermenting grapes," he says. He became a science teacher but began to plant grapes in 1983 on his Windsor-area property, opening a winery six years later. During an early Naramata vacation, he presented one of his Ontario reds to Hillside Cellars founder Vera Klokocka with the cocky assertion that the Okanagan was not suited to growing big reds. She produced a Cabernet Sauvignon (she was the first in the Okanagan to make this varietal). Sal changed his mind and started considering the Okanagan.

Since 2001, Sal has acquired an entire peninsula on the eastern bluffs above Lake Okanagan, only minutes north of Penticton. He planted about three hectares (7½ acres) initially, with room to triple his plantings. Not afraid to be original, Sal was the first in the Okanagan to plant Tempranillo, the leading red variety in Spain. He also planted red Bordeaux varieties and some Pinot Noir and intends to add Viognier, Sauvignon Blanc and Chenin Blanc. The initial winery is in a

SAL D'ANGELO

metal-clad barn on the property and the wine shop is on the ground floor of the family home. Longer-term plans call for the building of a gravity-flow winery.

OPENED 2007

979 Lochore Road
Penticton, BC V2A 8V1
T 250.493.1364
W www.dangelowinery.com

WHEN TO VISIT
Open Monday to Saturday
10 am – 6 pm and Sunday 11 am
– 5 pm May to October; and by
appointment.

PICNIC AREA

ACCOMMODATION
Vineyard View Bed and
Breakfast, with a chalet and
three suites.

MY PICKS

The flagship wine is a red blend called Sette Coppa, which means seventh measure. The wine takes its name from the nickname of Sal's great-grandfather, Donato, who persuaded the local flour mill to take every seventh measure as payment for grinding his grain when others were being assessed every sixth measure. Also, try the Pinot Noir, the Tempranillo, the Cabernet Merlot and the Tempranillo icewine.

DAYDREAMER WINES

Two of the signature wines from Daydreamer are Syrahs, a variety that practically runs in the veins of winemaker Marcus Ansems. Marcus's Australian family once owned a share of Mount Langi Ghiran, the legendary Shiraz producer in the state of Victoria, and his uncle, Trevor Mast, was a winemaker there. Today, Marcus owns Daydreamer with his wife, Rachel.

"One of my favourite wines in the world was made at my family winery," Marcus says. "It is just unique to that site . . . an atypical Shiraz. That wine was what inspired me to want to get involved with the industry." Born in 1974, he graduated in enology in 1996 from the University of Adelaide. He went abroad to gain experience, first with Simonsig in South Africa and then in Tuscany and the Rhône. He picked up his career in Australia briefly before a Canadian wine entrepreneur, Peter Jensen, recruited him in 1999 to run wineries in Ontario and Nova Scotia. Whilst in Niagara he met Rachel, an accountant with a talent in design and photography, before returning to Australia in 2002 as a consulting winemaker.

Rachel and Marcus moved to British Columbia in 2004, where Marcus became the winemaker for Blasted Church Vineyards and then, a year later, for Therapy Vineyards. Since late 2008, he has been the buyer for Hemispheres Wine Guild, a Canadian club for wine collectors.

Daydreamer is the culmination of a family winery dream that Rachel and Marcus share. The winery's Merlot-based blend is named Amelia, for their daughter. Daydreamer launched with about 1,000 cases including Chardonnay and the two Syrahs, one co-fermented with Viognier. "I like cool-climate Syrah," Marcus says. The wines come in two tiers, with the popular-priced wines under the Daydreamer label. For premium wines, he has revived the Marcus Ansems label that he first created while he was at Therapy.

MARCUS ANSEMS

They intend to remain a boutique winery, producing perhaps 2,000 cases a year. To keep the costs in check, they lease a quarter of their five hectares (12 acres) and they lease space in a new custom crush winery. "I have worked for other people and I have had other partners and lots of shareholders," Marcus says. "This is just my wife and I. We can do as little or as much as we want. It is a dream."

OPENED 2014

1493 Todd Road
Penticton, BC V2A 8T6

T   778.514.0026

W   www.daydreamerwines.ca

WHEN TO VISIT
By appointment only.

MY PICKS

No wines were available for tasting but I have always been impressed by the wines Marcus made for previous employers in the Okanagan.

DEEP ROOTS VINEYARD

The winery's name was prompted by the Hardman family's four generations on the Naramata Bench. Bryan Hardman's grandfather came here in 1919 after four years of military service, working initially with pioneer fruit grower Carl Aikins who once owned about 250 hectares (600 acres).

The Hardmans became major fruit growers as well; Bryan, who was born in 1950, once owned 20 hectares (50 acres) of apple trees. He was also an industry activist, serving as president of BC Tree Fruits, the Okanagan's apple marketing organization. It is famously tough to make a living with apples, even for a grower as progressive as Bryan who regularly embraced trendy new varieties like Gala and Fuji. "Behind any successful farmer around here, you will find his wife has a good job," Bryan quips. His wife, Debra, who has a master's in clinical psychology, manages the Ministry for Children and Families in the South Okanagan.

Bryan planted two hectares (five acres) of grapes in 1996 "just to see if I liked it." When he did, he gradually replaced his apple trees with vines and left the apple business entirely in 2010. Now he owns eight hectares (20 acres) of vineyard and manages another four hectares (10 acres).

He began thinking about a winery after his son Will, who was born in 1983, began working in the vineyards in 2006. In addition to studying winemaking at Okanagan College, Will has done crushes with wineries in New Zealand and South Africa. He also worked with Van Westen Vineyards, where Deep Roots made its 2012 vintage, a total of 13 barrels of Merlot, Malbec and Syrah. The new Tillar Road winery was completed for the 2013 harvest, at which point the winery added Chardonnay, Pinot Gris and Gamay Noir to its portfolio.

The winery launched with just over 1,000 cases of wine, most of which likely will be sold from Deep Roots' wine shop. The winery has

BRYAN AND DEBRA HARDMAN

the capacity to produce between 3,000 and 5,000 cases, with Bryan still selling some of his crop to CedarCreek, among other wineries. Almost all of the Deep Roots wines are estate-grown. "We're not going to release anything that we are not proud of," Bryan promises.

MY PICKS

No wines available for tasting at press time.

PROPOSED OPENING 2014

860 Tillar Rd.
Naramata. BC V0H 1N0
T 250.496.5681
W www.deeprootsvineyard.ca

ACCOMMODATION
Private one-bedroom cabin.

DESERT HILLS ESTATE WINERY

Twin brothers Randy and Jessie Toor, born in 1964 in Punjab, spent their summers working in Okanagan vineyards after coming to Canada. Having acquired a taste for the land, they bought a 10-hectare (25-acre) apple orchard in 1988 on Black Sage Road, one of the Okanagan's best vineyard areas. When they discovered that apples of only middling quality can be grown on Black Sage, they switched to grapes (mostly Bordeaux reds) in 1995. They named the vineyard Three Boys—their brother, Dave, is also a partner. Their sponsor was Langley's Chaberton Estate Winery, which needed a reliable supply of red grapes to supplement the white varieties in its own vineyard. Since 2005, they have added four other vineyards and now farm 28 hectares (70 acres).

The demand for their own wines has enabled them to increase production to 20,000 cases, ten times the modest volume with which they began. "It was a little dream to start a small winery," Randy says. The tasting room is still in a modest building next to the vineyard, at the end of a short but grand driveway. Behind it is a 241-square-metre (2,600-square-foot) addition built on top of a barrel cellar in 2005, for the extra tanks and new equipment required for the winery's growth.

Desert Hills is the Okanagan's largest producer of Gamay Noir. It was growing so much of that variety that, several years ago, a small Gamay block could be grafted to Zinfandel. That added another big red to a portfolio dominated by big reds, including a port-style wine called Ambassador.

The Toors have not forgotten their roots. Proceeds from tastings at the winery have been dedicated to a school in their home village in the Punjab. The funds are used for texts, supplies and teacher training. As well, the Toors helped finance a sports stadium at the school where they also support an annual soccer tournament.

RANDY AND JESSIE TOOR

MY PICKS

Everything. The wine to ask for, if it is not sold out, is the award-winning Syrah, which is remarkable for intense nutmeg spice in both the aroma and the taste. Other notable wines are Mirage (a Meritage blend), Malbec, Cabernet Sauvignon, Merlot, Gamay, Chardonnay, Pinot Gris, Gewürztraminer and Viognier.

OPENED 2003

4078 Black Sage Road
Oliver, BC V0H 1T1
T   250.498.6664
W www.deserthills.ca

WHEN TO VISIT
Open daily 10 am – 5:30 pm
April to October, and by
appointment.

DIRTY LAUNDRY VINEYARD

This winery set a new benchmark for slightly outrageous labels in 2009 when it released a red wine called Bordello. Naturally, the wine is a Bordeaux blend (Cabernet Sauvignon and Merlot) but the label extends the whimsical romp that began in 2005, when the winery changed its name from Scherzinger Vineyards to Dirty Laundry.

The winery was started a decade earlier by a former Bavarian wood-carver named Edgar Scherzinger who, on retiring in 2001, sold it to protegés Ron and Cher Watkins. To refresh the winery's image, Ron and Cher enlisted Bernie Hadley-Beauregard, the Vancouver marketer whose earlier successes included turning Prpich Hills Winery into Blasted Church Vineyards. Bernie uncovered the tale of a former Chinese railroad labourer whose Summerland laundry a century ago came to be called "the dirty laundry" because it fronted for a bordello.

Dirty Laundry was an instant hit; wines were sold in a matter of weeks. Needing to expand the tiny winery quickly (it was only making 2,000 cases a year), Ron and Cher first looked for partners and then sold the winery in the fall of 2006, to a group of four Albertans headed by Fort McMurray lawyer Bob Campbell. The lawyer has had a long love affair with Summerland, having owned a country house on the lake since 1977. He had just planted a vineyard nearby, with a winery in mind, when he was able to buy Dirty Laundry.

Production has grown to 18,000 cases a year, almost the capacity of the new winery that was built in 2010, and Dirty Laundry now is supported by more than 14 hectares (35 acres) of vineyards operated by its owners. The plantings are heavily tilted to Gewürztraminer and Pinot Noir, signature varietals in the wine shop.

The entertaining strategy of edgy "wink-wink, nudge-nudge" labels catches the fancy of wine tourists. The winery's best seller is its Woo Woo Vines Gewürztraminer, probably because a little touch of sweetness goes well with intimations of naughtiness.

WINEMAKER MASON SPINK (PHOTO BY STUART BISH)

MY PICKS

The top wines are spicy Gewürztraminers with equally spicy names: Madam's Vines, Woo Woo Vines and Threadbare Vines. Hush, as the rosé is called, is tasty. A complex blended white is called Secret Affair. The Bordello is a rich, concentrated red tasting of black currant, cherry and chocolate. Look for the port-style wine, released as "A Girl in Every Port."

OPENED 1995
(AS SCHERZINGER VINEYARDS)

7311 Fiske Street
Summerland, BC V0H 1Z2
T 250.494.8815
W www.dirtylaundry.ca

WHEN TO VISIT
Open daily 10 am – 6 pm mid-April to October; and Tuesday to Sunday noon – 4 pm November and December.

PATIO AREA AND PICNIC FARE

ACCOMMODATION
Bordello House vacation rental, with four bedrooms.

DOUBLE CROSS CIDERY

The trick to successful farming seems to be continual diversification. A fourth generation Okanagan farmer, Glenn Cross, born in 1958, started by leasing a pear orchard when he was 20. Within a decade, he had taken over his father Elwyn's 20-hectare (50-acre) Kelowna orchard, switching over the years to newer and higher-value apple varieties. "But the apple industry faltered," Glenn says. "It gets frustrating trying to make a living just on apples."

He reacted by opening a fruit stand in 2004 with his wife Loretta, who had just retired from 23 years with the Liquor Distribution Branch. They called the stand Function Junction for its strategic location at the busy intersection of Springfield Road and Highway 33. They grow produce for the stand and have developed a premium wholesale trade with restaurants and grocery stores for their produce and apple juice.

In 2011, when they thought of expanding to apple cider and fruit wine, they telephoned Richard Bullock, another apple grower, for advice. The Bullock family had opened the Raven Ridge Cidery on their East Kelowna orchard in 2003. To the surprise of the Crosses, the Bullocks had just decided to close Raven Ridge and sell the equipment. "We decided it was worth the gamble," Glenn says. "We ended up purchasing everything they had. We jumped into this rather quickly."

Moving forcefully is entirely in character for Glenn. He relaxes with backcountry snowmobiling in winter and spends summertime off-hours cruising on his 1998 Harley-Davidson motorcycle, a 40th birthday gift. "I guess it is the tough guy's bike," he says, explaining why he rides that machine rather than, say, a Japanese bike. "There's a T-shirt that says 'If I have to explain it, it is just not worth my time'."

This is not the first time the Cross family has flirted with wine. In the mid 1960s, Glenn's father owned Greata Ranch near Peachland for several years and wanted to plant vines until a government official

GLENN CROSS

advised against it. (CedarCreek Estate Winery subsequently planted a successful vineyard there in 1995.) His father then planted grapes on this Kelowna property, selling fruit to Calona Wines for several years before pulling them out. The fine southwest-facing slope here has room for almost seven hectares (17 acres) of grapes. In 2013, Glenn planted just over half a hectare of Pinot Gris.

OPENED 2012

3363 Springfield Road
Kelowna, BC V1P 1C6

T 250.765.2476

W www.function-junction.ca
/double_cross_cidery.html

WHEN TO VISIT
Open daily 9 am – 5:30 pm June
to mid-October; Saturday 11 am
– 4 pm and Sunday noon – 4 pm
November to May.

MY PICKS

At half the price of icewine, the four iced ciders here—three apple, one pear—are good-value dessert wines.

EAST KELOWNA CIDER COMPANY

A visit to the East Kelowna Cider Company, surrounded by apple trees, is to step back in time to an era when Kelowna was a community of orchards, not condominiums. This pastoral suburb still has historic apple orchards even if apple growing is not as lucrative as it once was. The value of Red Delicious apples is so low that packers in one recent year did not pay for the apples but billed growers for handling them. David and Theressa Ross, who own a 3.6-hectare (nine-acre) apple and peach orchard here, add value to their apples by making cider.

The driving influence, however, was David's interest in hard (alcoholic) cider. "Ever since he was 12, he has been concocting mixtures of moonshine, and that kind of stuff, just for the pure enjoyment of doing it," Theressa says of her husband. Now a logger, David was born in 1969 and grew up on this orchard, which has been in his family since his grandfather bought it in 1942. Ross Hard Apple Cider, the cidery's main alcoholic product, has Grandfather Ross on the label.

With her husband frequently away logging, Theressa, a hardworking young mother, has become an accomplished cider maker with a remarkable talent for improvisation. Rather than pressing the crushed apples, she extracts the juice by spinning the pulp in a converted dairy centrifuge and on the spin cycle of several washing machines. The only time this does not work well is when she makes ice apple cider. The sugar-saturated juice is extracted but the frozen pulp remaining in the spinners has to be practically chiselled out.

The Rosses grow dessert apples for cider. They do not care for the bitter taste that classic cider apples yield. The ice cider—the apple cider world's answer to icewine—is made with Golden Delicious and Braemar apples left on the trees to freeze naturally. Theressa contends that naturally frozen apples contain more sugar than artificially frozen apples because trees going into hibernation feed extra sugar into the fruit still hanging on them. "Yum, yum," she says of the taste of these

THERESSA AND DAVID ROSS

apples, which she has picked in temperatures as low as −20°C (−4°F). The ice ciders, available only at the winery, are dry on the finish. "A personal choice," Theressa says. "I like a dry cider."

MY PICKS

The Hard Cider is refreshing and, with about 6 percent alcohol, not too intoxicating. The non-alcoholic Soft Cider is also refreshing.

OPENED 2003

2960 McCulloch Road
Kelowna, BC V1W 4A5

T   250.860.3610

W www.eastkelownacider.com

WHEN TO VISIT
Monday to Friday 8 am – 5 pm
June to September, and by
appointment.

EAU VIVRE WINERY & VINEYARD

Dale Wright and Jeraldine Estin, busy with their careers in Saskatchewan, only began visiting wine country after Trina, their daughter, moved to the Similkameen Valley. "We got to know all the wineries around here," Dale says. "We would tour around the valleys and go home with half the truck full of wine for the winter until we could come back in the spring." Soon their Regina wine cellar was stocked almost exclusively with British Columbia wines.

Born in the Saskatchewan village of Rouleau in 1949, Dale, a professional geologist, has run his own oil well drilling company since 1984. Jeraldine, who has an education degree, is a college-level teacher and counsellor. They came to wine as consumers, and had dabbled in making country wines and kit wines before refining their palates on British Columbia wine, including wines made by Herder Vineyards.

They began looking at wine country property with retirement in mind. They bought the original site for Herder Vineyards when that winery moved to a different Similkameen location. Dale and Jeri liked the new house and also the potential of an equipped winery with a one-hectare vineyard, now planted with Gewürztraminer, Chardonnay and Riesling. Lawrence Herder got Eau Vivre off to a good start by making the debut 2007 vintage. Since then, several young winemakers have worked here, backed up by Dale. The current winemaker is Anthony Buchanan, a former sommelier with winemaking training from Washington State University and Okanagan College and hands-on experience at several Okanagan wineries.

The winery, which produces about 1,200 cases a year, has begun to make a name for itself with Pinot Noir, having twice won the Lieutenant Governor's Award for excellence in winemaking. The grapes have been purchased from vineyards in West Kelowna. The Pinot Noir planting at the Eau Vivre winery had to be removed after serious frost damage. The winery sources other varietals as well for its big reds,

Cabernet Franc and Malbec, and a blend of Bordeaux varieties and Syrah that carries the whimsical name Buddhafull.

Dale and Jeraldine also conceived their winery's unusual name. "We thought it would indicate something vague, the ungraspable," Jeraldine says poetically. Dale, a down to earth geologist, explains that "it is just a slang term for *water of life*."

MY PICKS

The portfolio is small but excellent. Standout wines include Riesling, Gewürztraminer, Pinot Noir, Cabernet Franc, Malbec and, of course, Buddhafull.

OPENED 2009

716 Lowe Drive
Cawston, BC V0X 1C2
T 250.499.2655
W www.eauvivrewinery.ca

WHEN TO VISIT
Open daily 10 am – 5:30 pm
May to mid-October, and by
appointment.

JERI ESTIN AND DALE WRIGHT

EDGE OF THE EARTH VINEYARDS

Although this winery, which Russ and Marnie Niles opened in 2002, is only six kilometres from the highway, the scenic but twisty country roads create the perception that it is off the beaten path. Russ met that perception head on when renaming the winery in 2009. "By the time people get here, they think they have gone off the edge of the earth," he says, laughing.

Hunting Hawk Vineyards, the winery's original name, was sold along with Hunting Hawk's second winery which Russ and Marnie operated for several years at the O'Keefe Ranch near Vernon. The city, which runs the ranch, declined to renew the winery lease.

After four years of stretching himself between two wineries, Russ was relieved to return to running just one. "This has become fun," he says. "This has become a lot of fun." Born in Victoria in 1957, Niles is the former editor of the now defunct *Vernon Daily Times*. He was drawn to wine as one of the original minority partners in Vernon's now closed Bella Vista winery. He launched his own winery after the closure of the *Daily Times*.

At the same time the owner of the local flying club alerted him that an aviation website had posted a job offer. Russ began writing for www.AVweb.com and eventually became editor of what he says is the world's largest general aviation website, with 200,000 subscribers. He also edits *Canadian Aviator* magazine and pilots his Cessna 140 around the Okanagan.

Russ relies on purchased grapes (such as Merlot, Pinot Noir, Pinot Gris and Gewürztraminer) as well as on his own 1.2-hectare (three-acre) vineyard. He is particularly enthusiastic about Maréchal Foch, grown in his vineyard and by any neighbours he can talk into it. "I just happen to love the grape," he says. "It makes fabulous red wine."

RUSS NILES

MY PICKS

How can you not sample the Foch when the winemaker is so enthusiastic about it? The rest of the portfolio changes to reflect the winemaking opportunities that come Russ's way. During a recent visit, the tasting room included a light Pinot Gris, a nicely-oaked red blend called Mostly Merlot and an organic Pinot Noir icewine, a winemaking first for Russ.

OPENED 2002
(AS HUNTING HAWK VINEYARDS)

4758 Gulch Road
Armstrong, BC V0E 1B4

T 250.546.2164

W www.edgeearth.ca

WHEN TO VISIT
Open daily 10 am – 5 pm
mid-March to October, and by
appointment.

8TH GENERATION VINEYARD

The singular name of this winery celebrates the eight generations of the family of winemaker and co-proprietor Bernd Schales that have been wine growers. However, it could also be called 10th Generation. The Frank family of Stefanie Schales, Bernd's wife, recently learned that their wine growing history in Germany goes back at least 92 years longer than the Schales family. They only confirmed that in 2009 after the Frank family went to church archives in Germany and found that the family has grown grapes since 1691.

Bernd and Stefanie brought the family tradition to the Okanagan in 2003. Bernd, born in 1972 and trained at Weinsberg, had spent 9 or 10 years managing a vineyard for his family's Weingut Schales in Flörsheim-Dalsheim. With Bernd's father and two uncles already in the business in Germany, the young couple struck out on their own, canvassing opportunities in South Africa, New York State and Ontario before being seduced, during a vacation, by the Okanagan's beauty. They bought an established four-hectare (10-acre) Okanagan Falls vineyard with a breathtaking view of Vaseux Lake, and subsequent purchases elsewhere in the valley have enabled them to double their vineyards.

Bernd's family sent him off to Canada with his grandfather's antique wine press, which was a godsend for the 2007 vintage. That summer, Bernd and Stefanie shelved original plans to attach a winery to their Okanagan Falls home when they were able to buy the building previously housing the highway-side Adora winery just south of Summerland. The building was empty (Adora moved its equipment elsewhere) and Bernd moved urgently to order new equipment because the grapes were ripening quickly. His grandfather's press, he discovered, was good for yet another vintage.

In 2010, when Berndt needed a bottle filler to increase the output of the winery's innovative sparkling wine, he bought a simple mechanical 1961 filler that had been in storage at a German winery. The frizzante

STEFANIE AND BERND SCHALES

wines, launched with 330 cases of a 2009 sparkling Chardonnay, have sold so well that they comprise a quarter of 8th Generation's entire 5,000-case production.

MY PICKS

The generations of experience in German wine country show in the fine Rieslings, whether dry, off-dry or late-harvest. The top-of-the-line is the elegant Riesling Selection. Bernd also has a sure touch with Pinot Gris, Chardonnay, Sauvignon Blanc and Pinot Meunier Rosé, along with Pinot Noir, Merlot and Syrah. The house specialities are Integrity and Confidence, the delightful white and pink frizzante wines.

OPENED 2007

6807 Highway 97
Summerland, BC V0H 1Z9

T   250.494.1783 (wine shop)
    788.476.6100 (office)

W www.8thgenerationvineyard.com

WHEN TO VISIT
Open daily 10 am – 6 pm May to mid-October; 11 am – 5 pm Easter Weekend and every Saturday in April; and by appointment.

ELEPHANT ISLAND ORCHARD WINES

Elephant Island raised the bar for fruit wines when Del and Miranda Halladay launched this winery. They retained winemaker Christine Leroux, whose entire training and experience had been in making grape wines. As a result, Elephant Island's fruit wines take the measure of grape wines any day. There are dry wines to go with food, sparkling wines for celebration, iced apple wines made just like icewine and fortified wines with cherries or currants as traditional as port. Most of the wines are made only with undiluted juice. "I know that it's a pretty common practice with fruit wine production to use water," Del says. "What better way to dilute flavours and dilute wine? We're doing everything we can to use the pure fruit and that's it."

This winery is tucked pleasantly amid the orchard that Miranda's grandparents bought years ago as a summer retreat on the Naramata Bench. The serene and shaded patio behind the wine shop is still a great spot for a picnic. The winery's singular name memorializes a family legend. When Catherine Chard Wisnicki, an architect and Miranda's grandmother, designed the house, her husband Paul (an engineer) scoffed that it was designed purely "for the eye." Having already been told the property would be a white elephant, she responded by calling the house "Elephant Eye-land".

Miranda, born in Powell River in 1973, is a geologist. Del, born in Victoria in 1972, went to Loyola College in Maryland on a lacrosse scholarship. He earned a marketing degree and a place on a professional American lacrosse team. Playing lacrosse, from which he retired in 2007, provided a "good part-time job" during the winter months as the winery became established.

Several years ago, Elephant Island launched two wines from grapes, reaching out to consumers who remain fruit wine sceptics. The Viognier is labelled "I Told You So" and the Cabernet Franc is labelled Naysayer. While the cheekiness rubs it in a bit with the sceptics, the quality shows off Del's accomplished winemaking.

MIRANDA HALLADAY

The pear wine, light and delicate, is a favourite of mine with a salad course. The Little King is a crisply dry Champagne method apple wine. The Pink Elephant is a sparkling apple wine with cassis dosage. The winery's tasty dessert products include the Stellaport, the Cassis and an immensely popular Framboise. And don't miss "I Told You So" or Naysayer.

OPENED 2001

2730 Aikins Loop
RR#1 S5 C18
Naramata, BC V0H 1N0

T 250.496.5522

W www.elephantislandwine.com

WHEN TO VISIT
Open daily 11 am – 4 pm April and late October; daily 10:30 am – 6 pm May to mid-October; and by appointment.

PATIO PICNIC AREA

ACCOMMODATION
The Tree House, with one studio suite.

EX NIHILO VINEYARDS

"Creating something from nothing"—one translation of Ex Nihilo from Latin—succeeds best if you hitch your wagon to a star. This winery debuted in 2008 by enlisting The Rolling Stones rock band as a partner in a brand of icewine called Sympathy for the Devil, the title of one of the band's most famous songs. Seldom has a new Okanagan winery opened with such extensive publicity.

Jeff and Decoa Harder run Ex Nihilo with partners from Alberta, Jay and Twila Paulson (with Jay since becoming the winemaker). The idea of linking up with the Rolling Stones came about after Jeff's younger brother James, who has a wine company in Napa, took them to a VIP dinner there. One of the wines that was served carried the band's signature "red tongue and lips" as a label. When Jeff dug further, he discovered Celebrity Cellars, an outfit that links celebrities to consumer products like wine. It took some doing, but eventually Jeff convinced Celebrity Cellars and the band to put the "tongue and lips" logo on a Canadian icewine. "Our gift to the wine world is icewine," Jeff says.

Jeff, a burly entrepreneur who formerly owned a pleasure boat manufacturer, was born in Edmonton in 1964. He got his first taste of the consumer beverage business as a partner in an apple cider venture in the late 1990s. Decoa, who was born in Innisfail, Alberta, in 1973, is a former skiing instructor with a marketing education who took up selling wine for Quails' Gate and then Mt. Boucherie. "I woke up one morning [in 2003] and said, 'Jeff, we have to find land'," she recalls. They bought their four-hectare (10-acre) property, formerly an orchard, in 2004 on a bench overlooking the Arrowleaf Cellars winery. Three years later, they planted Pinot Noir, Pinot Gris and Riesling. In 2013 they bought an adjoining block, also four hectares, and are planting the same varieties plus Chardonnay. In the elegant tasting room of the 697-square-metre (7,500-square-foot) winery, which was

DECOA AND JEFF HARDER

built in 2009, Ex Nihilo offers tastings of both its excellent table wines and its icewines.

The Paulsons are Alberta livestock dealers and high school friends of Jeff's. Among other things, they contributed Ex Nihilo's mascot, a fibreglass bull. It was inspired by bronze sculptures of animals at Napa's Cliff Lede Vineyards, whose owners are friends of the Paulsons. "We aren't quite at the bronze cow stage," Jeff laughs.

OPENED 2008

1525 Camp Road
Lake Country, BC V4V 1K1

T 250.766.5522

W www.exnihilovineyards.com

WHEN TO VISIT
Open daily 10 am – 5:30 pm May to mid-October; 11 am – 5 pm mid-October to Christmas and March to April; by appointment in winter.

MY PICKS

The dark Merlot is intense in berry flavours. Night is a fine Bordeaux blend. Several vintages of the winery's excellent Riesling won gold medals at the Riesling du Monde competition in France. The Pinot Gris and the Pinot Noir are both superb. Of course, the icewines make it on merit but are even more appealing to collectors of Rolling Stones memorabilia.

FAIRVIEW CELLARS

It may surprise those who relish the wines from Fairview Cellars that owner Bill Eggert does not consider himself a winemaker. He insists that he is a grape grower. Just don't ask him how he grows his grapes. "My wine is made in the vineyard and it is the vineyard secrets I keep to myself, not the winemaking secrets."

His secrets occupy a 2.4-hectare (six-acre) plateau overlooking the first tee of the Fairview Golf Club as well as two smaller plots south of Vaseux Lake (midway between Okanagan Falls and Oliver). The Fairview vineyard, which he began planting in 1993, is 50 percent dedicated to Cabernet Sauvignon, the variety that Bill calls "the workhorse" at Fairview. He also grows some on a leased neighbouring vineyard and contracts two acres of the variety at Inkameep Vineyards.

Fairview's vineyard also grows Cabernet Franc, Merlot and a row each of Syrah and Petit Verdot. The latter is the backbone of a wine called Bucket O' Blood, named for a saloon near the Fairview Townsite, the now vanished mining ghost town that inspired the winery's name. Recently, Bill planted a small block of Sauvignon Blanc, supplementing grapes he began buying in 2005 for the winery's only white. The Vaseux Lake properties, purchased in 2008, grow Pinot Noir. This marks Bill's foray into making wine with Burgundy grapes.

Born in Ottawa in 1957, Bill is the son of a mining engineer. He developed his passion for grapes on his uncle's Niagara vineyard and moved to the Okanagan in 1983 after failing to talk his uncle into switching from Concord grapes. Here, he became so adept at vineyard management that, in recent years, he developed and taught short courses on the subject at Okanagan College.

Bill's wines (he is in fact a pretty good winemaker) are a lot like Bill: bold direct wines that don't beat around the bush. His big Meritage is The Bear. A wine writer once referred to him as a madcap winemaker, so Bill blended Merlot and the two Cabernet varieties and called it

BILL EGGERT

Madcap Red. Expect to find at least one irreverently christened wine in the tasting room. A recent red blend, this one Cabernet-dominated, was called Two Hoots, primarily for the pair of owls that nest on Fairview's property every year. His first $100-plus red is appropriately called The Iconoclast.

OPENED 2000

989 Cellar Road
Oliver, BC V0H 1T5

T 250.498.2211

W www.fairviewcellars.ca

WHEN TO VISIT
Open Tuesday to Saturday
1 pm – 5 pm April to October.

MY PICKS

The Fairview reds are bold, sturdy in structure and capable of aging well. The winery's 2002 Cabernet Sauvignon is still drinking well a decade later. The 2005 Cabernet Franc, the first red Bill put under screw cap, is marvellously fresh. The Bear, with five Bordeaux varietals, and Madcap Red, with three, are complex and satisfying wines.

50TH PARALLEL ESTATE

The gleaming 30,000-case winery that is expected to open in 2014 is likely to win awards for its Toronto-based architects, the internationally established Zeidler Partnership Architects. The beauty has a purpose: drawing visitors to a location a bit off the beaten wine path. "So it has to be a destination," says winemaker Grant Stanley, who joined 50th Parallel in 2013 when the winery opened its first charmingly rustic tasting room.

The lead partners are Curtis Krouzel and Sheri-Lee Turner-Krouzel, wine enthusiasts from Alberta. They spent 10 years searching for a vineyard property before discovering, as Curtis says, "this beautiful piece of property that seemed to be sitting predominantly idle." The property is a sun-bathed slope stretching down to the eastern shore of Okanagan Lake. It is a bucolic 30-minute drive north from Gray Monk Estate Winery.

Born in 1975, Curtis grew up in Edmonton, earned a degree in engineering design technology and soon established his own company, designing plants for the oil and gas industry. With parents from the former Czechoslovakia and grandparents active in the Austrian wine industry, Curtis developed a passion for wine at the family table. When they began courting, one of the first things he told Sheri-Lee was that he was going to own a winery in the Okanagan.

There is a history of grape growing here. Jordan & Ste-Michelle Cellars, a winery then based in Victoria, bought grapes—mostly French hybrids but also Riesling and Bacchus—from this vineyard in the 1970s. Frank Whitehead, then a viticultural manager for the winery, remembers it as "good dirt." Ste-Michelle closed after being acquired by Brights Winery in 1981 and the vines were pulled out in 1988.

"It was 61 acres [24.5 hectares]," Curtis says. "It was about three times the size of the project I intended but I had always wanted to do something fairly world-class. So we set out on this mission

CURTIS KROUZEL AND SHERI-LEE TURNER-KROUZEL

GRANT STANLEY

to create a winery focused on Pinot Noir." Forty percent of the 13 hectares (32 acres) planted since 2009 is dedicated to Pinot Noir. The remainder is Pinot Gris, Riesling, Gewürztraminer and Chardonnay.

Grant became a 50th Parallel partner in 2013 after 10 years with Quails' Gate Estate Winery. Born in Vancouver in 1967, Grant trained in New Zealand where he made six vintages with a legendary Pinot Noir producer called Ata Rangi before returning to Canada. "As you know, Pinot Noir is near and dear to me."

OPENED 2013

17010 Terrace View Road
Lake Country, BC V4V 1B2
T   250.766.3408
W   www.50thparallel.com

WHEN TO VISIT
Open daily 10:30 am – 6 pm May
to October, and by appointment.

MY PICKS

Everything. Pinot Noir is the flagship wine, ably supported by Pinot Gris, Riesling, Gewürztraminer and rosé. A Chardonnay will join the portfolio in a few years.

FIRST ESTATE WINERY

It would be hard to find an Okanagan winery that has survived as many ownership changes at First Estate. In 2011 this historic winery was acquired by a Chinese businessman named Lu (his son, Lu Hong Quan, was studying business in Kelowna). After dabbling in wine exporting, the winery was leased in 2013 by winemaker Jason Parkes who proposes to make it an incubator for emerging wineries.

As the winery's name suggests, this was the Okanagan's first cottage winery. Soon after estate winery regulations were released in 1978, it was launched by Bulgarian-born Marion Jonn as Chateau Jonn de Trepanier (Cousins Place is a short street just off the end of Trepanier Bench Road). A year after opening, he sold the winery to Bob Claremont, the former winemaker at Calona. The winery operated under Claremont's name until going into receivership in 1986.

The third owner was Croatian-born Goldie Smitlener, a shrewd non-drinking real estate operator who called the winery Chateau Ste. Claire. It drifted along indifferently and was taken over in 1998 by Gary Strachan, now an Okanagan winery consultant, who coined the First Estate name. When the rundown facility defeated his efforts, it reverted back to Goldie and her partners in 2000 and closed for several years. The fifth owner, Calgary truck company executive Frank Silvestri, reopened the winery in 2004, with his Italian-born parents managing the property. After his father, Alf, died, the winery was sold to the Lu family who also struggled with the venerable facility.

Jason Parkes, the current operator, has one of the more colourful resumés in the industry. He was the leader of a "spacepunk" rock band from Kitimat called Glasshead. When music was not paying the bills, a vineyard job at Hainle Vineyards led to a flourishing winemaking career at Aces Wine, Serendipity Vineyards and Bounty Cellars. He makes wine at First Estate for several clients planning small premium wineries of their own.

JASON PARKES

If a wine shop is opened, Jason promises it will be casually rustic, perhaps with hot dogs on the barbecue. "What I like about this place," he says "is that I am up here with my dog and my music—which most people don't like—and I get to throw my heart into the wine the way I want to."

OPENED 1979

5078 Cousins Place
Peachland. BC V0H 1X2
T 250.767.9681

WHEN TO VISIT
By appointment only.

MY PICKS

No wines available for tasting at press time.

FORBIDDEN FRUIT WINERY

Half the farms in the Similkameen Valley are organic producers, with Steve Venables and Kim Brind'Amour among the pioneers. Their 57-hectare (141-acre) property, most of it still an untouched ecological sanctuary, has been farmed organically since 1977 and has been making organic wine since 2005.

Steve and Kim are self-described members of the "back to the land" generation. He was born in Victoria in 1952 and grew up in Indiana, where his father was deputy coroner. After two years studying science in college, Steve returned to the Okanagan to work in orchards. In 1977, he purchased the Sumac Road property, then raw land. Kim was born in Hull in 1963, the daughter of a market gardener; she formerly operated a health food store in Keremeos.

Their nine-hectare (22-acre) orchard is dedicated to tree fruits, including an astonishing 60 varieties of organic fruit that command premium prices. The winery was created initially to process so-called seconds (fruit with a less than perfect appearance), but Steve and co-winemaker Nathan Venables (their son) now dip into a diverse selection of produce because the portfolio has quadrupled. Forbidden Fruit now offers about 14 fruit wines, including a sparkling peach wine called Flirt that was created originally for a family wedding. As well, the winery makes five grape wines in its Earth Series and shares the proceeds with environmental causes.

Only a kilometre or so from the highway, this winery is a refuge at the end of a narrow, winding road down into the valley. The trees, including the majestic fir tree by the tasting room that Steve planted more than 35 years ago, provide shade on hot days. The tasting room is also the art gallery where Kim sells her attractive pottery, jewellery and paintings. Nathan, who is a carpenter by trade, has also begun making creative furnishings from wine barrels.

KIM BRIND'AMOUR AND STEVE VENABLES

MY PICKS

From dry to sweet, there are fruit wines for every palate. Pearsuasion, an oak-aged dry wine made from Asian pears, has delicious flavours of spice and ginger. Adam's Apple is a dry apple wine easily paired with main courses while Pomme Desiree is a luscious dessert wine with six apple varieties. Crushed Innocence is a delicately pure expression of white peaches. The tour de force among the Mistelles (fortified wines) is Cerise d'Eve, a port-style cherry wine. The grape wines are equally well-made, notably Cabernet Sauvignon, Merlot and a Bordeaux blend called Redemption.

OPENED 2005

620 Sumac Road
RR1, Site 33, Comp 9
Cawston, BC V0X 1C3

T 250.499.2649
  1.855.499.2649 (toll free)

W www.forbiddenfruitwines.com

WHEN TO VISIT
Open daily 10 am – 6 pm April to October, and by appointment.

LICENSED PICNIC AREA

FOXTROT VINEYARDS

Without doubt, Foxtrot Vineyards makes the most sought-after Pinot Noir in the Okanagan, meting it out a case at a time to the top restaurants in Canada and to a small number of private clients. The winery even has several customers in Britain who have paid an additional $830 air freight for wine that retails here at only $660 a case. "People who buy wine over $50 a bottle don't fret about the price," proprietor Torsten Allander has concluded from nearly a decade's experience selling wine.

An elegantly-mannered retired pulp and paper engineer, Torsten extends a lifetime of high achievement to wine growing. Born in Sweden, Torsten came to Canada in 1973 for a career with NLK Associates, a top pulp and paper consulting firm based in Vancouver and Montreal. In 2002, he and his wife, Elisabeth (the family calls her Kicki), retired to a 1.4-hectare (3½-acre) vineyard on Naramata Road planted entirely with Pinot Noir. After selling the grapes to another winery for a few years, Torsten enlisted Lake Breeze Vineyards in 2004 for a three-year winemaking trial with his grapes. "I wanted to convince myself before I invested a lot of money in a winery that we can produce a top wine that can compete on a world level," Torsten recalled.

The acclaim which the initial vintages received left no doubt about the quality of the Foxtrot Pinot Noirs. In 2008, Torsten and his winemaker son, Gustav, built a winery and cellar with the barrel capacity for 2,000 cases of wine. They will need to consider expansion in a few years because, in 2012, Torsten bought an adjoining two hectares (five acres) of orchard. The fruit trees are being replaced with Pinot Noir vines propagated from cuttings of Foxtrot's clone 115 Pinot Noir.

The winery makes Pinot Noir from the nearby Henricsson Vineyard as well, and plans to add Waltz Pinot Noir for wines made with other purchased fruit or fruit from young vines, releasing it under

TORSTEN AND KICKI ALLANDER

that vineyard's designation. In addition, Gustav also makes a premium Foxtrot Chardonnay. Gustav originally studied engineering until he was also seized by the passion for wine. His wife Nadine, an Okanagan native with a New Zealand enology degree, is a winemaker at Poplar Grove. Wapiti Cellars, a brand that the young couple created in 2010, has become a subsidiary label at Foxtrot Vineyards.

OPENED 2007

2333 Gammon Road
RR1, Site 9, Comp 15
Naramata, BC V0H 1N0

T 250.496.5082

W www.foxtrotwine.com

WHEN TO VISIT
By appointment only.

MY PICKS

The winery's Pinot Noirs are among the most elegant and suave examples of this variety from any Canadian producer. One buyer in 2013 compared it extravagantly to La Tâche and Richebourg. The winery's Burgundy-styled Chardonnay, first made in 2008, is arguably the Okanagan's most sophisticated.

GANTON & LARSEN PROSPECT WINERY

There must be an explanation for this winery's address since no winemaker, especially someone as lanky as Prospect's Wade Stark, lives in a post office box. Prospect is owned by Artisan Wine Company, a holding company whose best-known property is Mission Hill Family Estate Winery. That is where the Prospect wines have been made, and will continue to be made until (or if) the long-planned Prospect winery is built near Oliver.

Prospect was launched as a self-described "tribute to the Okanagan Valley." The complete name is Ganton & Larsen Prospect Winery; those names refer to two of Mission Hill's long-time growers. This was one device employed to root this virtual winery in the Okanagan.

Another effective device is building each wine label around British Columbia lore and history. For example, Prospect's wildly successful Pinot Grigio is called Ogopogo's Lair. This refers to a bend on the east side of Okanagan Lake where, according to legend, the mythical Ogopogo lake creature has its underwater cave. Another example: The Lost Bars Vidal Icewine refers to an 1896 robbery of three bars of gold from a mine near the Okanagan. Two bars are said to have been buried in the valley and the location was then lost. Altogether, Prospect celebrates Okanagan history on about a dozen different wines.

The label, which now includes 12 wines, has been so successful that, by volume, it would rank as a mid-tier winery. That speaks well for Wade's winemaking. Born in Guelph, Ontario, he became interested in wine while studying food engineering at the university there. After starting his career in a brewery laboratory, he moved to the Okanagan and, after working at Mission Hill, he became the inaugural Prospect winemaker in 2006.

WADE STARK (COURTESY OF MISSION HILL)

MY PICKS

Prospect's wines over-deliver in quality, considering that all are priced between $12 and $18 except for the icewine. The Census Count Chardonnay, the Pinot Grigio, the Sauvignon Blanc, the Riesling and the Merlot Cabernet stand out.

OPENED 2007

Box 474
Oliver, BC V0H 1T0

T   604.264.4020

W www.prospectwinery.com

WHEN TO VISIT
No tasting room.

GEHRINGER BROTHERS ESTATE WINERY

There is a definite house style here, with wines that are youthfully vibrant and bursting with flavour. In a rare practice, the winery releases both its white and red wines in the year after harvest, at their maximum freshness. For four years now, all bottles have been flushed with nitrogen before being filled and then closed with screw caps that lock in the fresh flavours. Walter and Gordon Gehringer stopped maturing Chardonnay, Pinot Gris and Pinot Blanc with oak, again to preserve pure, pristine fruit flavours. "These wines are better on their own," Walter decided. "Our personal preference won out."

That palate reflects the schooling of the brothers, Oliver-born sons of German immigrants. When their family conceived of a winery in 1973, Walter, who had just completed high school, was sent to Geisenheim University, Germany's leading wine school, to become its first Canadian graduate. Gordon, his younger brother, got his training at Weinsberg, another good German wine school. While they were studying in Europe, their family completed the climate studies that led to buying this Golden Mile vineyard property in 1981.

The winery's 10.5-hectare (26-acre) vineyard occupies a peninsula of glacial soil, sloping toward the east and the south. The shade from the mountains to the west shields the grapes from severe afternoon heat, allowing them to preserve fruity flavours and fresh acidity as they ripen. The terroir is especially suited to the winery's aromatic white wines, notably Riesling, Pinot Gris, Gewürztraminer, Schönburger and Sauvignon Blanc. The vineyard produces most of the grapes the Gehringers need to make about 30,000 cases each year.

For many years, the Gehringer whites usually had noticeable natural sweetness, much like many German whites. More recently, the wines have been finished dry or close to it, Walter alertly having picked up changes in consumer preferences during his stints serving wine in the Gehringer tasting room. The house style is consistently attuned to

WALTER GEHRINGER

popular tastes without any loss of finesse in the wines. The proof is in the winery's awards, particularly in a "Platinum" competition open only to wines of the Pacific Northwest which have already won gold in other competitions. Few wineries have as many Platinum awards (43) as Gehringer Brothers.

MY PICKS

All the wines are value-priced. My favourite whites include the zesty Sauvignon Blanc, the peachy Chardonnay, the elegant Pinot Gris. Flagship whites are the Rieslings, including the icewine. The budget-priced red here is Summer's Night, a soft, easy-drinking blend of Cabernet Franc and Pinot Noir.

OPENED 1986

876 Road 8
Oliver, BC V0H 1T1
T 250.498.3537
    1.800.784.6304 (toll free)
W www.gehringerwines.ca

WHEN TO VISIT
Open daily 9 am – 5:30 pm May to mid-October; Monday to Friday 9 am – 5 pm mid-October to May.

GOLD HILL WINERY

Gold Hill Winery arrived on the scene with a bang, winning a Lieutenant Governor's Award with a 2009 Cabernet Franc, one of the four wines with which it debuted. Numerous awards have followed, a credit to how well brothers Sant and Gurbachan Gill farm their 26 hectares (65 acres) of grapes.

Theirs is the classic immigrant success story. Sant, born in India in 1958, arrived in the Okanagan in 1984 with $6. Younger brother Gurbachan, born in 1967, followed him in 1989, the same year that Sant bought his first house in Osoyoos. After a few years of orchard work, the brothers began working in 1991 in vineyards owned by Kal Gidda, one of the principals at Mt. Boucherie Estate Winery. After a decade with Kal they became so adept at viticulture that today they farm not just their own land, but also take contracts to plant and manage vineyards for others.

The gold-hued adobe style winery, visible on the access road just beside the highway, is on an orchard that the brothers have owned since 1995. In 2007 the orchard was converted to grapes, and the award-winning Cabernet Franc came from that vineyard's first harvest—a variety in which Gold Hill now specializes. Since 2007, the brothers have expanded into all of the mainstream varietals, including Merlot, Cabernet Sauvignon, Syrah, Malbec, Pinot Gris, Chardonnay, Viognier and Gewürztraminer. They also own or lease smaller vineyards in Osoyoos, Okanagan Falls and Kaleden; the latter produces Pinot Noir for the winery. They have developed a high-elevation vineyard on the mountainside above the winery, planting Tempranillo and Sauvignon Blanc, among other varieties.

The winemaker for Gold Hill is consultant Philip Soo. Formerly a winemaker with Andrew Peller Ltd. in Port Moody, Phil, since 2006, has become one of the Okanagan's busiest consultants with a client

GURBACHAN (LEFT) AND SANT GILL

list that includes Dirty Laundry, Noble Ridge and Cassini Cellars. He crafts wines that are distinctive for each client, reflecting both individual vineyards and client preferences. The Gill brothers see him as a mentor. "Phil is a really nice guy," Sant says. "He explains lots of things to me when he comes here."

The Gill brothers sell most of their grapes to other wineries, currently producing about 2,500 cases at Gold Hill. The target is to cap Gold Hill at 5,000 cases a year.

OPENED 2011

3502 Fruitvale Way
Osoyoos, BC V0H 1T1

T 250.495.8152

W www.goldhillwinery.com

WHEN TO VISIT
Open daily 10 am – 6 pm April to October, and by appointment.

MY PICKS

The Viognier and the red wines here —Syrah, Cabernet Franc, Merlot, Pinot Noir—are powerful wines, usually with about 14 percent alcohol but with such concentrated fruit that this muscularity is not intrusive. The Chardonnay, the Pinot Gris and the Gewürztraminer are made in a refreshing fruit-forward style.

GRAY MONK ESTATE WINERY

One of the Okanagan's original estate wineries, Gray Monk evolved over 30 years from a small winery with a modest footprint to a grand winery styled like a European château. The wines also evolved. Initially a white wine house only, Gray Monk's portfolio now stretches from sparkling wine through reds to dessert wines.

The echoes of Europe here are authentic. George Heiss, born in 1939, grew up in Vienna and apprenticed with his father, a world champion hairdresser. His wife, Trudy, was born near Berlin. They met in Edmonton where both had hair salons. Hugo Peter, Trudy's father, began growing grapes in the Okanagan and George and Trudy followed him there, planting vines in 1972 for the winery they opened a decade later.

Today, they count themselves as one of the rare Canadian families with four generations in wine growing. Son George Jr., their German-trained winemaker, has taken over Hugo Peter's vineyard. His brothers, Robert and Steven, manage the winery while Robert's son, Kieran, has qualified as a viticulturist.

The Heiss family has had a profound impact on Okanagan wine growing. They were the first to import clones of Pinot Gris, Gewürztraminer and Auxerrois from Alsace. They facilitated the Becker Project, the eight-year trial of German vines that, by its conclusion in 1985, proved the viability of varieties now among the most important in the Okanagan. Alone among all the wine producers in North American, they nurture the hard-to-grow Rotberger grape to make notable rosé.

Now making about 80,000 cases a year, Gray Monk built its reputation with unoaked white wines that are expressive, fruit-driven and juicy on the palate. Winemaker Roger Wong joined the winery in 2005, making sparkling wines and reds. And after making reds for a decade with purchased grapes, Gray Monk made a big bet on reds by developing the Paydirt Vineyard, five hectares (12 acres) south of Oliver

GEORGE AND TRUDY HEISS
(PHOTO BY BRIAN SPROUT)

planted primarily with Malbec, Merlot and Cabernet Sauvignon. The winery made its first Meritage red blend in 2009.

MY PICKS

The quality of all Gray Monk wines is consistently high, and that includes its popular Latitude 50 wines, which are refreshing, easy to drink and affordable. The winery's flagship estate wine is Pinot Gris (the German name for that variety translates to Gray Monk). The winery's reserve wines are released under the Odyssey label. These are all delicious and well-priced for the quality. My favourite Odyssey wines include the Pinot Noir, the Merlot, the Cabernet Sauvignon, the Meritage and the Rosé Brut.

OPENED 1982

1055 Camp Road
Okanagan Centre, BC V4V 2H4
T 250.766.3168
   1.800.663.4205 (toll free)
W www.graymonk.com

WHEN TO VISIT
Open daily 10 am – 7 pm May to June; 9 am – 9 pm July to August; 10 am – 7 pm September to October; 10 am – 5 pm November to April.

RESTAURANT
Grapevine Patio
T 250.768.3168
Open daily 11:30 am for lunch and from 5 pm for dinner April to October. Contact restaurant for seasonal hours.

GREATA RANCH ESTATE WINERY

Greata Ranch, formerly a satellite of CedarCreek Estate Winery, is now emerging as the Fitzpatrick family's independent boutique specializing in sparkling wines. Senator Ross Fitzpatrick and his son, Gordon, retained ownership of Greata Ranch in 2014 when Mission Hill's Anthony von Mandl bought CedarCreek.

Greata Ranch's reincarnation as a sparkling wine producer had begun in the 2012 vintage. Darryl Brooker, who had moved from Ontario to become CedarCreek's winemaker in 2010, was struck by the potential of the Greata Ranch vineyard. "It is one of the best sparkling vineyards I have seen," Darryl says. The 16-hectare (40-acre) vineyard, shaded from the late afternoon sun by Mount Edna, is a cool terroir producing grapes with the fresh acidity that is ideal for sparkling wine.

The Pinot Noir–dominated cuvées that Darryl made (about 400 cases in 2012 and 600 cases in 2013), are now maturing in the Greata Ranch cellar. Darryl remained with CedarCreek but he is expected to handle the 2014 vintage before the Fitzpatricks recruit their own winemaker for the redeveloped Greata Ranch.

The wine shop closed for most of the 2014 and 2015 seasons for the construction of a striking new winery designed by Seattle architect Vassos Demitriou. One of the family's favourite architects, Vassos previously had designed the senator's lakefront home as well as the gleaming white CedarCreek winery. The Greata Ranch design incorporates more glass, emphasizing the 6,000-case winery's commitment to sparkling wine.

"We will also do a reserve Pinot Noir and reserve Chardonnay," Gordon says. (The winery previously made excellent reserves in 2006.) "We have the Gewürztraminer and will do a little late-harvest Gewürztraminer." Ehrenfelser and Pinot Meunier (the latter for sparkling wine) were planted several years ago while a hectare of Merlot

GORDON FITZPATRICK

was replaced in 2014 with Riesling.

Greata Ranch is an historic property that resonates emotionally with Ross. It is named for George H. Greata (pronounced *gretta*), an 1895 emigrant from Britain who planted fruit trees on this 44-hectare (109-acre) lakefront property. As a youth, Ross accompanied his father, a packing house manager, to buy fruit. The property became derelict after the hard winter of 1965 killed many trees. The Fitzpatricks bought it in 1994 to plant a vineyard, and the winery was opened a decade later in response to popular demand from travellers passing by on busy Highway 97.

OPENED 2003

697 Highway 97S
Peachland, BC V0H 1X9

T   250.767.2768

W www.greataranch.com

WHEN TO VISIT
Wine shop will reopen for 2015
Okanagan Fall Wine Festival.

MY PICKS

No wines available for tasting at press time.

HAINLE VINEYARDS & DEEP CREEK WINE ESTATE

In September 2012, Hainle Vineyards nearly became the third British Columbia winery to be destroyed by fire. A raging forest fire, which did damage a vineyard, came close enough to burn the roof and scorch the siding. "Someone asked me what I would do if the winery burns down," proprietor Walter Huber remembers. "I would just rebuild."

Walter, who was born in Munich in 1959, began developing vineyards near Peachland in 1991, buying this winery in 2002 from the legendary Hainle family. The late Walter Hainle and his German-trained winemaker son, Tilman, began making Canada's first icewines in the 1970s. Some of inventory passed to Walter Huber when he bought the winery. When a bottle of the rare 1978 icewine (the winery's first commercial production) was stolen from his truck, Walter considered insuring his remaining bottle for $1 million. He has retained icewine as one of this winery's specialties.

It is hardly surprising that Walter is deeply influenced by traditional European methods. He puts sub-appellations, like Appellation Peachland, on his labels even though they are not yet sanctioned in British Columbia. He makes wines in accordance with an 1856 wine purity law that echoes the famous Bavarian beer purity laws of 1516. And he prefers wines that are well-aged.

"Because of the fire, we have to release some of the wines early for cash flow," Walter lamented in the summer of 2013 as painters were restoring the winery's siding. "But I don't really like doing that. I like to release my whites when they are 3 to 5 years old, and my reds when they are 7 to 10 years old. What we are doing is old style European wine aging. The excise officer said we have a bigger library of old wines than Mission Hill and Jackson-Triggs together." Destruction by fire would have been an incredible tragedy.

WALTER HUBER

MY PICKS

The Pinot Noirs are powerful, yet elegant. The blended reds, some with Bordeaux varietals and some based on Zweigelt are bold. Lovers of older wines will be drawn to the library wines here, especially the mature dry Riesling.

OPENED 1988

5355 Trepanier Bench Road
Peachland, BC V0H 1X2

T   250.212.5944

W www.hainle.com

WHEN TO VISIT
Open daily 11 am – 5 pm April to
October, and by appointment.

HARPER'S TRAIL ESTATE WINERY

What makes this vineyard special is same thing that has enabled Lafarge to operate a cement plant nearby since 1970: the underlying limestone in the area, which is quarried for cement, also benefits grape growing. Ed Collett, who owns Harper's Trail with his wife, Vicki, points to the cliff above the south-sloping vineyards. "That whole sidehill is lime rock," he says.

This property on the north side of the Thompson River is about 16 kilometres (10 miles) east of Kamloops. Formerly, it grew hay and grazed cattle in what is quintessential British Columbia range country. The winery is named for Thaddeus Harper, the 19th-century American-born rancher who once owned the vast 15,569-hectare (38,472-acre) Gang Ranch, one of the first farms to use sturdy gang ploughs. Ed bought his modest slice of ranch country in 2007 after he had conceived the idea of developing a winery. He developed a taste for wine during travels to Chile on business for the mining equipment company he established in 1987.

The desire for a winery emerged during Okanagan wine tours. Ed remembers relaxing at a bed and breakfast overlooking a vineyard and remarking: "I've got to get myself one of these." He began planting vines in 2008. He currently has 11.7 hectares (29 acres) of vines and has plans for more in stages, as he and vineyard manager John Dranchuk determine what varieties will succeed. "You have to take baby steps," Ed notes. "We are further north [than most vineyards] but obviously, it is not a deterrent for us." The cold winters led to the removal of Merlot while a 2008 planting of Cabernet Franc succeeded so well that more was planted in 2012, followed with 2.4 hectares (six acres) of Pinot Noir and Gamay in 2013. Riesling, Pinot Gris and Chardonnay also are succeeding. Wind machines combat early autumn frost, while Ginseng shade-cloth on the vineyard's borders breaks the valley's

VICKI AND ED COLLETT

constant winds and propane cannons deter the birds. "All of this is new to the Thompson," the vineyard manager says. "This was the first vineyard with wind machines and bird bangers."

The first several vintages, which included three different Rieslings, along with Chardonnay, Pinot Gris, Gewürztraminer, a white blend, a rosé and a Cabernet Franc, were made for Harper's Trail at Okanagan Crush Pad in Summerland. That temporary wine-making facility is being replaced in 2014 by a new winery, and there are also future plans for a restaurant and for walking trails on the property. A tasting room opened at the vineyard in the summer of 2013.

OPENED 2012

2720 Shuswap Road East
Kamloops, BC V2H 1S9

T   250.573.5855

W www.harperstrail.com

WHEN TO VISIT
Open Friday to Sunday 11 am – 7 pm mid-May to mid-June; Monday to Thursday 11 am – 6 pm and Friday to Sunday 11 am – 7 pm mid-June to August; daily 11 am – 5 pm September to mid-October; Saturday 11 am – 5 pm January to mid-May.

MY PICKS

The limestone terroir gives an elegant discipline to all the wines, especially the Rieslings. The delicious Silver Mane Block Riesling is an off-dry Mosel-style wine while the Pioneer Block Riesling is austerely dry. The Cabernet Franc is a juicy, full-flavoured red.

HEAVEN'S GATE ESTATE WINERY

The Triple A Orchard, which Andy and Diane Sarglepp operated at this bucolic farm for 20 years, enjoyed close to a cult following for its peaches. "I had customers from day one, right to when I quit after 20 years," Andy says. "They would only buy from me because I had almost unsurpassed quality. I would grade harder and get rid of any flaws among the peaches. If you reached into one of my bins, you did not have to look at the fruit—it would be perfect."

The irony is that Andy stopped eating peaches about 15 years ago when his business lost its appeal. The orchard was "all peaches, of different varieties, so I was picking from the middle of July to the middle of September," he remembers. "I was busy picking peaches for two months straight."

In 2009, the Sarglepps replaced the orchard with 2.2 hectares (5½ acres) of grapes for a winery. "I wonder if the same thing will happen with wine," Andy says. Leaning against the Brazilian granite bar in the log cabin wine shop, he asks, rhetorically: "Will I dislike wine as much?"

Andy was born in Haney in 1965 and as an adult he began working in logging and sawmilling. His Estonian-born parents—his father had become a successful construction contractor in Canada after arriving impoverished after the war—bought this Summerland property about 25 years ago. Andy was asked to help develop the peach orchard. He fell in love with the Okanagan and stayed.

The grapes in the vineyard include almost one hectare (two acres) of Gewürztraminer, a variety very much at home in the Summerland terroir. Andy has also planted Merlot, Gamay and Sémillon; a planting of Sauvignon Blanc did not survive an early winter freeze. Because the vineyard yielded its first crop in 2011, Andy relied on purchased grapes for his initial vintage. He is likely to continue buying from other

ANDY AND DIANE SARGLEPP

growers, supplementing varieties not grown here.

For wine production, Andy put tanks and barrels in what had been the cool-storage facility for his peaches. With the help of consultant Christine Leroux, he made 13,000 litres (about 1,450 cases) in 2010, about two-thirds of it white. "That being the first year, I did not want to max out my capacity of my cellar," Andy said in the spring of 2011. "I wanted to go half throttle, learn my system, figure out the bugs if any. Next year, it will be game on, full steam ahead."

OPENED 2011

8001 Happy Valley Road
Summerland. BC V0H 1Z4

T 778.516.5505

W www.heavensgatewinery.ca

WHEN TO VISIT
Open daily 10 am – 5 pm May to October; and weekends noon – 4 pm April and November

MY PICKS

Andy thought that his Pinot Gris, with intense lime aromas and flavours, was his best debut wine; and I agreed. I have since been impressed with the Gewürztraminer, the Sauvignon Blanc/Sémillon, the rosé and the Merlot. Look for Revelation, a tasty blend of Malbec, Merlot and Cabernet Sauvignon.

HERDER WINERY & VINEYARDS

As this book was being published, the future of Herder Winery was uncertain. Founders Lawrence and Sharon Herder put the winery on the market in 2013 after Lawrence left the partnership to work elsewhere in the Okanagan.

The odds are that the new owners, when they can be confirmed, will continue with the Herder brand and wine portfolio, both of which are strong. The winery's flagship, Josephine, a blend of Merlot, Cabernet Sauvignon and Cabernet Franc, is an iconic wine sought by numerous collectors. Sharon Herder, who continued to manage the winery through the sale process, has been able to release the 2010 vintage of Josephine. The components for the subsequent two vintages are in the winery, should new ownership decide to continue the label.

It is unlikely there will be a 2013 Josephine, however, as most of the grapes in the Herder vineyard were sold to other wineries in that vintage. In addition, one of the components of Josephine, the Merlot from Bellamay Vineyards (a long-time Herder grower) was sold to another vintner. Fortunately, Sharon did bring in consulting winemaker Christine Leroux to produce modest volumes of Meritage, Pinot Noir and Chardonnay. In part, that ensured that the incoming owners have some 2013 wines from this excellent vineyard.

Lawrence, a San Diego native who operated a Paso Robles winery before coming to Canada, made wine for several Okanagan wineries before establishing in the Similkameen. The valley appealed to his interest in making big reds. The first Herder winery—now Eau Vivre—had a vineyard far better suited to growing white varieties. In 2008, the Herders moved their winery to Upper Bench Road, planting a site ideal for reds.

The 6-hectare (15-acre) vineyard was formerly an orchard on a mineral-rich, south-facing slope. It backs against a cliff that shields this sun-drenched property from cold northeast winds in winter.

The varieties that thrive here include Merlot, Cabernet Sauvignon, Cabernet Franc, Malbec, Petit Verdot, Viognier and Chardonnay. Historically, the winery also purchased Pinot Gris and other varieties not grown here.

The property came with a large three-storey house. In something of a European winery tradition, the family lived on the top floors while the wines were made and matured on the bottom floor. "Putting the winery downstairs gives me more peace of mind during crush," Lawrence once explained. The wine shop commands a stunning view over the Similkameen Valley.

MY PICKS

Josephine, if you can still find it.

OPENED 2004

2582 Upper Bench Road
Keremeos. BC V0X 1N4
T   250.499.5595
W www.herder.ca

WHEN TO VISIT
Open daily noon – 6 pm May to October. and by appointment.

SHARON HERDER

HERON RIDGE ESTATES WINERY

To open the Castlegar area's first winery, Paul Koodrin had to be very persistent. When he first applied for a blueberry winery license in the 1990s, the provincial regulators said there was no such category. The local regulators were no more supportive. For several years, Paul operated a thriving country store and restaurant beside the highway at Thrums. When he proposed adding a winery, the regional district told him that his zoning would not allow it. He sold the store, put the winery on hold and went back to his trade as a welder while he kept growing blueberries on his family farm, ultimately succeeding in opening the winery on the farm, where there are no zoning limitations.

Born in Nelson in 1943, Paul is a welder and pipefitter who has worked throughout British Columbia. The family roots, however, are at what is called Bluecrop Farms, the riverside farm near the village of Thrums, just north of Castlegar, which Paul established in 1984. Paul planted blueberries and, when the trial plantings thrived, he expanded to about 1.6 hectares (four acres). By 1990 the production was large enough that he installed a walk-in freezer for the crop, which he was selling locally.

Paul became an occasional home winemaker. He remembers that his first batch of blueberry wine was not appealing. "But I made another batch and it got better," he says. "Then I started working with different recipes and I got real nice wine from it. That's when we decided to build a winery." One of the recipes, he says, came from the University of Michigan (a blueberry state) but could have been from the playbook of an Amarone winemaker. He air-dried the berries to concentrate the sugar and the flavours, then fermenting the must with alcohol-tolerant yeast. "This is a port type with 18 percent alcohol," he said as we shared a well-aged bottle. For his commercial production, he gets help from consulting winemaker Christine Leroux from the Okanagan.

PAUL KOODRIN

The farm and the winery are beside the Kootenay River, a short distance north of where the river empties into the Columbia. The winery takes its name from the herons nesting nearby, at the river's edge.

MY PICKS

No wines available for tasting at press time.

OPENED 2011

1682 Thrums Road
Thrums, BC V1N 4N4

T 250.764.5413

W www.members.shaw.ca/pair/

WHEN TO VISIT
Open daily 9 am – 5 pm May to
October, and by appointment.

HESTER CREEK ESTATE WINERY

No Okanagan winery has transformed as thoroughly as Hester Creek, which was a bankrupt, ramshackle winery in 2004 when Prince George trucking magnate Curt Garland bought it. Today, after a $25 million investment, the wines are made in a completely modern 2,137-square-metre (23,000-square-foot) winery with grapes from one of the oldest and best vineyards in the South Okanagan.

Vines were planted here as early as 1968 by Joe Busnardo, an Italian immigrant who, realizing the site's potential, planted only premium European grapes when everyone else was still growing inferior hybrid varieties. Joe added a winery called Divino in 1983, running it until he sold the property in 1996 and relocated Divino to the Cowichan Valley on Vancouver Island.

The Okanagan winery was renamed Hester Creek, from a creek on the south side of the vineyard. The creek was christened by Judge J. C. Haynes, the first customs officer at Osoyoos in the 1860s, who had a daughter called Hester. The connection to the judge, although he was somewhat controversial, led the winery in 2011 to release an icon Bordeaux blend called The Judge.

The Judge crowns the pyramid of wines crafted by winemaker Rob Summers, who was recruited in 2006 to lead Hester Creek's turn-around. Born in Ontario in 1962, Rob had been the national winemaker for Andrew Peller Ltd. (among other posts). He discovered Hester Creek's potential while buying some of its grapes in 2003. He prizes the old vines from the late 1960s, which contribute intense flavours and mineral notes that are especially evident in the winery's sought-after Trebbiano and its Cabernet Franc Reserve.

The winery, with a capacity to produce about 30,000 cases a year, makes only 200 cases of The Judge along with small-lot reserves from Cabernet Franc and Merlot. It produces significant quantities of Pinot Gris, Pinot Blanc and red and white blends called Character, because,

CURT GARLAND

ROBERT SUMMERS

as the slogan has it, "character emerges from our land."

MY PICKS

Everything. Hester Creek makes just 700 cases annually of the Okanagan's only Trebbiano, a fruity Italian white. They make generous volumes of Pinot Gris and Pinot Blanc, including a late-harvest Pinot Blanc. Among the reds, The Judge is for collectors and special occasions. The Cabernet Franc Reserve and the Merlot Reserve are always outstanding. The two Character blends are under $20 each but over-deliver.

OPENED 1983
(AS DIVINO ESTATE WINERY)

877 Road 8, Box 1605
Oliver, BC V0H 1T0

T 250.498.4435
 1.866.498.4435 (toll free)

W www.hestercreek.com

WHEN TO VISIT
Open daily 10 am – 4 pm
January to April; daily 10 am –
6 pm May to June; daily 10 am –
8 pm June to mid-October.

RESTAURANT
Terrafina
T 250.498.2229
Open daily 11.30 am – 10 pm
May to mid-October; Wednesday
to Saturday 11.30 am – 10 pm
mid-October to December and
March to April, with brunch on
Sundays.

ACCOMMODATION
The Villa, with six mountainside
Tuscan-style guest suites.

HIDDEN CHAPEL WINERY

When an increasing number of wineries started setting tasting room fees, Hidden Chapel proprietor Deborah Wilde decided the fees here would go to a charity (as some other wineries have also done). She chose to direct the fees to South Okanagan Women in Need. "I think that is the best way to do it," she says. "We as wineries don't need the money . . . well, we need the money, don't get me wrong, but people would rather give for charity than give to the wineries."

That is refreshingly down to earth. Perhaps it is also in harmony with the tiny white chapel, barely large enough for eight people, secluded among trees at the rear of this property, the inspiration for the winery name. It was a serious chapel for a previous owner and still is, popularly used for weddings or simply as a place where a visitor can rest and meditate.

The winery was founded on a 1.2-hectare (three-acre) vineyard of Cabernet Sauvignon in 2005 by Lanny Kinrade, who was Deborah's active partner at the time. Grape grower Swaran Chahal, who has a vineyard next door and another in Osoyoos, also grows fruit for Hidden Chapel.

Lanny helped launch the winery in 2010 but left the partnership two years later to return to one of his other trades, home building. His handicraft remains, however. The underground barrel cellar, with a capacity of 60 to 90 barrels, has taken the place of what formerly was a swimming pool. The tasting room nearby exudes a warm welcome, thanks to its bright paintwork and the antique quality of its doors, salvaged from a Vancouver office that was being demolished.

The chapel provides constant inspiration. The labels feature an embossed chapel which, because of its white on white presentation, seems to be hidden. The wine names also draw on images around the chapel. The winery's debut 2009 white was a Sauvignon Blanc called White Wedding. It was joined by such labels as Nuns on the Run,

DEBORAH WILDE

The Flying Nun, Chapel Blend, The Collection, Merry Monk, Holy Smoke, Shotgun Wedding, Blushing Bride and St. Vincent (one of the patron saints for winemakers).

As this book was being completed, Deborah listed the winery for sale for $1.59 million. At the time of publication, no sale had been completed.

OPENED 2010

482 Pinehill Road
Oliver, BC V0H 1T5

T   250.490.6000

W www.hiddenchapelwinery.com

WHEN TO VISIT
Open daily 10 am – 5 pm mid-April to mid-October, and by appointment.

MY PICKS

White Wedding is crisp and aromatic. The red wines are all well-made. Trilogy is the name of the winery's Meritage. Nuns on the Run is a full-bodied blend of Syrah and Cabernet Sauvignon reminiscent of some Australian reds. The Cabernet Sauvignon is one of the best in the Okanagan.

HILLSIDE ESTATE WINERY

Among the delicious wines here, Duncan McCowan, the winery's president, singles out three flagship wines. Muscat Ottonel, the delicately spicy white wine, and Old Vines Gamay Noir both rely on vines that were planted here in 1984 by Hillside's founders, Vera and Bohumir Klokocka. Mosaic is the elegant Bordeaux blend that was created in 2002 and, since the 2006 vintage, has been made only with Naramata Bench grapes.

After Bohumir's death, Vera sold the winery in 1996 to a Calgary businessman. It had previously operated from a heritage cottage. In 1997, the new owner gave Penticton architect Robert Mackenzie the first of his many commissions to design a winery. The winery timber frame design mirrors a grist mill with a 22-metre (72-foot) tower looming over Naramata Road. When the winery went over budget, a large group of Albertan investors (as many as 95) took over in 1998 to complete the project and add the 160-seat bistro. Duncan, a wine-loving geologist and oil industry entrepreneur, was one of the 1998 investors. As the winery needed cash infusions over the years, he became a substantial shareholder, twice serving as president.

Since he took control a second time in 2011, the winery pared its large portfolio and, after peaking at a 12,000-case annual production, has set 9,000 to 10,000 cases as its annual target. The winery owns or controls about 16 hectares (40 acres) of vineyard, most of it on the Naramata Bench. Winemaker Kathy Malone, who joined Hillside late in 2008, believes that some of the Okanagan's best grapes are grown on the Bench. Born in New York and with a chemistry degree from the University of Victoria, Kathy made wine at giant Mission Hill for almost two dozen years before switching to Hillside for a more "hands-on" cellar experience.

DUNCAN MCCOWAN

KATHY MALONE

MY PICKS

The Muscat Ottonel, the Gewürztraminer and the Pinot Gris offer crisp and refreshing flavours. The winery's bold reds include the spicy Old Vines Gamay, the intense Reserve Merlot, the peppery Syrah and the yummy Pinotage, tasting of black cherries and coffee. The flagship Mosaic has a style quite reminiscent of fine Bordeaux.

OPENED 1990

1350 Naramata Road
Penticton, BC V2A 8T6

T   250.493.6274
    1.888.923.9463 (toll free)
W www.hillsideestate.com

WHEN TO VISIT
Open daily 10 am – 6 pm April to
November; daily 11 am – 4 pm
December through March

RESTAURANT
The Barrel Room Bistro
Open daily for lunch and dinner
April to mid-December.

HOUSE OF ROSE WINERY

House of Rose celebrated its 20th anniversary in 2013 by winning a double gold for its trademarked Winter Wine, judged the top dessert wine in the 2013 All Canadian Wine Championships. This medal, along with two golds, a silver and a bronze at that spring's Northwest Wine Summit, indicates how much the wines have improved since Aura Rose and spouse Wouter van der Hall took charge in 2009.

The winery was founded by Aura's father, Vern Rose, a retired school-teacher from Alberta. He bought this property in 1982 after a trip to New Zealand where his interest in viticulture was ignited by time spent as a vineyard volunteer. He was one of very few Okanagan vintners who remained loyal to the heritage varieties that most others removed in the 1988 pullout. House of Rose still grows both Okanagan Riesling and De Chaunac in its 2.2-hectare (5½-acre) vineyard, along with Verdelet for icewine and Maréchal Foch, almost the only red hybrid to make a comeback in British Columbia. Vern's winemaking style was eccentric; he often turned to creative blending to cover up the occasional oxidized wine. But he also was shrewd: when he began making icewine, he could not technically use the term because he was not using VQA-eligible grapes. So he called it Winter Wine, promptly getting a trademark to keep the name exclusive to House of Rose.

His clientele loved him. Always garbed in a Tilley hat, Vern injected memorable enthusiasm into vineyard tours and marathon tastings. The summer of 2003, when Vern turned 76, sapped that enthusiasm after the Okanagan Mountain Park forest fire threatened his Rutland neighbourhood three times, forcing evacuation of the winery and sharply curtailing the usual number of visitors. He considered selling the winery but, before a buyer emerged, Vern was incapacitated by a stroke.

The winery stayed in the family when Aura stepped in. Aura, who runs her own healthcare communications company, became involved with House of Rose in 1996 as the bookkeeper. She and Wouter, a

Dutch-born child welfare consultant, refocused the sprawling wine portfolio at House of Rose and, as the medals show, brought a more settled style to the wines.

They have, however, not lost Vern's legendary panache for welcoming visitors. The anniversary celebrations included unveiling a six-metre (20-foot) high metal rose. Wouter maintains that it is the largest rose in Canada.

OPENED 1993

2270 Garner Road
Kelowna. BC V1P 1E2

T   250.765.0802
     1.877.765.0802 (toll free)
W www.houseofrose.ca

WHEN TO VISIT
Open daily 10 am – 6 pm April to October; Tuesday to Saturday noon – 5 pm November to March.

PICNIC AREA

MY PICKS

The Maréchal Foch is one of the Okanagan's best. Many other wines here are still creative blends. Cool Splash is a fruity Riesling and Pinot Gris blend. Award-winning Hot Flash is a blend of Syrah, Maréchal Foch and Pinot Gris Sweet Reserve. Sweet Mystery is an off-dry blend of Pinot Noir and Maréchal Foch. The varieties in Winter Wine White and Winter Wine Rosé are a winery secret.

HOWLING BLUFF ESTATE WINES

Former stockbroker Luke Smith planned to grow mostly premium Bordeaux-style reds until his vineyard set him straight. "After nine years of farming, I am starting to see the patterns of the vineyard," he said in the spring of 2011 when he started converting most of the property to Pinot Noir.

He has kept enough of the Bordeaux varietals to make Sauvignon Blanc but he is phasing out the finely crafted Sin Cera, as the Bordeaux red blend is called. It means "without wax" and was the term used by Roman sculptors when marble they used had no imperfections that needed to be covered with wax.

Luke's switch to Pinot Noir is terroir driven. "I have come to the conclusion that you have the possibility of making a world class Bordeaux blend with just Naramata Bench grapes one out of four years," he says. "In three out of four years you have a chance of making a world class Pinot Noir on the Bench, because of the weather. So why would I fight that?" In fact, Howling Bluff has won the Lieutenant Governor's Award of Excellence twice with Pinot Noir.

A broker in Vancouver, Luke moved to the Okanagan in 2003 to turn an orchard on the Naramata Bench into a vineyard. A university economics graduate, he now tends about 15,000 vines. "Every single post put into the vineyard I have touched three times," he says. "I put the irrigation in. There is nothing here that I haven't done." Since then, his son Daniel, besides mentoring in viticulture with Sal D'Angelo, a nearby winemaker, has joined his father in farming their Summa Quies Vineyard.

In April 2008, nearing his 50th birthday, Luke decided he had juggled two careers long enough and retired as a broker to focus on his winery. That year, he also retained a winemaking consultant, Chris Carson, a Canadian trained in New Zealand and a Pinot Noir zealot.

LUKE SMITH

By the time that vintage was over, Luke had become just as passionate about Pinot Noir.

"I have people asking, as I interplant with Pinot Noir, 'How can you afford to do it?' I can't really afford to do it," Luke admits. "But I set out to make a world-class wine and I am not going to stop halfway through it."

MY PICKS

The portfolio here is focused: crisp Sauvignon Blanc, silken Pinot Noir and the vanishing Sin Cera. When the wines are estate-grown, they have begun to appear with the label, Summa Quies. Roughly translated, that means "attaining peace".

OPENED 2007

1086 Three Mile Road
Penticton, BC V2A 8T7

T   250.490.3640

W www.howlingbluff.ca

WHEN TO VISIT
Open daily 11 am – 5 pm May to October, and by appointment.

HUGGING TREE WINERY

Walter and Cristine Makepeace moved 13 times during their careers with the RCMP. In 2005, just before Walter retired from the force, they settled down in the south Similkameen Valley, buying a highway-side organic apple and peach orchard near Cawston where they could finally put down roots for themselves and for their three children. Nine years later, the property has blossomed into a family-operated estate winery that includes daughter Jennifer and sons Brad and Wes.

Walter, who was born in Vancouver in 1953, joined the RCMP in 1975. His wife Cristine, whom he had met in high school in Surrey, joined the force soon after. At the time of their retirement, Walter was the staff sergeant in charge of the South Okanagan and Cristine, who joined the RCMP in 1990 (and who had previously run the Keremeos detachment), retired in 2013 as a sergeant posted at the Vancouver headquarters.

Their interest in wine burgeoned after they were posted to Oliver in 1993. Walter says "the bug" was put in his ear by Randy Toor, one of the owners of Desert Hills Estate Winery and then an auxiliary RCMP constable. "He was just getting into grape growing and he said, 'Walt, you should buy a vineyard'," Walter remembers. A volunteer spot at a winery during a wine festival motivated him even further. "I worked the till one of the days," Walter says. "There was a lineup. Everybody was standing there with credit cards and money in their hands and they all had smiles on their faces. I said, 'I have got to become a part of this'."

Their search for a vineyard ended when George Hanson, the owner of Seven Stones Winery, directed them to a 24-hectare (60-acre) property located almost across the highway from Seven Stones. Half of the property was orchard; the other half was raw land. (A pair of entangled willow trees on the lawn inspired the winery's name.) Walter planted

WALTER, CRISTINE, BRAD AND JENNIFER MAKEPEACE

grapes on the second half in 2007 and 2008 and now has an eight-hectare (20-acre) vineyard, all of it in Bordeaux reds except for a modest block of Viognier. Syrah planted unsuccessfully on another four hectares (10 acres) was removed, making room for a white varietal in the future, as well as for a winery cellar.

Walter contracted Serendipity Winery to make the wines in 2011 (50 cases of Cabernet Sauvignon) and in 2012 (1,400 cases). Both Walter and Brad, his son, have taken viticulture and winemaking courses at Okanagan College. Brad is the emerging winemaker, a career choice flowing from the family's roots decision. Brad was a professional snowboarder, rock musician and bartender in Whistler until he decided to move to the farm. "I wanted to support my dad's dreams," Brad says. "And when I spent time here, I got addicted to the lifestyle and the valley and the beauty."

MY PICKS

No wines available for tasting at press time.

PROPOSED OPENING 2014

1002 Highway 3
Cawston. BC V0X 1C3

T 250.499.2274
   250.499.2201

INNISKILLIN OKANAGAN VINEYARDS

Few winemakers have had a more intimate relationship with a vineyard than Sandor Mayer has had with Inniskillin Okanagan's Dark Horse Vineyard, which he planted in 1990. He has won international medals for the Dark Horse Cabernet Sauvignon and Meritage wines.

The sunbathed nine-hectare (22-acre) vineyard still inspires new wines, which owe their distinctive flavours and longevity in bottle to the rugged granitic soil. The most recent release is a pure Cabernet Franc, a variety that had always been blended in Meritage until its standout quality demanded it should be released on its own. He is also working on a blend from the vineyard's whites, which include Marsanne, Roussanne, Chardonnay and Pinot Blanc. The only white he planted that did not flourish on this warm site was Gewürztraminer. Those vines were grafted over to Tempranillo in 2005 and Sandor soon was making an exceptional red wine.

Born in Hungary in 1958, Sandor began making wine with his father when he was 14 and, after getting a degree in winemaking, worked with a major research institute there. "In Hungary, I was involved in different trials and made wines with many different varieties," he recalls. No winemaking jobs were available when Sandor and Andrea, his wife, came to the Okanagan in 1989, so he took a job replanting the Dark Horse Vineyard, replacing the hybrid varieties that had been pulled out the year before.

Until recently, he worked in what could only be called a heritage winery. The original Vinitera Estate Winery had 11 horizontal wine tanks tunnelled into the hillside, perhaps the only buried horizontal tanks in any Canadian winery. In 2014 Constellation Brands, the current owner, moved Inniskillin's wine production and the tasting room to the much more modern Jackson-Triggs winery.

Because Constellation is the largest owner of vineyard land in the

SANDOR MAYER

South Okanagan, Sandor is also able to access additional varieties, such as Pinot Gris, from the cooler McIntyre and Whitetail vineyards above Oliver. Sandor made the Okanagan's first Zinfandel in 2002 from vines in Constellation's Bear Cub Vineyard. "It is planted on a well managed site with drip irrigation," he says. "The fruit quality is soaring."

MY PICKS

All the wines are consistently reliable. The standouts are found in the Discovery Series, including the Zinfandel, the Tempranillo and the tangy Chenin Blanc; and in the new Reserve range. Other notables are the Riesling and Tempranillo icewines.

OPENED 1979
(AS VINITERA ESTATE WINERY)

7857 Tucelnuit Drive
Oliver, BC V0H 1T2

T   250.498.4500
    1.866.455.0559 (toll free)

W www.inniskillin.com

WHEN TO VISIT
Open daily 9:30 am – 6 pm July and August; 10 am – 5 pm March to June and September to mid-November; 11 am – 4 pm mid-November to February.

INTERSECTION ESTATE WINERY

Bruce Schmidt describes sales and marketing as the "talent base" he has applied to a variety of fields since earning a physics degree at the University of British Columbia in 1975. He has worked in pharmaceuticals, advertising and financial consulting, but his heart is in the wine business. "I have always been connected in some way to someone who is selling wine, making wine, or whatever," he says. "I have always been interested in a vineyard." The passion has come together at Intersection Estate Winery, so named because it is at the intersection of Road 8 and Highway 97.

A Kelowna native, Bruce began his wine career in 1978 with Nabisco Brands, the company that then owned Calona Vineyards. There, he put his formidable marketing talent behind Schloss Laderheim, the iconic Calona brand that became the top selling white wine in Canada in the early 1980s. He left in 1985 to run an advertising agency for a couple of years and then moved on to consult with start-up companies, mostly in science, something he continues to do.

He also kept a finger in wine, heading a group of investors that helped finance Blue Mountain Vineyard & Cellars in 1992. "Blue Mountain has been a great teacher of how you do things right," he says. In 2005, Bruce bought this highway-side four-hectare (10-acre) orchard. Since then, he has planted 20,000 vines and has transformed a sturdy packing house into a winery. Most of the vineyard is planted to Merlot and Intersection makes several wines from that variety: a rosé; a soft, fruity table wine; unfiltered, age-worthy wines from different blocks in the vineyard; and a muscular Amarone-style made from air-dried grapes.

Winemaker Dylan Roche, an urban geographer who was born in Vancouver in 1976, developed his passion for wine while working as a bicycle mechanic and guide in Burgundy. After earning a winemaking

RYAN AND BRUCE SCHMIDT

DYLAN ROCHE

diploma there, he worked in Bordeaux and Burgundy wineries before returning home in 2011 after 10 years away. "I am pleasantly surprised here," he says. "The more I taste here, the more I find that the shape of the wines is closer to what we tasted in France than it is to [New World] wines."

OPENED 2012

450 Road 8
Oliver, BC V0H 1V5

T 250.498.4054

W www.xwine.ca

WHEN TO VISIT
Open daily 11 am – 5 pm April to October, and by appointment.

MY PICKS

Everything, including the rosé. The whites are Miles's Edge White, a Viognier-based blend, and Sauvignon Blanc. The reds are Milepost Red, Unfiltered Merlot, Cabernet Franc and Vin de Paille Merlot, the Amarone-style red.

INTRIGUE WINES

On a flight to a family vacation in the Maritimes, winemaker Roger Wong and his wife, Jillian, were kicking around names for their new winery when someone observed that wine is "intriguing." They settled on that as the name for the venture they opened in 2009 with partners Ross and Geri Davis. Ross owns a Kelowna data centre and Geri is the controller at Gray Monk Estate Winery.

Roger, who was born in Vancouver in 1965 and has a geography degree, started making wine at home at 17. When he was 30, he quit his government job (technical records keeper for the Department of Energy, Mines and Resources) to volunteer with Tinhorn Creek for the 1995 crush. They hired him, promoting this keener through the vineyards and cellars and through courses at the University of California. In 1998, Roger took over as winemaker at Pinot Reach Cellars, a Kelowna winery that became Tantalus Vineyards in 2004. In 2005 he moved to Gray Monk to make the red and sparkling wines.

Roger's first independent label was Focus Wines, concentrating on Riesling, a variety he believes is well-suited to the North Okanagan. He made the first Focus Riesling in 2002 but the venture stalled in 2003 when smoke from forest fires saturated Kelowna vineyards and ruined the grapes. The dream was reborn after Roger and Jillian found Ross and Geri to be kindred souls. "We all have the passion," Geri says. On their two properties near Wood Lake (near Oyama), the couples in 2008 planted 6.9 hectares (17 acres) of vines, the majority being Riesling. In the 2010 vintage, Roger reintroduced a Focus Riesling in a portfolio of Intrigue wines that includes crisp whites, solid Merlots and a sparkling wine.

The winery occupies a wing of Ross and Geri's house. The wine shop nearby, a favourite with the growing number of residents in suburban Lake Country, includes a pleasant picnic area.

ROGER WONG

The Focus Riesling is a classic dry Riesling built for aging while the regular Riesling is a refreshing charmer. The Pinot Gris, the Gewürztraminer and the white blend are expressive and fruit-forward. The Merlot is a generous wine with ripe berry flavours. The newest wine in the portfolio is a sparkling rosé called I Do.

OPENED 2009

2291 Goldie Road
Lake Country, BC V4V 1G5
T 877.474.3754
W www.intriguewine.ca

WHEN TO VISIT
Open daily 10 am – 6 pm
March to December, and by
appointment.

PICNIC AREA

JACKSON-TRIGGS OKANAGAN ESTATE WINERY

Winery tours are not offered here for a good reason: visitors would get lost amid the towering tanks and stacks of barrels in this sprawling winery. But the elegant hospitality centre, opened in 2006, definitely deserves a visit. Jackson-Triggs has a large portfolio of award-winning wines, many of which can be tasted and purchased here.

The key to all of the awards is the vineyards. Since 1998, Vincor Canada—now Constellation Brands, the parent of Jackson-Triggs—has planted nearly 400 hectares (1,000 acres) of vines, on Black Sage Road, on the Osoyoos Lake Bench and near Okanagan Falls. These professionally managed vineyards are among Canada's best.

All of the vineyards produce premium fruit. However, with the experience of several vintages, Jackson-Triggs has been able to pinpoint superior blocks, one of which is now called the SunRock Vineyard. About 40 hectares (100 acres) in size, it lies on a gentle south-facing slope on the north shore of Osoyoos Lake. The defining feature, and the genesis of the name, is a massive rock block at the northern end of the vineyard. It soaks up sunlight and gives the vineyard the hot microclimate preferred by Shiraz and Cabernet Sauvignon vines. A 2004 vintage SunRock Shiraz whipped a tough field of Australian and other New World wines to be judged the best of variety at the 2006 International Wine & Spirits Competition.

The red wine–maker at Jackson-Triggs Okanagan is Brooke Blair, who came here in 2004. Born in 1978 at Mount Gambier in Australia, she trained at the University of Adelaide, starting out in commerce before switching to wine, in part because winemakers get to travel. Her favourite grape variety? "I love working with Shiraz," she confides.

The white wines and the icewines are made by Derek Kontkanen. Born in Midland, Ontario, in 1978, he has a master's degree in enology, and wrote his thesis on icewine fermentation. It shows in the focused purity of the Jackson-Triggs Riesling icewines.

DEREK KONTKANEN AND BROOKE BLAIR
(COURTESY OF JACKSON-TRIGGS)

MY PICKS

The winery has three tiers. Value-priced wines are offered in the Reserve tier. The Grand Reserve is a sharp step up in intensity and price and includes an award-winning sparkling Entourage Grand Reserve. The SunRock tier is reserved for four special releases from the SunRock Vineyard—Chardonnay, Cabernet Sauvignon, Meritage and Shiraz.

OPENED 1981
(AS BRIGHTS WINES)

7857 Tucelnuit Drive
Oliver, BC V0H 1T2

T   250.498.4500
     1.866.455.0559 (toll free)

W www.jacksontriggswinery.com

WHEN TO VISIT
Open daily 10 am – 6 pm July
to August; daily 11 am – 4 pm
September to June.

JOIEFARM

Now producing about 14,000 cases a year, JoieFarm has been remarkably successful since Michael Dinn and Heidi Noble launched it with just 840 cases from the 2004 vintage. For all its growth, JoieFarm has retained a tight focus on wines inspired by Alsace and Burgundy. "The superiority of the Burgundian varietals to our terroir is undeniable," they wrote in 2013, "but of equal importance is their compatibility with the cuisine of the Pacific Northwest."

The Gewürztraminer-based wine they call A Noble Blend is inspired by the Edelzwicker blends of Alsace. They started with three varieties in the debut Noble Blend but have increased that to six, making a much more refined and complex wine. A red blend called PTG is modelled on the Pinot Noir/Gamay blend called Passe-Tout-Grains in Burgundy. Among the other wines are Pinot Noir and Chardonnay, the classics of Burgundy.

Their commitment and focus arises from previous experience in the restaurant trade. Michael, born in Victoria in 1967, is a history major who started serving in restaurants when he was in university. His 14-year career as a server and sommelier in top Vancouver restaurants inspired a burning ambition to make wine in the Okanagan. Heidi, born in Toronto in 1974, began cooking at 14. She has degrees in philosophy and literature but turned down an academic scholarship to enroll in a chef's school. Like Michael, she also worked in a top Vancouver restaurant. The couple, who married in 2001, met through a sommelier school.

Their intimate knowledge of restaurants put JoieFarm on a fast track. "Because I was working in them, I knew the power of restaurants to expose the wines to the public," Michael says. "They are always the early adopters. By focusing our business model on dealing with the trade first, it allowed us to build a significant reputation quite quickly."

The JoieFarm winery was built in 2007 amid Michael and Heidi's

MICHAEL DINN AND HEIDI NOBLE

one-hectare (2½-acre) Naramata Bench vineyard, which is entirely devoted to Moscato Giallo for the winery's delicate Muscat wine. For most of its grapes, JoieFarm relies on what Michael and Heidi called "committed" growers. In 2013, when the winery adopted the term "En Famille" for a new reserve range, the labels included growers in the family behind those wines.

OPENED 2005

2825 Naramata Road
Naramata. BC V0H 1N0

T 250.496.0073
   1.866.422.5643 (toll free)

W www.joie.com

WHEN TO VISIT
No tasting room or wine shop.

MY PICKS

Every Joie wine is quite simply delicious, with clean, fresh fruit flavours and vivid aromas, reflecting exceptional winemaking by Heidi and Robert Thielecke, who joined JoieFarm in 2009.

KALALA ORGANIC ESTATE WINERY

Kalala is the town in the Punjab where Karnail Singh Sidhu, this winery's owner, was born in 1968. Translated, Kalala means "miracle place" and Karnail honours this on the winery's labels, which show a wolf and lamb with their heads together affectionately. Legend has it that these animals lived in serene harmony at this place in the Punjab.

Kalala's pastoral Glencoe Road property is perhaps too remote, for in 2013 Karnail bought property and planted a small vineyard on Greenbay Road, not far from Quails' Gate Estate Winery. "We'll sell a lot more wine there than we do here," Karnail believes. At the time of this writing, Karnail was deciding whether or not to move Kalala there, while keeping the Glencoe property for Dostana and 3 Cru (the labels that he developed with partners in 2011).

When Karnail came to Canada in 1993, his diploma in electrical engineering was not recognized, so he relied on his 25 years experience as a farmer for employment in the Okanagan. In 1996, he joined the pruning crew at Summerhill Pyramid Winery. That was the beginning of a 10-year career there, during which he emerged as a leader in organic viticulture in the Okanagan. The company he set up in 1997 with two brothers, Kalala Agriculture, has provided supplies and expertise for many organic grape growers in the valley.

Karnail's winery gets fruit from his organic vineyards at Westbank and near Oliver in the South Okanagan. The south-facing Westbank property, one of the highest elevation vineyards in this part of the Okanagan, is well suited to the cool-climate varieties planted here, including Pinot Noir, Pinot Gris and Gewürztraminer. Karnail has a significant planting of Zweigelt, an Austrian red from which he has made table wine, icewine and, most recently, sparkling wine.

In a return to his roots, Karnail began to export Kalala wines to India in 2013, culminating a marketing approach dating from a 1997 trip to

KARNAIL SINGH SIDHU

explore the market there for Canadian icewine. He even considered planting a Himalayan vineyard just for icewine. Subsequent visits revealed both a rising number of quality Indian wineries and a rising demand for the kind of table wines that Kalala makes.

MY PICKS

The Pinot Gris and Gewürztraminer are refreshing whites. The Merlot, Pinot Noir and the Zweigelt, while aged in barrels, show attractive fruit flavours that are not submerged in oak. Wine prices here are affordable.

OPENED 2008

3361 Glencoe Road
West Kelowna, BC
V4T 1M1

T 250.768.9700
   1.866.942.1313 (toll free)

W www.kalalawines.ca

WHEN TO VISIT
Open daily 10 am – 6 pm April to October; Wednesday to Sunday 11 am – 5 pm November to March; and by appointment.

KANAZAWA WINES

The distinctive Diamond Flower (*hanabishi* in Japanese) has a deeply personal meaning for winemaker Richard Kanazawa. The diamond-shaped flower was the symbol, or *kamon*, that always appeared on his mother's kimono. Now it honours her memory on the labels of his finely crafted Okanagan wines.

Richard was born and grew up in Langley, British Columbia. He explored his heritage as a young man by going to Japan and playing rugby professionally. On returning to Langley, he found a job delivering wine for the Domaine de Chaberton Winery, and it was there that his interest in wine blossomed. Since there was no winemaking school in British Columbia, he began studying food technology at the British Columbia Institute of Technology and started looking for a winery job.

"I had a lot of experience at Domaine but I couldn't get a job as a cellar hand in the Okanagan if my life depended on it," he recalled later. "I thought if I can't get a job here, what do I have to do to further my career? Going overseas was my best opportunity." In 2002 he enrolled at Charles Sturt University in Australia in a program that enabled him to get winery work experience. One of those wineries was Simon Gilbert. Richard started as a cellar hand but was quickly promoted to the laboratory. After he returned to Canada in 2004, his beefed-up resumé won him the winemaker's job at Red Rooster. He was there three vintages making, among other wines, a Malbec that won a Lieutenant Governor's Award of Excellence. He moved on to Blasted Church Vineyards in 2008 and then Lang Vineyards in 2012, making award winners at both wineries.

He also determined that he and Jennifer, his wife, would develop their own label. That was a gutsy decision for two reasons: one, they started on a shoe string; and two, several of his employers objected to Richard creating his own label while he was making prize wines for them. The Kanazawa wines, which debuted in 2010 with 900 cases, have been made under various other winery licenses. With effective distribution in select wine stores and restaurants, the winery has since doubled production. "I promised Jennifer we would never grow over 5,000 cases," says Richard, who expects to grow into his own licensed winery by then.

MY PICKS

The labels of the excellent wines echo Richard's Japanese heritage as well as his opportunistic winemaking. Ronin, the bold red, was a Bordeaux blend in 2010 and a Syrah in 2011. Nomu is a Viognier Sémillon blend. Pika Pika is an elegantly dry sparkling wine.

OPENED 2010

P.O. Box 72
Naramata, BC Canada V0H 1N0

T 250.486.7424

W www.kanazawawines.com

WHEN TO VISIT
No tasting room.

RICHARD KANAZAWA

KETTLE VALLEY WINERY

When they launched Kettle Valley, chartered accountant Bob Ferguson and geologist Tim Watts intended to limit production to three wines: Chardonnay, Pinot Noir and a Bordeaux blend called Old Main Red (named for their Naramata vineyard where most of the grapes grow). And they believed they would never make more than 5,000 cases a year. Yet today, the winery makes about 10,000 cases a year and has spawned a companion label, Great Northern Vineyards, from its five-hectare (12-acre) Similkameen property.

The portfolio now is close to 30 wines, including many single vineyard wines expressing individual terroirs. One of Kettle Valley's best Pinot Noirs is grown in the Hayman Vineyard, which the partners planted in 1988. Production averages about 80 cases a year. The winery's legendary Barber Cabernet Sauvignon—again about 100 cases a year—comes from a two-hectare (five-acre) vineyard that the partners have farmed since 2000 for businessman Dave Barber. Although he died in 2010, his family still use the summer retreat while Kettle Valley manages the vineyard.

Wines like the Barber Cabernet are something of a labour of love, made from grapes cropped so sparingly that the selling price of the wine barely covers the costs. "It is because we enjoy doing it," Bob explains. "To make money on growing things like Cabernet Sauvignon and Petit Verdot in this region, you would have to be charging way more money than the market would bear."

The winery was named for the Kettle Valley Railway, whose railbed above the Naramata Bench is now a well-used hiking trail. Railway history and lore has been exploited in naming the wines. Adra Station, a reserve Chardonnay, takes its name from a station on the line. Naramata Bench Reserve EXTRA 4079, a red blend, is named for the last train over the Coquihalla Summit in November 1959 before a series of washouts

TIM WATTS (L) AND BOB FERGUSON

closed the Kettle Valley service forever.

In the same vein, the Similkameen vineyard was named for the Great Northern Railway that once operated in that valley. There is a steam locomotive on the Great Northern labels, similar to Kettle Valley's labels. The winemaker for Great Northern Vineyards is Andrew Watt, Tim's son and a 2010 winemaking graduate from Lincoln University in New Zealand.

OPENED 1996

2988 Hayman Road
RR 1 Site 2 Comp 39
Naramata, BC V0H 1N0

T 250.496.5898
　1.888.496.8757 (toll free)

W www.kettlevalleywinery.com

WHEN TO VISIT
Thursday to Monday 11 am
– 5 pm April to October; and
by appointment. Groups of
eight or more should make
appointments.

MY PICKS

Everything. The red wines, including Pinot Noir, are bold, full-flavoured and can be aged at least 10 years. The flagship is Old Main Red, a seamless blend of Merlot, Cabernet Sauvignon and Cabernet Franc, touched up with a dash each of Malbec and Petit Verdot. From the Great Northern portfolio, look for the Viognier, Syrah and Zinfandel.

KISMET ESTATE WINERY

The Dhaliwal brothers had farming in their blood before coming to the Okanagan. "When I was 14 years old, I was driving a tractor on a farm," says Sukhwinder (Sukhi for short). "We came from the farming area in India, the Punjab." He came to the Okanagan, where he had relatives, in 1989 at the age of 20. His brother, Balwinder, born in 1974, joined him in 1993. Both have worked in, and managed, vineyards ever since for major producers including Mission Hill and Vincor.

They bought their first property in 1996 and planted grapes the following year. "After that, we never stopped," says Balwinder (who sometimes goes by the name of Bill). Now, they operate about 52.6 hectares (130 acres) of vineyards in the South Okanagan and sell grapes or manage vineyards for well-known wineries such as Laughing Stock Vineyards and Black Hills.

Growing grapes obviously introduced the brothers to wine. "We didn't drink wine when we were in India," Suhki says. "As soon as we started dealing with those wineries, we starting getting some free wine." In time, that led them to open their own winery as well. Suhki explains why: "The first thing is that we grow good quality fruit; and we think if we make our own wine, we can make very good quality wine. We have all the varieties. Secondly, I think we can make a little bit more money. And the third thing is that we really would like to have our own winery. That's our hobby."

It is a pretty serious hobby that is designed to grow into making 5,000 cases a year, with a processing facility amid the vines and a wine shop beside the highway. The consulting winemakers have the benefit, Suhki says, of many varieties, including rare blocks of Grenache and Mourvedre.

The brothers called the winery Kismet, meaning luck. It seems appropriate since they have made their own luck for years.

SUKHWINDER AND BALWINDER DHALIWAL

MY PICKS

Kismet debuted with two well-priced whites— an aromatic blend of Sauvignon Blanc, Sémillon and Muscat called Saféd (meaning "clear") and a delicious Viognier. The reds are blends incorporating Malbec, Merlot, Cabernet Franc, Petit Verdot and Syrah.

OPENED 2013

9580 Road 20
Oliver, BC V0H 1T0

T 250.408.9800

W www.kismetestatewinery.com

WHEN TO VISIT
Open daily 10 am – 5 pm.

KRĀZĒ LEGZ VINEYARD & WINERY

Its "Roaring 1920s" motif differentiates this winery from its peers. That decade was the golden era for the Charleston, a provocative dance whose high kicking steps inspired this winery's name, Krāzē Legz, pronounced *crazy legs*. That decade also encompassed Prohibition in the United States and much of Canada. Citizens got around the ineffective ban on alcohol by patronizing unlicensed bars called speakeasies, whose locked doors usually had keyholes or peepholes for screening the patrons. There is a keyhole in the door of this winery's tasting room, although visitors need not say "Joe sent me" or a similar 1920s password before entering.

The wines, whose labels feature jazz dancers, are branded around the musical terms and colloquial language of the 1920s. While the Charleston was the era's most popular dance, other wines take their namesake from the Cakewalk, the Lindy Hop and the Black Bottom Stomp (the latter is a Jelly Roll Morton song). The label for Bee's Knees—slang for excellence—was inspired perhaps by the knees of Bee Jackson, a World Champion Charleston dancer. To add to the theme, background music in the Krāzē Legz wine shop is comprised mostly of vintage 1920s jazz and, on occasion, the tasting room hosts wear flapper-style fashions.

The winery is run by Susan and Gerry Thygeson, who was a marketer of food products in his previous career. Born in Bonnyville, Alberta, in 1957, Gerry began his career in 1980 with Okanagan Dried Fruits, a Penticton company that became a national success. He joined a similar company in Seattle in 1996, got a marketing degree there and was a marketing vice-president for several American food companies before returning to the Okanagan in 2007 to plant the Krāzē Legz vineyard at Kaleden. He and Susan, an equestrian as well as an equine photographer, bought this 5.6-hectare (14-acre) orchard in 1995. It now grows

GERRY AND SUSAN THYGESON

Merlot, Cabernet Franc, Chardonnay and Pinot Blanc.

Krāzē Legz was the first winery in Kaleden, an attractive village laid out in 1909 on the western shore of Skaha Lake. According to *A Traveller's Guide to Historic British Columbia* by Rosemary Neering, the town's name celebrates the site's pastoral beauty. The name combines the first syllable of *kalos*, Greek for "beautiful," with "Eden." There have been vineyards here since at least the 1970s but, despite the easy access from highway, no winery until Krāzē Legz opened in the fall of 2010.

The keyhole in the door is embossed on the back of every Krāzē Legz wine bottle. "We feel eventually it will be our Nike Swoosh," Gerry says. "It will be consistently the most recognizable part of our marketing."

OPENED 2010

141 Fir Ave
Kaleden, BC V0H 1K0

T 250.497.6957

W www.krazelegz.com

WHEN TO VISIT
Open daily 10 am – 6 pm
May to mid-October, and by appointment.

MY PICKS

The excellent wines still come with memorable period labels, including The Bee's Knees Pinot Blanc and the Charleston Chardonnay. In 2014, the winery also began releasing wines under a more conservative label, Skaha Vineyard.

LA FRENZ WINERY

When he conducts tours of the La Frenz vineyards, proprietor Jeff Martin is likely to offer visitors a chance to smell a handful of earth. "That's alive," he says. In 2012, before he planted vines in his newest Naramata Road vineyard, he had livestock grazing on previously planted fall rye. The object was to get organic matter and bacteria into the soil. "The smell you get from the earth turns up in the fruit; and it is particularly noticeable in reds," Jeff says. "We're farming not only for the health of the vineyard but for the flavour of the soil."

That thinking also governed the guidance that was given to New Zealand–born winemaker Andrew Leitch when Jeff hired him in 2013 to replace Scott Robinson (who left to work on a doctorate). "I am looking for vineyard designated wines that totally reflect the effort that is going into the vineyard," Jeff says. "It is the French model."

Jeff is a New World winemaker who has acquired French values. At the age of 20, Jeff started in 1977 with the McWilliams winery in Australia. He and Niva, his wife, came to the Okanagan in 1994 where his winemaking skills put Quails' Gate Estate Winery on the map before they opened La Frenz Winery. (La Frenz is the surname of Jeff's paternal grandfather.)

When Andrew returned to Australia in 2014, he was succeeded by Dominic McCosker, who was born in Australia in 1976. Dominic, a biology graduate, had been dividing his time between working in agricultural laboratories and travelling, until opting for the Okanagan after a trip there in 2007. A job in the vineyards at Tantalus led to the Okanagan College winemaking program and two vintages in Australia. He returned to the Okanagan to spend four years as a cellar master and assistant winemaker at CedarCreek, and two years as the winemaker at St. Hubertus. Dominic was drawn to La Frenz by the opportunity to learn from Jeff's 40 years of experience as a winemaker and to work with a broad range of varieties.

JEFF MARTIN

DOMINIC MCCOSKER

He inherits a portfolio of elegant, award-winning La Frenz wines and an employer with uncompromising standards. "I have come to the opinion [that] there is just no place for average wine," Jeff declares. "Why would I want to do average? It's way easier to sell the better wines."

MY PICKS

Everything, from the exceptional whites, the delicious reds and the extraordinary fortified wines.

OPENED 2000

(Tasting Room)
1525 Randolph Road
Penticton, BC

(Mailing Address)
740 Naramata Road
Penticton, BC V2A 8T5

T   250.492.6690

W www.lafrenzwinery.com

WHEN TO VISIT
Open daily 10 am – 5 pm
May to October; weekends
10 am – 5 pm November; and
by appointment.

LAKE BREEZE VINEYARDS

Lake Breeze calls itself a "wine farm"—the quaint South African term for a vineyard. Founder Paul Moser, a South African entrepreneur, put the stamp of that country on Lake Breeze with the winery's white-washed Cape-style architecture, a small block of Pinotage grapes and with winemaker Garron Elmes.

Garron Elmes, then a 23-year-old graduate of the leading South African wine school, arrived to make the first vintage in 1995. The winery has been through four ownership changes but Garron, now a Canadian citizen, has remained to make every vintage. "I am almost more Canadian than I am South African," he says. In 2013, Garron was also named president of the winery.

The disciplined portfolio, about 20 wines, has achieved a quality so consistent that eliminating the winery's Seven Poplars label has been considered. While consumers perceive it as the winery's reserve tier, it usually is applied to limited-production wines (like the 50 to 60 cases of Pinotage made each year). "It gives us somewhere to put the special stuff," Garron says of the label. "But then we believe that all the wines are good." The winery's reputation was built initially with its white wines, especially Pinot Blanc. This variety has been growing on the 4.85-hectare (12-acre) farm since 1985 and the older vines produce wines with more intense flavours. The winery also buys grapes, mostly from the Naramata Bench, with Pinot Noir from a Summerland grower. Cabernet Sauvignon from an Oliver grower enables Garron to make both a Meritage and a premium red blend called Tempest.

Lake Breeze now makes an average of about 12,000 cases a year, having more than tripled its production since 2001 when a partnership of two Alberta business couples bought the winery. Calgary investment banker Drew MacIntyre and his wife Barbara, who have built a Tuscan-style home next to the winery, became the sole proprietors in 2011 after acquiring the interests of their partners.

GARRON ELMES

MY PICKS

Everything. The Winemaker Series whites include one of the Okanagan's best Viogniers, an ageable Riesling and a delicious white blend called Windfall. Tempest is the winery's collectible Bordeaux red. Look especially for the winery's Pinot Blanc, one of the best in the Okanagan, and for the Seven Poplars Pinotage.

OPENED 1996

930 Sammet Road
PO Box 9
Naramata, BC V0H 1N0
T 250.496.5659
W www.lakebreeze.ca

WHEN TO VISIT
Open daily 11 am – 5:30 pm
May to October; weekends
noon – 4 pm in November;
Friday to Sunday noon – 4 pm
in April; and winter visits by
appointment.

RESTAURANT
The Patio
T 250.496.5659
Open daily 11:30 am – 3:30 pm
May to mid-October;
reservations only for groups
of eight or more.

LANG VINEYARDS

There is no doubt that Lang Vineyards, one of the original farm gate wineries, is back on its feet. Its iconic Farm Reserve Riesling 2011 was judged the best white wine at the 2013 All Canadian Wine Awards. A few weeks earlier, the same vintage was judged Best of Varietal at a major Okanagan wine competition.

The winery was founded by Günther and Kristina Lang, who had moved from Germany in 1981, buying a four-hectare (10-acre) property with a vineyard and an exceptional view. The winery had an enviable reputation when it was purchased in 2005 to anchor the growing Holman-Lang winery group. When the group went into receivership five years later, Lang Vineyards was purchased by a Chinese mining executive called Yong Wang. He has revived the brand, putting the Lang family back into the winery by naming Mike Lang, Günther's nephew, as the general manager.

Mike and his winemakers have returned the winery to its traditional focus, anchored by the Riesling and Maréchal Foch in the vineyard. The mature vines enable the winery to make about 900 cases of the legendary Farm Reserve Riesling. The red wines include about 1,500 cases of Maréchal Foch from vines more than 50 years old. The ripe and slightly off-dry wine developed a cult following soon after the first vintage was made in 1989. The winery also makes a solid Pinot Noir, a variety that can be so challenging that Richard Kiltz, the winemaker for the 2012 vintage, calls it a "high maintenance girlfriend." In 2013, when Richard moved to another winery, he was succeeded by Lawrence Herder, a veteran vintner more comfortable with Pinot Noir.

Lang Vineyards also is well regarded for its Riesling icewine and for two dessert wines that Günther developed in 1995 to supplement his icewine offerings. The red Original Canadian Maplewine is Pinot Noir to which 15 percent maple syrup has been added. The white Original

MIKE LANG

Canadian Maplewine is Chardonnay with about 20 percent maple syrup. The precise percentage is a trade secret. The wines have taken the Lang brand into many duty-free shops.

The Maplewines, which sell for less than half the cost of icewine, are carefully crafted so that the maple flavours are subtle and the sweetness is moderate. The white, in fact, is crisp and lively.

MY PICKS

The Farm Reserve Riesling is one of the Okanagan's best Rieslings. Try the Maréchal Foch, which the winemaker— and the fans of the wine— believes can compete with any vinifera. Maplewines are unique and delicious.

OPENED 1990

2493 Gammon Road
Naramata, BC V0H 1N0

T   778.514.5598

W www.langvineyards.ca

WHEN TO VISIT
Open daily 10 am – 5:30 pm daily May to October, and by appointment.

LARCH HILLS WINERY

Jack and Hazel Manser made two tours of the Okanagan before buying Larch Hills in mid-2005. "I like a green country," Jack says, explaining why they chose not to settle in the desert landscape of the South Okanagan. Born in eastern Switzerland in 1957, Jack had a 20-year career there as a forester before coming to Canada in 1992. After operating a mixed farm in Alberta, he settled on wine growing as a farming business with more potential. He and Hazel, a former nurse, are industrious, running this 6,000-case winery with just one other employee.

Geographically, Larch Hills is just beyond the northern end of the Okanagan Valley. The non-irrigated six-hectare (15-acre) vineyard (the highest-elevation vineyard in British Columbia at 700 metres or 2,297 feet) was planted by Hans and Hazel Nevrkla. Like the Mansers, they settled on this heavily forested property because of its verdant richness. After clearing some of the south-facing slope, Austrian-born Hans, a prize-winning home winemaker, succeeded as a professional vintner with early-ripening varieties chosen to suit this northern location. The three primary white varieties in the vineyard are Ortega, Siegerrebe and Madeleine Angevine. After selling, Hans tutored Jack through several vintages. "Hans made really nice wines," says Jack, who has clearly raised the bar since taking over.

For Jack, managing the vineyard is the easy part of owning a winery. "Driving a tractor is nothing new to me. In forestry, I planted thousands and thousands of trees. Putting a plant in the ground does not scare me." He increased the vineyard's plantings of Ortega and Siegerrebe. The slope still has more than 25 hectares (62 acres) of land with vineyard potential, provided the forest is cleared.

HAZEL AND JACK MANSER

MY PICKS

The dry Ortega, crisp and fruity, is one of British Columbia's best examples of this variety. Other favourites in this cheery tasting room include the vivid Siegerrebe, the whimsically named Mad Angie (who can get their tongue around Madeleine Angevine?) and Tamarack Rosé. The rosé is a fruity blend of St. Laurent and Lemberger grapes, with a rose petal aroma and flavours of strawberries. The Lemberger, Merlot, Maréchal Foch and a blend called Grandview Bench are so well-made that in 2013 they were sold out by mid-August. The wines all are priced at less than $20 and everything is open in the tasting room.

OPENED 1997

110 Timms Road
Salmon Arm, BC V1E 2P8

T   250.832.0155
    1.877.892.0155 (toll free)
W   www.larchhillswinery.com

WHEN TO VISIT
Open daily 9 am – 5 pm
year-round; in winter, check
road conditions first.

LARIANA CELLARS

The winery name is a tribute to Larry and Anna Franklin, the parents of Carol Scott, who owns this winery with her husband, Dan. Larry Franklin was a shareholder in Shannon Pacific Vineyards, a large Black Sage Road vineyard until it was broken up after the 1988 vine pull out. During one vintage, Carol was assigned to keep the starlings away from the grapes with a bird gun. In another vintage, she helped pick grapes. She also hauled grapes to the family home in Burnaby where her father made wine.

Those experiences planted the seed for this winery even as the Scotts, both born in 1963, pursued careers in Burnaby—Don as a millwright, and Carol as a travel agent. They moved to Osoyoos in 1989, taking over a campground that her parents had established in 1968. The recreational vehicle sites, which they still operate, take up the lakeside half of the four-hectare (10-acre) property. The vineyard, which began to replace apple and cherry trees in 2007, occupies the top half.

Planting vines was Carol's passion. "It took a few years to get Dan on board," she admits. "It was kind of a dream to plant grapes. I finally convinced Dan and we cleared the land. It was a new tractor that convinced him." They planted Viognier, Cabernet Sauvignon and Syrah. When the hard winters of 2008 and 2009 mortally damaged the Syrah, that variety was replaced with 2,500 Carmenère vines. Now, they purchase Syrah for Lariana's red blend.

The Scotts, who intend to limit production to about 1,200 cases a year, built a plain-Jane winery with a modest tasting room. They invested instead in top-flight equipment, including the California-made concrete egg, in which Carol and consulting winemaker Senka Tennant make Lariana's Viognier. Stainless steel tanks are half the price but whites made in concrete eggs—several larger Okanagan wineries have them—show richer texture.

Lariana is the Okanagan's southernmost winery, tucked snugly against the 49th parallel. In fact, winery visitors take a street that winds to the east of the massive American customs post.

MY PICKS

The exceptional Viognier and the companion red blend are well-grown and well-made.

OPENED 2013

8310 2nd Avenue
Osoyoos, BC V0H 1V1

T   250.498.9259

W www.larianacellars.com

WHEN TO VISIT
By appointment only.

DAN AND CAROL SCOTT

LASTELLA

This winery has atmosphere to spare. The name, LaStella, was inspired by the twinkling constellations in the clear night sky of the South Okanagan. The wines take their names from Latin musical terms (because a former partner was a classical music lover). The secluded Tuscan-style building is nestled at the bottom of a vineyard with 122 metres (400 feet) fronting on Osoyoos Lake. Sean Salem, who owns the winery with wife Saeedeh, becomes lyrical when speaking of the birdsongs he has heard while relaxing here. The ambiance also makes this winery a favourite South Okanagan wedding venue.

LaStella and its sister winery, Le Vieux Pin near Oliver, are operated by Enotecca Wineries and Resorts, the Vancouver holding company set up by the Salems to make Okanagan wine. Some of the LaStella wines, made by French-trained winemaker Severine Pinte, reflect the Italian theme of the architecture. One notable example is Moscato D'Osoyoos, an intensely aromatic white inspired by Piedmont's Moscato d'Asti.

Currently, LaStella's flagship reds are two terroir-driven and intensely-flavoured Merlots. Allegretto is produced from own-rooted vines growing on sun-bathed sand in Osoyoos. Maestoso, a $100 wine, is from a vineyard on the Golden Mile where the clay and alluvial till in the soil contributes to the wine's remarkable depth. Collectible wines like these are offered first to LaStella's wine club (just sign up) and are also among the wines that LaStella has been exporting.

The winery allows its fans to get as fully involved as they wish. At vintage time, the call goes out for volunteers to help pick grapes and sort them on the crush pad. Even with a start time of 6 am, the atmosphere, the food and ultimately the wine appeal to genuine enthusiasts.

SEVERINE PINTE

MY PICKS

Maestoso is one of the Okanagan's most expensive red wines but also one of the most memorable. Other delicious reds include Allegretto (Merlot), Fortissimo (a Bordeaux blend) and La Sophia (Cabernet Sauvignon). Rounding out the portfolio is Vivace (Pinot Gris), Leggiero (unoaked Chardonnay) and La Stellina (Merlot rosé).

OPENED 2008

8123 148th Avenue
Osoyoos, BC V0H 1V0

T 250.495.8180

W www.lastella.ca
www.enotecca.ca

WHEN TO VISIT
Open daily 10 am – 7 pm
May to October; 11 am – 5 pm
November to April (appointments encouraged).

LICENSED PATIO

LAUGHING STOCK VINEYARDS

One of the Okanagan's most collected wines is Laughing Stock Portfolio, a Bordeaux blend capable of aging in a good cellar. The winery believes that the inaugural 2003 vintage peaked in 2013 and calculates that later vintages will need 11 or 12 years to peak.

Their previous careers in the investment business inspired David and Cynthia Enns to christen their flagship wine Portfolio. They owned Credo Consulting, a mutual funds advisor, and continued running it for four years while getting the winery established. "I never worked so hard in my life," says David, who was born in 1957. "The investment business forced me to be on a plane a week a month, all over North America, while building the winery. That was the perfect storm of way too much work and pressure." The cheeky response to those who questioned their career switch was to call the winery Laughing Stock.

The fingerprints of the investment business are all over Laughing Stock. The opening in September 2005 was called the Initial Public Offering. Every bottle is encircled with ticker tape showing the trading value of certain shares on the days when the grapes were picked. Red and white blends are called Blind Trust because the varietal composition is hidden under neck capsules. Some varietals are released as "Small Caps" wines. As a result, many Laughing Stock wine clients work for the sort of corporations that David and Cynthia once advised. "I think our wine is the most corporately gifted wine in Canada, without a doubt," David says.

The clever marketing is backed up by winemaking continually stretching for improved quality. Cellar tools now include three concrete eggs from France and two clay amphorae from Italy. David ferments wines in these as well as in 500-litre oak puncheons, standard oak barrels and stainless steel tanks. Blending the separate ferments adds complexity, he believes.

DAVID ENNS

"We do 1,400 cases of Pinot Gris," David says. "I will have four different ferments just to make a $20 Pinot Gris. Our Pinot Gris is consistently complex. The commitment to quality hasn't stopped since day one."

OPENED 2005

1548 Naramata Road
Penticton, BC V2A 8T7

T   250.493.8466
W www.laughingstock.ca

WHEN TO VISIT
By appointment only.

MY PICKS

Everything including the Syrah, the Blind Trust twins, the Chardonnay, the Pinot Gris and Viognier. And keep an eye out for the single-vineyard Pinot Noir to be released under a proprietary label from a small Naramata vineyard David and Cynthia planted in 2013.

LEFT FIELD CIDER COMPANY

The urge to make cider came to Kate Garthwaite "out of left field" and that explains the name of this family cidery on the historic Rey Creek Ranch in the Nicola Valley. Kate, then a fundraiser and now a human resources manager, started to make cider in her Vancouver kitchen. "I did not know you have to put water in the airlock so, needless to say, it did not work out well," she says and laughs.

Nothing if not determined, she took several cider-making courses in Washington State. "Then I thought if I am serious about this, I should go where the cider is," Kate says. "Fifty percent of the world's cider comes from a couple of counties in England. So I moved to Hertfordshire and got a job with a wonderful craft cider–maker there named Mike Johnson at Ross-on-Wye Cider and Perry. I spent a year there, working and learning, and that is how it came about."

Upon returning to Canada in 2011, she enlisted sister Theresa Pederen to do the marketing and parents Gordon and Debbie Garthwaite to build the cidery on a ranch with 1,100 head of cattle, which the family has operated since 1952. "Cattle ranching is all I have ever done, until the girls sucked me into cider making," Gordon says. He is just as serious about it as his daughters, having also taken a course in Washington State.

While the Nicola Valley is marginal for apple growing, provincial rules require basing a land-based cidery or winery on an orchard or vineyard. The Garthwaites have planted about 1.2 hectares (three acres) of heritage apples on winter-hardy Russian rootstock. Meanwhile, they are sourcing cider apples from growers in the Okanagan and Similkameen valleys.

The two carbonated ciders produced here are called Little Dry and Big Dry; one is less dry than the other. Both are sold in brown half-litre bottles, not unlike the English ciders that Kate admires. "We are

THE GARTHWAITE FAMILY: GORDON, THERESA, KATE AND DEBBIE (COURTESY OF LEFT FIELD CIDER)

marketing it as something to drink by the pint, not as a wine alternative," Kate says. "We don't want to discourage wine drinkers from drinking it. I like wine and I like cider."

MY PICKS

Both Little Dry and Big Dry are crisp and refreshing and taste a lot like authentic English ciders.

OPENED 2012

8821 Highway 97C
PO Box 731
Logan Lake, BC V0K 1W0

T   250.448.6991

W www.leftfieldcider.com

WHEN TO VISIT
Open weekends 10 am – 6 pm and Friday afternoons May long weekend to Labour Day; and by appointment.

LE VIEUX PIN

The Robert Mackenzie–designed winery is said to resemble a small French railroad station with its drooping overhang of a roof, shading the walls from the blistering Okanagan sun. The winery's French name was inspired by the old pine tree on the nearby ridge overlooking the town of Oliver. The compact winery is designed to produce about 3,500 cases a year. The owners believe it would be difficult to hand-craft quality wines at much larger volumes. LaStella, its sister winery, is built for a similar capacity. Both are owned by Enotecca Winery and Resorts of Vancouver.

Enotecca has acquired vineyards of its own and works with select growers. "Because we had such a small volume of production, I could not believe that we would not have our own vineyards," says Sean Salem, who owns Enotecca with his wife, Saeedeh. "Then we would have our own way of growing grapes. That would allow us to keep the quality where it is today."

Le Vieux Pin's four-hectare (10-acre) property, a former orchard, was planted in 2005, chiefly with Syrah, along with a small plot of Viognier. Recently, the winery has added Marsanne and Roussanne vines. As these vines come into production, Le Vieux Pin is converting some of its portfolio to Rhône varietals. In its initial vintages, this winery's reputation was built with Sauvignon Blanc and Pinot Noir. The final Pinot Noir vintage was 2008. Some of those vines were then grafted over to Syrah. The only Pinot Noir still in the line is the very popular rosé, Vaïla, named for a former vineyard manager's daughter.

The winery also has changed its labels, phasing out such labels as Belle and Périgée (both Pinot Noirs) and Époque and Apogée (both Merlots). For the most part, the new releases highlight the varietal name on the labels, with Équinoxe designating the reserve tier. Petit Le Vieux Pin is the second label for value-priced wines.

SEVERINE PINTE

MY PICKS

Everything in the Équinoxe range, especially the Syrah, the Cabernet Franc, the Merlot, the "Ava" Viognier Roussanne blend and the Chardonnay. Vaïla is an excellent dry rosé. The Petit tier of wines is anything but petit in quality.

OPENED 2006

5496 Black Sage Road
Oliver, BC V0H 1T0

T   250.498.8388

W www.levieuxpin.ca
    www.enotecca.ca

WHEN TO VISIT
Open daily 10 am – 7 pm
May to October; daily 11 am
– 5 pm November to April;
appointments recommended.

PICNIC PATIO

LIQUIDITY WINES

This location was destined for a winery. It commands a vineyard view similar to the neighbouring Blue Mountain Vineyard & Cellars' stunning vista. (Blue Mountain founder Ian Mavety once grew grapes in this slope.) A previous owner built what looked like a winery in waiting, a sprawling adobe-style home now renovated as Liquidity's tasting room. About 2005, the property was acquired by Arizona housing developer Gordon Pekrul, one of several where he planned wineries until the properties went into bankruptcy in 2009. The Allendale Road property was purchased by Vancouver businessman Ian MacDonald and his partners, wine-loving Calgary business people.

Ian is Liquidity's hands-on manager because of his interest in viticulture. Born in Montreal in 1954, he is the grandson of a farmer. He worked in Calgary in the 1980s as a vice-president of sportswear maker Sunice, an official supplier to the 1988 Winter Olympics. "I fell in love with the Olympics," Ian says. He formed a company called Moving Products, which has supplied non-athletic uniforms at nearly every Olympics since then. "We are the only company on the planet providing the logistics for uniforming large numbers of people at the Olympic games," he says.

The Allendale Road vineyard had 10 acres of mature vines, notably Pinot Noir; another 10 acres on the prime south-facing slope has been replanted. The other varieties here include Viognier, Chardonnay, Pinot Gris, Merlot, Cabernet Franc and a little Cabernet Sauvignon. After taking over, Ian upgraded all the irrigation, installed moisture sensors and a weather station, and had the soils analyzed.

After working with consultants for two years, Liquidity named Matt Holmes, the former winemaker at Tantalus Vineyards, as its vineyard and winery manager. Matt was born in Australia but is now a Canadian citizen. Just 28 when he joined Tantalus in 2005, he has a winemaking

IAN MACDONALD

MATT HOLMES

degree from Charles Sturt University and experience with wineries there, in New Zealand and in the United States. He made Liquidity's first two small vintages in 2010 and 2011 at a nearby winery while designing the winery that Liquidity moved into for the 2012 vintage.

"Our goal is not to be a big operation" Ian says. "It is more about the quality, long-term, than about the quantity." The adobe-style home originally on this property was redeveloped in 2013 to include a spacious tasting room and bistro with one of the finest vineyard views in the Okanagan.

OPENED 2012

4720 Allendale Road
Okanagan Falls, BC V0H 1R2

T 778.515.5550

W www.liquiditywines.com

WHEN TO VISIT
Open daily 11 am – 6 pm June to October.

BISTRO
Open daily 11 am – 9 pm May to October.

MY PICKS

Everything, including the Pinot Noir, the Viognier, the Chardonnay and a Champagne-style wine called Bubbly.

LITTLE FARM WINERY

Rhys Pender's total immersion in the wine industry began at age 14 with an after-school job stocking shelves in a Canberra wine store. "I wasn't that interested [in wine] but you do learn something by default," says Rhys, who, with partner Alishan Driediger, opened up Little Farm Winery in 2012.

Rhys was born in the Australian capital in 1975. Immediately after university, where he had studied sports administration, he jetted off to Europe and began taking in the food and wine culture. He did temporary office work for about a year in London where he met Alishan, who was from Vancouver. They began travelling to French wine country; and Alishan took a French cooking course.

The food and wine passion had taken hold. In 1998, shortly after they moved to Vancouver, Rhys and Alishan both enrolled in a professional culinary school, leading to restaurant and wine retailing jobs. As well, Rhys began taking wine courses until he had earned a diploma from the Wine and Spirits Education Trust. "We got the wine bug and decided to move to the Okanagan in 1999," Rhys says. They worked at three different wineries—in tasting rooms, vineyards and cellars—before returning to Vancouver. Rhys managed a wine store while Alishan began studying university-level winemaking, including courses from the renowned University of California.

They returned to the Okanagan in 2003 and, after an interlude managing tasting rooms, opened a bakery and a catering company in Kelowna. The bakery was successful but so much work (they were starting a family) that they sold it to their baker. Rhys started consulting and teaching wine courses while studying to become a Master of Wine by 2010. While all that was going on, they moved to Cawston in 2008, and planted Chardonnay and Riesling on a 1.6-hectare (four-acre) vineyard. Their initial harvest in 2011 enabled them to launch Little Farm Winery

ALISHAN DRIEDIGER AND RHYS PENDER

with a total of 56 cases.

"We'll probably only ever make about 500 or 600 cases a year," says Rhys, currently the only winery owner in British Columbia with the prestigious MW designation. "We know better than to think we are going to make much money from doing this. It was just the fact that we had to do everything from scratch."

OPENED 2012

2155 Newton Road
Cawston, BC V0X 1C1

T 250.499.8891

W www.littlefarmwinery.ca

WHEN TO VISIT
No tasting room.

MY PICKS

The Chardonnay, Riesling and Cabernet Franc rosé are cerebral dry wines reflecting Alishan's minimalist style of making wines with limited intervention.

LITTLE STRAW VINEYARDS

Some wineries have given up trying to break down consumer resistance to Pinot Auxerrois, a resistance likely based in its obscure pronunciation, since the grape produces excellent white wines. (It is pronounced *ox-er-wah.*) Peter Slamka, the winemaker at family-owned Little Straw, remains an Auxerrois stalwart.

The gnarled plants at the top of Little Straw's six-hectare (15-acre) vineyard are Auxerrois vines imported from Europe in the 1970s. These provide the grapes for the winery's Old Vines Auxerrois. Peter also has a younger, but still mature, Auxerrois planting for a very special ice-wine described as "crème brûlé" in a glass. These wines are available primarily in the winery where, Peter has found, resistance melts away when the wines are tasted.

The vineyard was established in 1969 by Peter's father, Joe, a machinist who came to Canada in 1948 from what was then Czechoslovakia. The family—Peter, who was born in 1954, has two younger brothers—planned their winery after farm gate winery licenses were created in 1989. The winery opened in 1996 after Peter had spent nearly a year touring wine regions around the world. In 2004, the winery changed its name to Little Straw, a direct translation of *slamka* from the Slovak language.

The current two-level winery, replacing the remodelled farm building that served Peter through a dozen vintages, opened in 2006. "I don't mind working hard but I don't like hard work," he quipped as he moved into the spacious and efficient new winery. A second-floor mezzanine, after serving briefly as an art gallery, has become a popular lounge where visitors can enjoy food, wine and great views of the Okanagan.

The choices in the wine shop, besides Auxerrois, include Viognier, Sauvignon Blanc, Riesling, Pinot Noir, Syrah and Maréchal Foch. Peter

PETER SLAMKA

has also created a second label, La Petite Paille (French for "little straw"). When he has time, Peter prefers to meet visitors in the tasting room. "To me, that's the best part of the business," he says. "I like being out front, selling wine."

MY PICKS

Tapestry is the winery's popular white blend. Other favourites include the medal-winning Sauvignon Blanc, the Viognier and the Old Vines Auxerrois. The Pinot Noir is always reliable. The winery also makes some wine with South Okanagan fruit, notably a blend of Merlot, Cabernet Sauvignon and Syrah.

OPENED 1996
(AS SLAMKA CELLARS)

2815 Ourtoland Road
Kelowna, BC V1Z 2H7
T 250.769.0404
W www.littlestraw.bc.ca

WHEN TO VISIT
Open daily 10 am – 6 pm April to October; and noon – 4 pm November to March.

RESTAURANT
The Barrel Top Grill
T 250.300.4206
Open daily 11:30 am – 4:30 pm during high season; weekends until late fall.

LIXIÉRE ESTATE WINERY

Balvir Grewal is not afraid of work. Born in India in 1958, he recalls that he took responsibility for himself when he was 11. He joined his brother in Canada in 1978, spending five years working in a lumber mill before switching to orchard jobs in the Okanagan. In time he acquired an eight-hectare (20-acre) orchard near Oliver. When he got, as he puts it, "fed up" with fruit trees, he sold the orchard and, in 1996, he bought a 1.8-hectare (4½-acre) Kaleden vineyard from the estate of Nick Brodersen.

Nick was a German-born electrical contractor and motel operator who had dreamed of a vineyard since the 1960s but kept being told that the Okanagan was apple country. Finally, he bought this highway-front property and in 1981 planted it entirely with Gewürztraminer. He initially sold the grapes to Sumac Ridge and later to Gray Monk. Unfortunately, the vines were all planted on east–west rows, giving them inconsistent exposure to the sun. When he took over, Balvir, found once again that he had a lot of work to do. He replanted everything in north–south rows making the grapes more evenly exposed to the sun. He changed the vineyard mix to Pinot Gris as well as Gewürztraminer, and continued to sell to Gray Monk.

Balvir purchased a second 2.8-hectare (seven-acre) vineyard nearby. When that proved too much work, he sold it in 2006 to Gray Monk and bought one half the size close by. Here, he grows Pinot Gris and Chardonnay. The downsizing decision is explained by the fact that Balvir also has two other jobs—a full-time job in a manufactured homes plant and a part-time job as a school janitor. He manages to juggle it all with help from his family, all with full-time jobs of their own.

The family opened Lixiére cautiously, giving it a name inspired by the word, "elixir". They hired consulting winemaker Phil Soo to make about 500 cases of Lixiére for the 2012 vintage. Future growth will be determined by demand, with most grapes still going to Gray Monk.

BALVIR GREWAL

MY PICKS

The winery launched with three white wines and one rosé in the portfolio, reserving its reds for 2014. The Gewürztraminer and the Cabernet Franc rosé were the stars of the first vintage.

OPENED 2013

266 Highway 97
Kaleden, BC V2A 5C7

T   250.497.8887
    778.878.7184

WHEN TO VISIT
Open weekdays 2 pm – 6 pm,
and on weekends 10 am – 6 pm
May to October; and by
appointment.

LOCK & WORTH WINERY

In the spring of 2012, Lock & Worth moved into the buildings formerly occupied by Poplar Grove Winery and its sister producer Monster Wines, after the latter two had relocated to larger wineries overlooking Penticton. The partners are Ross Hackworth, the owner of Nichol Vineyard, and Matthew Sherlock, his sales director. The winery was launched as Clean Slate but, after a trademark conflict with a German wine brand, the partners switched to a name crafted from their surnames.

They took over the former Poplar Grove winery so that Ross could capture some of the wine tourists that never get to Nichol Vineyard at the far northern end of Naramata Road. "People are spent out, drunk out and burned out by the time they hit the Naramata border line," Ross says. "They have already hit 12 wineries. If people are only going to do the bench for one day, very few of them, unless they know Nichol, start there, just as few make it to the end."

There is another reason for Lock & Worth—it permits Ross to stretch his winemaking talents. Nichol Vineyard limits its production to just six varietals, with perhaps a few blends. "At Lock & Worth, I like to try different things," Ross says. "I don't want to encumber the Nichol brand with three or four new varietals. It confuses things."

From the vineyard of Gitta Sutherland (who operates the cheese company here), Lock & Worth is able to source well-grown Merlot and Cabernet Franc from mature vines. A rugged vineyard near Oliver supplies Sauvignon Blanc. "We pick and choose," Ross says. "We figure out where we would like to get fruit and then go in and start knocking on doors." The winery launched with a blended white, an easy-drinking Merlot and rosés from Cabernet Franc and Gamay. A premium Cabernet Franc was aging in barrel. The initial production target is about 2,000 cases a year.

MATTHEW SHERLOCK

Matthew Sherlock is also the sales director for Lock & Worth. He has a bachelor's degree in English and Dramaturgy but shortly after his 2006 graduation he plunged into wine. While managing a large private wine store in Vancouver, he earned a diploma from the Wine & Spirit Education Trust, subsequently becoming a wine educator.

MY PICKS

Merlot and Cabernet Franc show the intensity of flavour that 20-year-old vines produce. White Slate is an excellent Sauvignon Blanc/Sémillon blend while Red Slate is light and cheerful Gamay.

OPENED 2012

1060 Poplar Grove Road
Penticton, BC V2A 8T6

T 250.492.4575

W www.lockandworthwinery.com

WHEN TO VISIT
Open daily 11 am – 5 pm May to mid-October.

FOOD SERVICES
Poplar Grove Cheese Company operates from the same site, with cheese available for purchase.

LUSITANO ESTATE WINERY

To name their winery, Fred and Fernanda Ganhao simply dipped into their Portuguese heritage. Lusitano derives from Lusitania, the name applied by the Romans to indigenous peoples in central Portugal. While they are only a small percentage of Portugal's modern population, the name occasionally is applied to expatriate Portuguese. It is better known today as the name of Lusitano horses, a breed of beautiful show horses.

Fred and Fernanda both were born in central Portugal. He came to Canada in 1966 at age 11, to join relatives already living in Osoyoos, and Fernanda immigrated later, in 1978, to marry Fred. 1978 was also the year the couple bought an orchard near Vaseux Lake, north of Oliver, which they operated for 25 years before selling. Several times during that period, Fred suggested switching to growing grapes but his cautious wife talked him out of it.

"We sold the orchard in 2003 and we were semi-retired for three years," Fernanda says. However, retirement was not appealing after a life full of activity and they looked for ways to re-engage with agriculture. In 2006 they bought a rural Okanagan Falls property that enchanted them. "When you come up the driveway, it feels like you are closer to the sky," she says. "You have a beautiful view of the valley."

The property included a meadow where the previous owner kept horses, though most of it was covered with pine trees. Fred proposed replacing the trees with vines and, this time, Fernanda agreed. In the spring of 2007 the couple planted close to 25,000 vines in a 5.5-hectare (13½-acre) vineyard. The major varieties here are Pinot Gris, Merlot and Pinot Noir, with smaller blocks on Chardonnay, Sauvignon Blanc and—on a sunbathed south-facing slope—Cabernet Sauvignon.

After several years of selling their grapes, Fred and Fernanda retained consulting winemaker Philip Soo to make their debut 1,200 cases in the 2013 vintage. They continue to sell about half of their crop while

FERNANDA AND FRED GANHAO (COURTESY OF LUSITANO)

easing their wines into the market. "We did not want to go too far ahead of ourselves," says Fernanda, who has not lost all her caution.

She looks forward to selling wines from the Lusitano tasting room. "When we had the farm, we had a fruit stand," she says. "I enjoyed being out there, meeting new people every day. When you have good products, you can see the smile on peoples' faces."

OPENED 2014

2318 Rolling Hills Road
Okanagan Falls, BC V0H 1R2

T   250.497.7055

W   www.lusitanowinery.com

WHEN TO VISIT
Open daily 9:30 am – 6 pm May to October.

MY PICKS

No wines available for tasting at press time.

MARICHEL VINEYARD

For viewing the extraordinary beauty of Naramata Bench, few places are better than Richard and Elisabeth Roskell's home, overlooking the three hectares (7½ acres) of Syrah and Viognier vines they have planted since 2000. The sculptured vineyard dips sharply down a slope, pauses for a rise, resumes on the top of the rise and then disappears toward the lake. Richard, an excellent photographer, has posted his calendar-quality images of the vineyard on the winery's website.

The Roskells acquired this magical property after several years of searching Okanagan properties. It belonged to a pair of absentee German investors who were estranged from each other. The Roskells sent several purchase offers to their agent in British Columbia without getting a reply. So Elisabeth, who was born in Germany, searched German telephone listings until she located the reclusive owners. After six months of difficult negotiation, the Roskells finally bought the property late in 1999.

This is a new career for both. Elisabeth formerly owned a dental laboratory. Richard, born in North Vancouver in 1952, was an Air Canada pilot until retiring early in 2005, fed up with jet lag. "The thought of doing another seven years of long-haul flying did not appeal to me," he says. "I really wanted to stretch out into something different."

A niche producer, Marichel (a contraction of several family names) makes only Syrah and Viognier. "I'll be surprised if we ever make it to 1,000 cases a year," Richard said in his first year. The wines were so well received that in his second year he said that Marichel would expand "all the way up to 1,000 cases [but] we are not going to get big. We are going to stay personally focused on the vineyard and in the winery, and we will stay faithful to the terroir it comes from, and that will be the Naramata Bench." Production has since edged its way up as high as 4,000 cases as Richard has been able to source grapes elsewhere in the Bench as well. Eventually, it will be for someone else to decide

ELISABETH AND RICHARD ROSKELL

whether or not to grow beyond this. As this book was being written, Marichel Vineyard was for sale for $3.98 million.

MY PICKS

The Viognier is vibrantly fresh while the Syrah is rich and peppery, with a concentration that reflects Richard's decision to keep his tonnages low. The lower-priced Syrah "Côte-Rôtie" from purchased grapes is good value.

OPENED 2007

1016 Littlejohn Road
RR1 S11 C73
Naramata, BC V0H 1N0

T 250.496.4133

W www.marichel.ca

WHEN TO VISIT
Open during wine festivals and select summer weekends; and by appointment.

MAVERICK ESTATE WINERY

The origins of this winery go back to Uniondale, a small agriculture town in South Africa, and the friendship between the town's bank manager and its doctor. Schalk de Witt, the doctor, has a daughter, Elzaan. One of her playmates when she was five was Bertus Albertyn, the bank manager's seven-year-old son. Elzaan also got a medical degree at Stellenbosch University, after her father moved to Canada in 1990. Meanwhile, Bertus had become a winemaker. They met again during a de Witt family vacation in South Africa, fell in love and married.

Meanwhile, Schalk (rhymes with "skulk") had invested in two Okanagan properties for vineyard. Having a winemaker in the family triggered the launch of Maverick. "When Bertus came into the picture, obviously, that was the way to go," Schalk says. "There is more profit in making wine than in selling grapes."

A 1976 medical graduate from Stellenbosch University, Schalk brought his family to Canada because they feared civil war in apartheid South Africa. He drove through the southern Okanagan on the way to a locum's posting in Castlegar and was immediately attracted. "Even the natural vegetation—the sagebrush and the antelope brush—reminded me of the drier areas of South Africa," he says. Toward the end of a long career in general practice in Alberta, he began searching for property. In 2006 he purchased 19.4 hectares (48 acres) of raw land adjacent to the Osoyoos Larose vineyard near Osoyoos. Three years later, he purchased a former organic farm beside the highway, and tapped his son-in-law's expertise to plant three hectares (7½ acres) of vines in 2011.

When Bertus, born in 1978, finished his enology degree at Stellenbosch University, he started at a large wine cooperative before joining family-owned Avondale Estates in 1994 as winemaker. He came to the Okanagan early in 2009 when Elzaan began a medical practice in Osoyoos. He was Burrowing Owl Winery's winemaker until mid-2013, when he left to concentrate on Maverick.

BERTUS ALBERTYN

SCHALK DE WITT

The Highway 97 vineyard, where a wine shop opens in 2014, is planted to Pinot Noir, Shiraz, Sauvignon Blanc and a little Chardonnay. The other property, which has just enough water to support six hectares (15 acres) of vines, will be planted in 2014 with similar varieties and perhaps Chenin Blanc. That is a major varietal in South Africa and is so admired by Bertus that he also makes Pinot Gris in what he considers a Chenin Blanc style.

SALES BEGAN 2013

3974 Highway 97
Oliver, BC V0H 1T0

T   250.498.1202

W www.maverickwine.ca

WHEN TO VISIT
By appointment only.

MY PICKS

Everything, beginning with Origin, a clever blend of Sauvignon Blanc and Gewürztraminer. The Sauvignon Blanc is sophisticated, the Pinot Gris is crisp. Rubicon is a superb Syrah/Cabernet Sauvignon Blend while the port-style Syrah is rich and full of flavour.

MEADOW VISTA ARTISAN FARM WINERY

During Meadow Vista's first four years, Judith Barta spent a lot of time searching for a partner to finance the meadery's move from its dingy original home in an industrial park. The low point came when a Chinese businessman, who agreed to invest $2.5 million in Meadow Vista, was involved in a car accident that put him into a coma. The high point came when, through a friend's introduction, Judith found a Calgary businessman to be her silent partner. By the end of 2013, Meadow Vista had become a land-based winery on two hectares (five acres) of property with a house, thornless blackberries, an edible flower garden and fifty beehives.

Judith is used to solving business problems. Born in Cobourg, Ontario, in 1971, she started her first business, a boat cleaning company in Belleville, when she was 19. She recreated the company in Kelowna in 2006 and ran it successfully for three years before selling it to open the meadery. In between stints at polishing yachts, she was also a wine consultant, a massage therapist and the operator of a spa and wellness centre. "It is this entrepreneurial thing," she says. "I love what I do." She still receives a few massage clients at the meadery.

While she was solving problems, Alan Marks, her consulting winemaker, was helping her craft innovative meads. Joy, her meadery's sparkling wine, may be the only sparkling honey wine in Canada made by the traditional Champagne method.

Before launching Meadow Vista, she sketched out two grape winery concepts before deciding the Okanagan was glutted with grape wineries. "I entered the market with products that are different," Judith says. Joy is just one example. The wines are all made with organic honey. Because honey has its own preservative properties, the wines are all sulphur-free, a boon to consumers sensitive to sulphur, a common wine preservative.

JUDITH BARTA (COURTESY OF MEADOW VISTA)

MY PICKS

Don't come looking for a lot of sweet wines. Except for Libra, a delightful dessert mead made with apricots, the wines are dry and food-friendly. Cloud Horse is dry with a floral fruitiness reflecting the flowers from which the honey was made. Some call this tasting "nature in a glass". Mabon is flavoured with coriander, cinnamon, cardamom, nutmeg and cloves and is a bit like drinking spice cake. Joy is crisp, with flavours of honey and yeast.

OPENED 2009

3975 June Springs Road
Kelowna, BC V1W 4E4

T 250.862.2337

W www.meadowvista.ca

WHEN TO VISIT
Open daily 10 am – 5 pm, and
weekends noon – 4 pm.

MEYER FAMILY VINEYARDS

Meyer Family Vineyards began making premium Chardonnay wines, coming to market in early 2008, with just 600 cases from a 1.6-hectare (4,000-acre) Naramata vineyard. It did not take owners John Meyer and Janice Stevens very long to realize the winery needed to be larger. By the end of 2008, they had purchased a larger second vineyard near Okanagan Falls. Pinot Noir, a natural partner to Chardonnay, was added to the portfolio, along with the popular Gewürztraminer that came with the vineyard. Shelving plans for a Naramata Bench winery, they opened their winery at Okanagan Falls, utilizing buildings from a previous stillborn winery project on the property.

Born in Calgary in 1958, Jak Meyer (he uses his initials in place of his given name) entered the wine business after previous careers in the investment business and in real estate development. His passion for wine began in the 1990s with an infatuation for top-flight Cabernet Sauvignon wines from California. "Why would anybody drink anything else?" Jak remembers thinking.

His conversion to Burgundian varieties was driven in part by his vineyards, notably the mature Chardonnay on the Naramata Bench, and in part by Chris Carson, the winemaker he hired in 2008. Born in Edmonton, Chris was drawn to winemaking in 1997 while, as a backpacking student in New Zealand, he worked in a vineyard. That led to a winemaking degree from Lincoln University. Starting in 2001, he did Pinot Noir crushes in California, Burgundy, New Zealand and the Okanagan before joining Jak's team. Here, Pinot Noirs and Chardonnay dominate the portfolio. "We are trying to raise the bar," Jak says. "There are not too many guys that are specializing."

Each year, the winery dedicates a Chardonnay in tribute of an individual or an institution, with a cheque paid to the appropriate charity. The Tribute wines so far have honoured the Emily Carr Institute of Art and Design with the 2006 vintage; artist Bill Reid with the 2007;

CHRIS CARSON

JAK MEYER

and hockey star Steve Yzerman with the 2008. Canadian rodeo champion Kenny McLean, who once lived in Okanagan Falls, was honoured with the 2009 vintage and Sonja Gaudet, a Canadian Paralympic curler, with the 2010. Winnifred Mary Stewart, an Edmonton woman who pioneered programs helping people with developmental disabilities, was the 2011 honouree.

OPENED 2008

4287 McLean Creek Road
Okanagan Falls, BC V0H 1R1
T 250.497.8553
W www.mfvwines.com

WHEN TO VISIT
Open daily 10 am – 5 pm May to
October, and by appointment.

MY PICKS

The McLean Creek Chardonnay, the Tribute Chardonnay and the ultra-premium Micro Cuvée Chardonnay are world-class wines. Under Chris Carson's hand, an exceptional range of Pinot Noirs have emerged, crowned by the Micro Cuvée Pinot Noir. Don't miss the bargain-priced Rosé and Gewürztraminer.

MISCONDUCT WINE COMPANY

As Richard da Silva tells the story, the partners behind this winery are members of a "clandestine syndicate" called The Uncrushables. He and his wife, Twylla Field, are the partners that the public sees. The others are friends and members of the da Silva family, farmers and grape growers in the Okanagan since arriving from Portugal in 1956.

Keeping the names of partners confidential is mostly about marketing the 1920s image of gangsters, hot jazz and good times that Misconduct uses to differentiate itself from other wineries. Some of the labels recall Prohibition-era gangsters. "The St. Valentine's Massacre Rosé is a play on the story behind the St. Valentine's Day Massacre," Richard says. In 1929 gunmen associated with Al Capone shot seven men linked to a rival. "The wine is the bleed from seven of our varietals, representing the seven guys that Al Capone whacked."

The period antiques in the wine shop, which opened in 2011, reinforce the winery's 1920s image. It occupies a house built about that time and now expanded with practical renovations, including a shaded deck overlooking the vineyard and the adjacent city of Penticton beyond the vines.

Richard was born in 1971, and grew up on a farm. "The reason the winery is called Misconduct Winery is that in my early 20s, I was a nightmare to society," Richard admits. "I was one of those guys who was a rebel." The one thing he did not rebel against was the wine culture that his family brought from Portugal. "In my culture," he says, "wine is always viewed as a companion to whatever else is going on. You would enjoy the wine but also you enjoy the atmosphere. We could get into detail about oak and clones and varietals and terroir and all this kind of stuff. Growing up with our family, that was never discussed. It is something you make and you enjoy it with food, at weddings, at funerals, whatever. We want the winery to reflect that philosophy."

RICHARD DA SILVA

MY PICKS

Misconduct has two tiers of wine. What Richard calls "blends for the working joe" are released under the Bugsy or the Bootleg Series. The Big Take is a solid Bordeaux blend; Misfit is a delicious blend of Chardonnay/ Chenin Blanc and Viognier; and Massacre Rosé is quite good if you get beyond the gruesome story. Misfit's upper tier, the Suspect Series, is reserved for varietals such as Viognier and Syrah.

OPENED 2008

375 Upper Bench Road North
Penticton, BC V2A 8T2

T 1.800.851.0903

W www.misconductwine.com

WHEN TO VISIT
Open daily 11 am – 5 pm, with extended hours during the wine festival.

RESTAURANT
The Kitchen at Misconduct
T 250.462.4157
Open Wednesday to Sunday
11:30 am – 3:30 pm and
Thursday to Sunday 5:30 pm
– 9 pm.

MISSION HILL FAMILY ESTATE WINERY

In a relay, the best runner anchors the team. In Mission Hill's portfolio, the anchor is Oculus, the winery's ultra-premium red wine. Investments in vineyards and in the winery have lifted the quality consistently since the first Oculus vintage in 1997. Over two years beginning in 2005, Mission Hill installed state-of-the-art winemaking equipment in a dedicated cellar for premium wines within its vast winery. "That significant investment in equipment allowed us to really elevate what we could do as winemakers with premium red grapes," winemaker John Simes says.

At the same time, parallel improvements in vineyards enabled Mission Hill to get the best from each block through precision viticulture, which includes annual flyovers with aerial cameras to identify any blocks that need help. "The vineyards are absolutely critical," John says. "When you are offering wines at $50–$100 a bottle, you have got to know the vineyards."

All the wines have benefitted from the Oculus project. The Martin's Lane Pinot Noir 2011, which the Decanter World Wine Awards in 2013 named the world's best Pinot Noir under £15, was made with the gentle winemaking equipment originally installed for Oculus.

It is hard to believe there were dirt floors here in 1981 when Anthony von Mandl acquired Mission Hill. The first wine to raise the bar was Mission Hill's 1992 Chardonnay, one of the first wines made by John after he arrived from New Zealand. The wine went on to achieve a "best in the world" award at the International Wine & Spirit Competition, putting Mission Hill and the Okanagan on the map.

After that award, the winery began buying vineyards. Today, it owns almost 400 hectares (1,000 acres) throughout the Okanagan, some in locations producing the best Bordeaux reds for Oculus and companion Legacy wines; and others in the best terroir for premium Pinot Noir

ANTHONY VON MANDL (COURTESY OF MISSION HILL)

JOHN SIMES
(COURTESY OF MISSION HILL)

and Riesling for the Martin's Lane label. "As the vineyards get more mature, we are looking at making wine specifically from certain regions, and working with the varieties with which we think we can do more with," John says.

MY PICKS

Everything. Oculus is the rising tide that lifts all tiers, including Legacy, Select Lot Collection, Reserve and entry-level Five Vineyards.

OPENED 1966

1730 Mission Hill Road
Westbank, BC V4T 2E4

T 250.768.7611

W www.missionhillwinery.com

WHEN TO VISIT
Open daily 10 am – 6 pm
(5 pm in winter). In addition
to free tastings, the winery
offers deluxe tours and private
tastings, some with lunches.
Charges apply. Consult website
for details.

RESTAURANT
Terrace
T 250.768.6467
Open daily for lunch May to
October, weather permitting.

MOCOJO WINERY

Kon Oh came to Canada from South Korea at 16 when his family moved to Alberta, and it was his father's background in agriculture that eventually brought Kon to wine. In Korea, his father was a leader in the 4-H club, an international agricultural youth movement. That brought him into contact with 4-H members in Alberta. "He got a taste of western culture and lifestyle and he decided to immigrate to Canada," Kon says.

The family settled in Lacombe. "When we were going to school, my father started a little vegetable garden and we were supplying mostly Korean stores in the city," Kon says. "We were growing radishes and cabbages, and stuff like that, for Korean people. We started with a little greenhouse in the early 1980s."

After a stint in retail, Kon picked up the family's bent for agriculture. "The farming life started with vegetables," he recalls. "I was not really thrilled to grow vegetables. It is a lot of work. I spent a year of research to develop the fresh-cut flower business in the greenhouse. We did that for 10 years, growing fresh-cut roses, competing with the South American cut flower–industry."

He and his wife Dianne—she is of Dutch agricultural stock—built a successful business, even with the disadvantage of heating a greenhouse in Alberta's winters. "We were working pretty much 24/7 cutting roses," Kon remembers. Ready for a change in lifestyle, they closed the flower business in 2008 and bought an established vineyard near Naramata.

The number of visitors they hosted that summer led them to develop a bed and breakfast, and the enthusiasm of wine touring guests prompted the opening of a winery. "The amount of wine that was purchased by our guests, it was crazy!" Dianne says. There also was the need to add value to the vineyard's production. "You know what the vineyard can bring in financially after five harvests," she says. "We would like to be a little more self-sufficient."

For winemaking, Kon has been mentored by winemaker Richard Kanazawa, a neighbour and a friend. The debut production in 2013 was 700 cases, including Maréchal Foch, Gewürztraminer, Viognier and Malbec. The wines are marketed under the Mocojo label, a name created from the first syllables of the names of their three children. And Kon is not planning to get much bigger than 1,000 cases, leaving time for a new interest—being a lieutenant in the Naramata fire department.

MY PICKS

No wines available for tasting at press time.

PROPOSED OPENING 2014

1202 Gawne Road
Naramata, BC V0I 1N0
T 250.496.4063
W www.mocojowines.com

WHEN TO VISIT
By appointment.

ACCOMODATION
Bed and breakfast suite.

KON OH (COURTESY OF MOCOJO WINERY)

MONEY PIT WINERY

Scott Stefishen laughs when asked to explain this winery's cheeky name. "Everyone in the industry says if you own a vineyard or a winery, it's a money pit," he says. "It doesn't end."

If there is anyone who has figured out how to keep the pit from getting too deep, it is Scott. He launched this winery in his garage in Oliver under a three-year permit from the town (renewable for three more years), limiting his annual production to 575 cases. His commercial license relieves him from the cost of buying a vineyard while allowing him to buy grapes both in British Columbia and in Washington State, where grape prices (but not grape quality) can be significantly lower.

He does not intend to stay small forever. "As soon as we have product and sales, the bank can look at us for debt financing," he says. "Either we will take out a small loan, purchase another building and keep our commercial license; or purchase vineyard land and switch over to a land-based license. The end game plan is to own our own land."

Born in North Vancouver in 1979, Scott's interest in wine was sparked during a French vacation that started in the Beaujolais region in 2000. In 2004 he and Kristie, his wife, went to Perth in Australia, where she enrolled in Curtin University's world-renowned physiotherapy program. Scott, who had been taking business courses, switched to the university's winemaking and enology program. "I decided I didn't want an office job," says Scott, who worked at two Australian wineries before he and his family came back to Canada in 2008.

The couple pursued their careers in Oliver. Kristie opened a physiotherapy clinic and Scott worked at Road 13 and then at Burrowing Owl Winery. Ultimately, he decided to open his own winery, giving him the flexibility to help look after their two children while establishing the Money Pit brand at a pace that prevents the pit from consuming him. "My target is 5,000 cases, but that is about 20 years out," Scott says.

He has chosen to launch Money Pit with moderately-priced blends.

The white is a blend of Sémillon, Sauvignon Blanc and Chardonnay. The reds include a Meritage, a Syrah-Malbec blend and a Cabernet Sauvignon/ Cabernet Franc blend.

MY PICKS

Markup, the winery's white blend, is an excellent value at $15. The red blends, College Fund and Catch 22, were not available for tasting but, given the wines he made at Burrowing Owl, the Money Pit wines will hardly disappoint.

OPENED 2013

860 Fairview Road
Oliver, BC V0H 1T6
W www.moneypitwines.ca

WHEN TO VISIT
No tasting room.

SCOTT STEFISHEN

MONSTER VINEYARDS

The Monster Vineyards winery makes wines that, with playful labels, celebrate the enduring myth of Ogopogo, the Okanagan's answer to the Loch Ness monster. There have been enough alleged sightings over the years to give a sliver of credibility that a prehistoric creature dwells in the dark vastness of Okanagan Lake.

Created in the 2006 vintage with sales beginning the following year, it is a sister label to Poplar Grove, producing a value-priced portfolio to compliment Poplar Grove's exclusive portfolio. Both wineries draw almost entirely on grapes grown in the 30 hectares (75 acres) of vineyard owned by Barbara Holler, whose husband, Tony, is the majority partner in the wineries. As those vineyards approached full production, the Monster winery was built in 2011 on the site of a former Penticton apiary.

In contrast to the architectural showpiece Poplar Grove Winery on the hillside above, the homely lines of the Monster facility hide the leading edge winemaking equipment inside. It not only makes all of the Monster wines, but most of the Poplar Grove wines as well. Stefan Arnasen, the senior winemaker, has all of the tools a winemaker could want including a superbly equipped laboratory. Stefan, who was born in Port Moody in 1970, developed a keen appreciation of laboratories during three years at Andrés Wines and two at RJ Spagnols in New Westminster before he joined Poplar Grove in 2008.

There is a deep winemaking team here. Stefan is one of three at Monster and Poplar Grove. Nadine Allander (whose husband is winemaker at Foxtrot Vineyards) joined in 2010. Kitson Stewart, a member of the family that owns Quails' Gate, joined in 2011. Both Nadine and Kitson are winemaking graduates of Lincoln University in New Zealand.

STEFAN ARNASEN AND NADINE ALLANDER

Tony Holler has described the Monster wines as "fun wines that people can enjoy on a patio in the afternoon." The Monster concept was created by cutting-edge Vancouver marketer Bernie Hadley-Beauregard. "We did not want to refer to Ogopogo but we wanted the wines to come in interesting bottles," Tony says. "We had a graphic artist in London do all the images on the bottle. The images glow in the dark as well. It's a fun bottle and the wine is very good."

OPENED 2007

1010 Tupper Avenue
Penticton, BC V2A 8S5

T   250.493.9463

W www.monstervineyards.com

WHEN TO VISIT
Open daily 11 am – 6 pm May to October.

MY PICKS

This portfolio does not break the bank, it just delivers flavour. Try the Riesling, the rosé and Monster Cabs, an excellent Bordeaux blend.

MONTAKARN ESTATE WINERY

Gary Misson, after several years of making kit wines, made his first dry table wine in 1984 with Concord grapes growing on a trellis at his house. "It was not very palatable," he says. "It was too foxy. I gave the wine to a Romanian friend who distilled it. He said it was the best moonshine he had ever made."

In spite of that experience, winemaking joined photography as serious hobbies for Gary. Born in Campbell River in 1957, he spent 25 years sailing on tugboats and other coastal vessels. He still has a shaggy seaman's beard even though he tired of the sea years ago and earned a diploma in agricultural engineering in 2003. Between classes, he vacationed in Thailand and met his wife, Monty—Monty is short for Montakarn, which explains the winery's name.

When she found Vancouver's damp climate too cold after Thailand, they decided to put Gary's diploma to work on an Okanagan farm (he had a sister already living in the valley). In 2003, they bought a four-hectare (10-acre) orchard near Oliver. "I was finishing school," Gary remembers. "I didn't want to go back to the boats and tow logs and stuff."

After several years of growing peaches and apricots, his wine interest kicked in. "I have been making wine for myself since I was 20," he says. In 2009, he planted about three hectares (seven acres) of Merlot, Malbec, Syrah, Cabernet Franc and Chardonnay. Despite vine damage from the bitterly cold 2009 winter, Gary pressed ahead to make wines with consultants Philip Soo and then Daniel Bontorin. The winery's initial release is close to 1,000 cases.

The red-roofed winery is just off Black Sage Road, with wine shop windows giving a commanding view looking west over the Okanagan Valley. The winery's outward design reminds some of the neighbouring Le Vieux Pin winery, if only because both have large overhanging roofs that protect against the hot sun. "It is a completely different building,"

GARY MISSON

Gary says. "They have got a hip roof. Mine goes the other way. I don't think I copied them."

MY PICKS

Gary believes the Okanagan's strength is in blended wines. The wines reflect that. The whites are well-crafted blends of Chardonnay, Sauvignon Blanc and Viognier. The red combines Merlot, Syrah, Cabernet Franc and Malbec.

OPENED 2013

5462 Black Sage Road
Oliver, BC V0H 1T1

T   250.498.3240
    250.498.7709

W www.montakarn.ca

WHEN TO VISIT
Open daily 10 am – 8 pm May to October.

MONTE CREEK RANCH ESTATE WINERY

Hybrids Marquette, La Crescent and Frontenac have joined the lexicon of varietals in British Columbia with the development of this winery. Bred at the University of Minnesota, these varietals have been engineered to survive winters as frigid as those experienced occasionally at Kamloops. In an abundance of caution, Gurjit Sidhu, the owner of Monte Creek, also has installed wind machines for added protection against late spring and early autumn frost.

Since 2010, Monte Creek has planted about 14 hectares (35 acres) on two vineyards: a south-facing slope called Lion's Head on the north flank of the Thompson River; and a windswept plateau south of the river and beside the highway (where the winery and wine shop are located). In addition to the Minnesota hybrids, Monte Creek also has a large block of Maréchal Foch. On the Lion's Head slope, Riesling, Pinot Gris and Gewürztraminer are grown.

The first commercial production from this vineyard, about 23 tons in 2013, was vinified for Monte Creek by Eric von Krosigk, the winemaker at Summerhill Pyramid Winery. The wines are promising, in part because the hybrids, which have big berries when grown in eastern Canada, produce small berries with concentrated flavours in the Kamloops climate and soils. Marquette, which the University of Minnesota says is a "grandson" of Pinot Noir, is medium-bodied with good flavours. La Crescent, which has some Muscat in its ancestry, yields a fruity white. "We have at least two very strong ones," Gurjit says of the gamble on Minnesota hybrids.

The Sidhus are immigrants from the Punjab in India who have already succeeded in horticulture in Canada. Gurjit was just three when his father Gurdev moved the family to British Columbia in 1969. Unable to use his law degree here, he started a small plant nursery in Mission in 1975. Today, Sidhu & Sons Nursery Ltd., specializing in producing

GURJIT SIDHU

shrubs and trees for landscaping, is one of Canada's largest nurseries.

In 2001, the Sidhus expanded to growing blueberries, quickly becoming one of the largest producers in the Fraser Valley. Soaring land prices sent Gurjit, who has a diploma in horticulture, looking for cheaper farmland in the interior to plant more blueberries. In 2007 he bought Monte Creek Ranch and then the Lion's Head Ranch on the north side of the river, almost directly across the valley. Because the Thompson River Valley is not ideal for blueberries, he turned to grapes and a groundbreaking trial of hybrids that could open wine growing possibilities in British Columbia's cooler regions.

MY PICKS

No wines available for tasting at press time.

OPENED 2014

2121 East Trans-Canada Highway
Kamloops, BC V2C 4J0

W www.montecreekranch.com

WHEN TO VISIT
Wine shop expected to open in 2015.

MOON CURSER VINEYARDS

In the crowded field of Okanagan wineries, Moon Curser Vineyards differentiates itself with innovative wines from varietals that almost no one else grows. These include Arneis, an Italian white; Tannat, a red identified with Uruguay; and Touriga Nacional, the great Portuguese red. Soon, the winery may offer a Dolcetto after planting that Italian red in 2013.

Another example of how owners Chris and Beata Tolley think outside the box was their decision in 2011 to rechristen the winery and put edgy gothic labels on the bottles. The couple—she is a former chartered accountant, he a former software engineer—decided that the winery's original name, Twisted Tree, was bland and too similar to other winery names. With the help of marketing consultant Bernie Hadley-Beauregard (of Blasted Church and Dirty Laundry fame), they researched South Okanagan history and discovered a tale of gold smuggling.

"Moon Curser is a synonym for a smuggler," Beata says. "The whole idea is that the wine is all about the place. We picked Osoyoos for the sunshine and the heat. We wanted something that talked about the location but we did not want to do it in the traditional way. There is a history of gold smuggling that took place here during the gold rush of the 1800s. The smugglers would curse at the moon because the border agents would catch them" in its light. The labels echo this story: Dead of Night, an excellent blend of Tannat and Syrah, features a fox and an owl with a lantern.

Moon Curser makes excellent wines with mainstream varietals but Chris cannot resist pioneering new varietals. A few years ago, a neighbour, a fruit packer of Portuguese heritage, planted a small vineyard with just over a hectare (three acres) of Touriga Nacional, a notoriously late ripener. The young vines were decimated by an early freeze in

BEATA AND CHRIS TOLLEY

2009 but the surviving vines, harvested in November, produced a ton and a half of the ripest fruit Chris bought in 2011. Chris bought the vineyard and replaced the ailing Touriga Nacional with mainstream varieties, but not before propagating Touriga cuttings for his own 2014 planting.

MY PICKS

Everything. The labels might telegraph novelty but these are elegant and interesting wines—dry, full-flavoured whites and intense, age-worthy reds.

OPENED 2006
(AS TWISTED TREE VINEYARDS & WINERY)

3628 Highway 3 East
Osoyoos, BC V0H 1V6

T 250.495.5161
W www.mooncurser.com

WHEN TO VISIT
Open daily 10 am – 5 pm May to October, and by appointment.

MORAINE VINEYARDS

Oleg Aristarkhov crossed Canadian wine off his list after he tasted his first in Edmonton when he and his wife, Svetlana, were new immigrants there in the 1990s. "I have liked wines all of my life," says Oleg, an oil industry electrical engineer who was born in 1965 in western Siberia. He established a business involving instrumentation for the oil industry and came to Edmonton to enlist partners and technology to support his Russian business.

"When we came to Canada, I went to a store and I bought a Canadian wine," Oleg recalls. "It was red. As immigrants, we did not have much money, so I probably bought something cheap. I can't remember but the wine was awful." He stayed away from Canadian wine for years until visiting Okanagan wineries during a family vacation. The wines, he discovered, were vastly improved.

The Aristarkhovs then bought a Naramata Bench property for a vacation home. It was not long before Oleg and Svetlana, who had lived in Edmonton about 15 years, decided to live in the Okanagan year-round. "We asked ourselves what is the reason for living in Edmonton?" Oleg says. "I can run my business from any place in the world." His neighbour is vintner Sal D'Angelo. Oleg quickly tapped Sal's expertise in vineyards and, by 2010, had planted almost 1.6 hectares (four acres) of Pinot Noir on what he called the Sophia Vineyard, after one of their daughters.

That fall, the Holman-Lang group of wineries went into receivership. The last of the group's seven wineries, which opened in 2008, was called Zero Balance Vineyards. Oleg's native entrepreneurship had not been snuffed out by growing up in the Soviet Union. "After Holman went under, I thought it was a good business opportunity to pick up that winery," Oleg says. The winery is right on Naramata Road with a seven-acre vineyard now named Anastasia, for the other daughter. Oleg bought the winery in 2011, renaming it Moraine for the glacial soil on

OLEG AND SVETLANA ARISTARKHOV

Naramata Bench.

In 2012, Oleg secured New Zealand–born Jacqueline Kemp to make the wines. After working at the renowned Akarua winery there, she moved to the Okanagan with husband Chris Carson (of Meyer Family Vineyards). Here, she juggled consulting with raising a young family. "She is crazy about quality," Oleg says. "It is what I like."

OPENED 2012

1865 Naramata Road
Penticton, BC V2A 8T9

T 250.460.1836

W www.morainewinery.com

WHEN TO VISIT
Open daily 10 am – 6 pm May to November.

MY PICKS

The appealing whites include Pinot Gris, Chardonnay, Gewürztraminer and Viognier. Several of the wines are interesting blends. Cliffhanger White is Pinot Gris and Viognier, Cliffhanger Red is Gamay and Syrah and Red Mountain is Malbec and Cabernet Franc.

MT. BOUCHERIE ESTATE WINERY

Nirmal and Kaldep Gidda, brothers who own this winery with their families, are among the largest non-corporate owners of vineyard in British Columbia, with 121 hectares (298 acres) in the Okanagan and Similkameen Valleys. "We are proud of being farmers and growers, first and foremost," Nirmal says. "Having your own vineyards [means that] you can control the quality of the grapes that come into the winery." And it shows in the deep and well-crafted selection of wines offered in the tasting room.

The Gidda saga in British Columbia began with their immigrant father, Mehtab, a one-time Punjabi farmer who planted the family's first vineyard in 1975 near Westbank. He flourished as a farmer but did not let his three sons join in the farming enterprise until they acquired a professional education. The eldest, Sarwan, studied business administration. Nirmal got a science degree and Kaldep became a heavy-duty mechanic.

Strategically, they acquired or developed vineyards in three different terroirs—Westbank, where the winery was built, the Similkameen Valley and Okanagan Falls. Sarwan left the partnership in 2008, taking some of the Westbank vineyards with him for his own winery. The remaining Gidda brothers more than replaced that acreage by planting a significant new Okanagan Falls vineyard. They grow an alphabet soup of grape varieties, from Bacchus to Zinfandel and Zweigelt, providing winemaker Jim Faulkner with an enviable range of options. Jim, who was born in 1962, developed an interest in wine during years managing nightclubs. He started his winemaking career in the cellar at CedarCreek Estate Winery, moved to Summerhill and then Church & State before joining Mt. Boucherie in 2009.

After opening in 2001, Mt. Boucherie first attracted notice with its flagship Pinot Gris, its Gewürztraminer and its budget-priced Pinot Noir. The winery has since added big reds and complex white blends

KALDEP AND NIRMAL GIDDA
(COURTESY OF MT. BOUCHERIE)

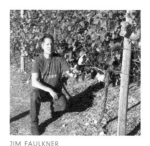

JIM FAULKNER

under a premium tier called Summit Reserve. Recently, a super-premium tier called Family Reserve has been created for small-lot wines, starting with Zinfandel, Cabernet Sauvignon, Syrah, Pinot Noir and a blend called Summit White. Members of the Mt. Boucherie Wine Club (registration is free) get advance notice when special wines are released.

OPENED 2001

829 Douglas Road
Kelowna, BC V1Z 1N9

T   250.769.8803
    877.684.2748 (toll free)

W www.mtboucherie.bc.ca

WHEN TO VISIT
Open daily 10 am – 6 pm May to October; and 11 am – 5 pm November to April.

PICNIC AREA

MY PICKS

Every time I taste the wines here, my list of recommendations grows. The whole portfolio is impressive, including the Chardonnay, Sémillon, Pinot Gris and Gewürztraminer among the whites; the Pinot Noir, Cabernet Franc, Merlot, Syrah, Blaufränkisch and Zweigelt among the reds.

NAGGING DOUBT WINES

Searching for a wine name and a label, Rob Westbury turned to Vancouver marketing guru Bernie Hadley-Beauregard, a creator of many cutting edge labels. "We kicked around a bunch of names," Rob recalls. "Finally he said, 'You know Rob, this is really your nagging doubt. This is that dream you have wanted to fulfill all your life and it has been nagging at you and you are finally getting to that dream'."

A human relations executive, Rob launched Nagging Doubt as a virtual winery. The early vintages, starting with just 150 cases of wine in 2010, were made for him in a licensed winery under the direction of winemaker Mark Simpson. Succeeding vintages have been made at Mark's BC Wine Studio at Okanagan Falls. For the 2014 vintage, Nagging Doubt plans to move to its own 5.6-hectare (14-acre) property in East Kelowna where Rob and his wife, Abbey, have just planted a new vineyard.

Born in Edmonton in 1969, Rob has degrees in psychology and telecommunications management, equipping him for a career that took him all over North America with an international consulting firm. "I've always enjoyed wine, ever since I was legal to drink," he says. "The tipping point was I had an assignment in San Francisco. I remember going to Napa and Sonoma almost every weekend. I just woke up one morning and thought, 'I could definitely do this for a living'." By using a custom crush winery and mentoring with a winemaker, Rob could start with limited resources and build the brand. He moved from Vancouver to a human relations job in Kelowna in 2012, pursuing a career he enjoys at the same time as he follows his passion for wine.

Rob's target is to grow Nagging Doubt to 2,000 cases a year, with a tight focus on just four wines—a red blend, a Pinot Noir, a Chardonnay and another white to be determined. "One of the reasons I got into winemaking is that I love French wine, good Burgundian wine," Rob says. "I have always wanted to make a Chardonnay and I have always wanted to make a Pinot Noir."

MY PICKS

The Pull is what Nagging Doubt calls its fine Merlot-anchored red blend. The Chardonnay and the Pinot Noir also are well-crafted wines.

SALES BEGAN 2011

4525 Sallows Road
Kelowna, BC V1W 4C2

W www.naggingdoubt.com

WHEN TO VISIT
No tasting room.

ROBERT WESTBURY (COURTESY OF NAGGING DOUBT)

NICHE WINE COMPANY

Several elements came together to suggest Niche as the name of this winery that James and Joanna Schlosser opened in 2011. The vineyard is off the beaten path, well up a mountainside at an elevation of 706 metres (2,316 feet), with only one other vineyard nearby. "The property appears to be an ecological niche at certain times of the year," says James as he waxes lyrical about the colourful dragonflies in August.

And the winery is small enough that two people can fit it in together with other careers. "When you look up the definition of niche, it is about fit," Joanna says. "We feel this business fits with our life, and our wine fits with everything we do."

The four-hectare (10-acre) vineyard is on a farm owned since 1978 by James's parents, Jerold and Kathleen Schlosser, both of them Kelowna lawyers. Jerold began planting vines about 1997, starting with two clones of Pinot Noir, now the dominant variety grown here. James, who was born in Vancouver in 1975, began working in the vineyard after completing a science degree at the University of Victoria. His father seized on this apparent aptitude for grapes by enrolling James in the winemaking program at Brock University, where he earned a master's degree in enology. Since James returned to the Okanagan in 2002, the selection of varieties in the vineyard was increased to include Gewürztraminer, Chardonnay, Pinot Blanc, Riesling and Maréchal Foch and he began making trial lots of wine. At the same time, his background in science has taken him to a parallel career as a technology development officer with the British Columbia Cancer Agency.

Joanna, who was born in North Vancouver, is equally adept at juggling several interests at once. During a 13-year career as an Air Canada flight attendant, she also earned a communications degree from Simon Fraser University. More recently, she has studied graphic design, equipping herself to develop websites for Niche and for other wineries.

JAMES SCHLOSSER

James makes the Niche wines in a rustic former stable, a charming wooden building constructed entirely without nails. The building underlines the artisan ideals that James brings to winemaking. He declares on the website: "Our wines are made without fancy equipment, and instead benefit from gravity, smarts, and a few strong hands."

OPENED 2011

1901 Bartley Road
West Kelowna, BC V1Z 2M6

T 604.733.1100

W www.nichewinecompany.com

WHEN TO VISIT
By appointment only.

MY PICKS

The rosé, the Chardonnay, the Pinot Noir and the Riesling all display the bright flavours and crisp acidity of high-altitude vineyards. The Foch's soft tannins make it an easy-drinking red.

NICHOL VINEYARD

A few years ago, Ross Hackworth noticed an alarming trend with the winery's customer list. Wine release announcements were bouncing back because long-time buyers, some on the list since the early 1990s, were dying just as he was increasing production. To attract younger consumers to the Nichol brand, he began in 2011 to sell wine to restaurants in 20-litre steel kegs, one of the first wineries to do so. Restaurant wine by-the-glass programs target younger consumers. "The buzz was fantastic," Ross says. And he hired a sales director, Matt Sherlock, who was then an under-30s sommelier and wine educator. "We are finally seeing some younger traffic come to the winery," Ross said in 2012.

Ross inherited the aging customer list when he bought the winery from founders Alex and Kathleen Nichol, who retired in 2002. In fact, Ross probably was on the list. "I knew the Nichol wines," Ross says. "I'd been drinking them for years."

Born in California, Ross was 10 years old when his parents bought the Penticton-area orchard in 1973 where he grew up. A business graduate from the British Columbia Institute of Technology, Ross was previously a sales vice-president in the Vancouver office of a Japanese pulp and paper giant. Corporate entertaining educated his wine palate but, tiring of the job's extensive travel, he was drawn back to Naramata.

Since taking over the winery, Ross has doubled production to about 3,500 cases, all with Naramata Bench grapes. The winery's 4.5-hectare (10-acre) vineyard has been supplemented with grapes from nearby vineyards, some planted with the same varieties Nichol was already growing: Syrah, Cabernet Franc, Pinot Gris and Pinot Noir. "We are absolutely invested in Naramata," Ross says. "That has been my plan from day one. A lot has to do with the fact that I grew up out here. Every year, I appreciate the benefit of being out here."

ROSS HACKWORTH

MY PICKS

Everything. The Syrah can be a big, brooding south-of-France red in the best years and light and peppery in cooler years. The Cabernet Franc and the Pinot Noir are deep, concentrated wines. The 9 Mile Red and 9 Mile White are excellent blends. The pink-hued Pinot Gris, intense in flavour, is a deliciously eccentric take on this varietal.

OPENED 1993

1285 Smethurst Road
RR1 Site 14 Comp 13
Naramata, BC V0H 1N0

T 250.496.5962

W www.nicholvineyard.com

WHEN TO VISIT
Open daily 11 am – 5 pm May to mid-October; and on weekends 11 am – 5 pm mid-October to April.

NK'MIP CELLARS

This winery, on a hilltop surrounded by eight hectares (20 acres) of vines, recalls a Santa Fe pueblo. Architect Robert Mackenzie captured two themes in his design: the simulated Spanish style of Osoyoos and echoes of the aboriginal culture of New Mexico. Nk'Mip (pronounced *en-ka-meep*) is North America's first aboriginal winery, owned by the Osoyoos Indian Band in a joint venture with Constellation Brands. The winery anchors a development of luxury condominiums, a golf course and a superb interpretation centre where the band shares its culture with visitors.

Winemaker Randy Picton, who acquired his winemaking prowess at CedarCreek before being recruited by Nk'Mip, crafts the wines with winemaker Justin Hall and assistant winemaker Aaron Crey, both members of First Nations bands. They make wines with grapes from the winery vineyards and from the band's Inkameep Vineyard at Oliver. Since it was established in 1968, the Inkameep Vineyard has become one of the Okanagan's best. Randy gets grapes from the vineyard's top sites, hand-tended by the vineyard's most experienced crew. When Randy asks the vineyard for special favours, he gets them—and repays the favours by making award-winning wines.

You can sample the wines in the winery's exceedingly smart tasting room or sign up for tutored tastings, one of which features wines served in Riedel stemware. Nk'Mip makes both a regular and a reserve tier. Rather than using the term "reserve" for a wine produced on a reserve, Nk'Mip dips into the Salish language to dub its upper tier wines as Qwam Qwmt, meaning "achieving excellence." How is it pronounced? Even the winery's personnel use a shortcut—Q Squared.

RANDY PICTON

Everything including the $50 flagship red, Mer'r'iym, which means marriage; all five Bordeaux varietals are blended in this wine. The sophisticated Q Squared wines are all intensely flavoured and the "regular" wines are anything but regular. Don't miss the crisp Pinot Blanc and the elegant Riesling icewine. I scored the 2012 icewine 100 points.

OPENED 2002

1400 Rancher Creek Road
Osoyoos, BC V0H 1V6

T   250.495.2985

W   www.nkmipcellars.com

WHEN TO VISIT
Open daily 9 am – 6 pm May
to early January; 9 am – 8 pm
July to August; and 9 am – 5 pm
January to April.

RESTAURANT
The Patio at Nk'Mip
Open for lunch daily 11:30 am –
5 pm late April to early October;
and Long Table dinners Fridays
and Saturdays at 6:30 pm July
and August.

NOBLE RIDGE VINEYARD & WINERY

This winery took root in 1998 in Europe where Jim and Leslie D'Andrea visited numerous wineries during a three-month family sabbatical. Jim was already a wine enthusiast with a growing library of viticulture books. In Châteauneuf-du-Pape, they met a former accountant who had switched careers to manage a winery and to enjoy the appealing lifestyle.

Born in Welland, Ontario, in 1954, Jim moved to Calgary in 1982 to join the law firm, Bennett Jones LLP. He now heads the firm's employment practice group and has written two books on that discipline. He continues to practise law, even when that involves dealing with clients by cellphone from the vineyard. Leslie, born in Toronto, has a master's in health administration and worked extensively in that field until switching her skills to the administration of Noble Ridge. The winegrower in Châteauneuf-du-Pape served as their model as professionals changing careers.

They looked at vineyard properties in France and Ontario before focusing on the Okanagan, a region that they believed held the promise for producing great red wines. In 2001 they purchased a 10-hectare (25-acre) hilltop property on Oliver Ranch Road with a small planting of Cabernet Sauvignon, Merlot and Chardonnay. They filled out the vineyard with Pinot Noir and Pinot Gris. On top of the ridge that gives this winery its name, they placed an elegant wine shop with views of Vaseux Lake.

They seized the opportunity to expand in 2006 by purchasing the neighbouring vineyard on the east side of Oliver Ranch Road. "Being able to obtain some land in our area is of great importance to us," Jim says. "We are strongly of the view that the Okanagan Falls 'appellation' is a premiere wine-growing region." The sturdy barn on the property, a few hundred yards from the wine shop, was transformed into a good production facility.

LESLIE AND JIM D'ANDREA

Noble Ridge is an estate producer relying exclusively on its own grapes. Its vineyards, when fully planted, will allow the winery to cap its annual production of about 6,000 cases. "Our goal was to make premium quality wine," Jim says. "After travelling the world and tasting various wines, I was convinced that Canada also can make very good wines."

MY PICKS

Everything. The flagship wine is a premium Bordeaux blend called The King's Ransom, made only in top vintages. The 120-case production of the 2009 King's Ransom is only the second. If you miss out on this wine, you will be more than pleased with the Meritage, the Pinot Noir, the Chardonnay, the Pinot Grigio and the elegant sparkling wine called The One.

OPENED 2005

2320 Oliver Ranch Road
Okanagan Falls, BC V0H 1R2
T   250.497.7945
W   www.nobleridge.com

WHEN TO VISIT
Open daily 10 am – 5 pm May to mid-October; and Friday to Sunday 10 am – 5 pm mid-October to April.

PICNIC AREA WITH PICNIC FOODS AVAILABLE

OKANAGAN CRUSH PAD WINERY

Driven by colourful personalities, Okanagan Crush Pad Winery is one of the valley's most innovative wineries. As the first successful custom crush winery, it has been the incubator for new wineries, offering expert winemaking with such leading edge tools as the first egg-shaped concrete fermenters in the Okanagan. Most recently, it has begun planting a totally biodynamic vineyard in the almost virgin soil of the Garnet Valley north of Summerland.

The lead personalities are Christine Coletta, a former executive director of the British Columbia Wine Institute, and Steve Lornie, her husband. A builder, he erected the winery on their Switchback Vineyard in Summerland, where they have grown Pinot Gris since 2009. Their original intent was to sell the grapes until Michael Bartier, another personality, talked them into making wine. At the time, Michael was Road 13's winemaker. Subsequently, he became head winemaker at Okanagan Crush Pad where, among other accomplishments, he also launched Bartier Brothers (with his brother, Don).

A fourth personality is Tuscan winemaker Alberto Antonini, a consultant recruited by Vancouver wine expert David Scholefield, a fifth personality at Crush Pad. Alberto recommended the concrete fermenters based on traditional Roman winemaking technology. "Concrete is a nice environment," he says. "When you smell an empty concrete tank, you smell life. You smell something which is important for making a premium wine. If you do the same with a stainless steel tank, you smell nothing." At least three other wineries have installed concrete eggs since Crush Pad brought in the first six from California.

A fifth personality is Chilean Pedro Parra, a self-described "terroirist" who consults on terroir to clients around the world. He is the guiding hand behind Crush Pad's Garnet Valley project where 24 to 32 hectares (60 to 80 acres) will be planted, primarily with Pinot Noir, starting in 2014.

CHRISTINE COLETTA

MICHAEL BARTIER

In addition to its own Haywire label, Crush Pad has made wine for producers such as Bella Wines, Harper's Trail, C. C. Jentsch Cellars, Platinum Bench, Perseus, Sage Hills and Bartier-Scholefield.

MY PICKS

The Haywire Pinot Gris (notably the Wild Yeast Ferment Pinot Gris) and Pinot Noir are both excellent. Both Haywire and Bartier-Scholefield have very tasty rosé wines.

OPENED 2010

16576 Fosbery Road
Summerland, BC V0H 1Z6

T 250.494.4445 (ext. 1)

W www.okanagancrushpad.com

WHEN TO VISIT
Open daily 10:30 am – 5:30 pm
June to September; select
weekends in the shoulder
season; and by appointment.

OLIVER TWIST ESTATE WINERY

Their friends were not surprised when Bruce and Denice Hagerman sold the Oliver Twist winery in 2012. It is entirely in character that they would move on to fresh adventures in their activity-packed lives. "I like to do different things," Bruce says. "I once asked an old lady about the things she did in her life, and what it was she regretted. She said, 'Sonny, it is not the things I did in my life that I regret, it is the things I didn't do.'"

The chance to move on occurred after the Hagermans had mentored Gina and Trevor Mitchell for several years. "We were bottling one day," Gina remembers. "Bruce and Denice said, 'Why don't you buy the winery?'" Given her heritage, she did not need to be asked twice. Her maternal grandfather, Joe Fernandes, left Madeira in the 1960s to establish an orchard in Osoyoos. Gina grew up around wine. When she and Trevor married in 2008, they made their own Gewürztraminer and Merlot for their 350 guests.

That sparked Gina's winemaking career, starting with the assistant winemaker course at Okanagan College in 2009 and a crush and a half at Cassini Cellars (until she went on maternity leave). She helped Denice and consultant Christine Leroux with the 2011 crush at Oliver Twist. She completed her rapid rise as a winemaker by taking over Oliver Twist in 2012.

"I came into this not knowing a thing about winemaking," Trevor admits. Born in Duncan, British Columbia, in 1976, Trevor came to Osoyoos in 1993 when his parents bought an orchard. He and Gina subsequently managed an orchard but his real passion is building hot rods. The couple own a custom autobody shop in Osoyoos although they leased it to another operator after taking over Oliver Twist.

The winery is now making about 5,000 cases annually, getting fruit from its own seven-hectare (17-acre) vineyard and from

GINA AND TREVOR MITCHELL

purchased fruit. "I am making a lot of red wine," Gina says. "I like reds." She has also begun to make special small-lot wines, some of which—like an oaked Chardonnay—are offered exclusively to members of the wine club that Oliver Twist established in 2013.

OPENED 2007

398 Lupine Lane
Oliver, BC V0H 1T1

T   250.485.0227

W www.olivertwistwinery.com

WHEN TO VISIT
Open daily 10 am – 5.30 pm.

MY PICKS

The whites (including the flagship Kerner which is called Oliver's Choice) and the Merlot rosé (called Patio Passion) are attractively fresh and fruity. The Merlot, Cabernet Sauvignon, Merlot Reserve and Syrah are full-flavoured, drinkable and often complex. If you have a sweet tooth, try the Rosado Splash, an off-dry Syrah rosé, or the Pinot Splash, a late-harvest Pinot Gris.

ORCHARD HILL ESTATE CIDERY

In the midst of wine country, Orchard Hill offers the wine tourist a distinct change of pace. This was the South Okanagan's first apple cidery, making its products with fresh fruit grown right there.

It was established by Gian Dhaliwal and his son, Ravi, who operate a roadside orchard and fruit market. The orchard primarily grows apples, but also has cherries and other tree fruits. For some time, the Dhaliwal family has sold their fruits and vegetables at the Sunshine Valley Fruit market. The cidery opened in 2006, adding value to the apples and giving passing motorists another reason to stop and linger.

Three ciders, all vintage dated and branded "Red Roof", were offered when Orchard Hill opened. Okanagan Bubbly is a semi-sweet cider made refreshing with its effervescence. Summer Sipper is a medium-dry cider with a little more body than the sparkling version. Extra Dry cider, according to the Dhaliwal family, "is unlike any other dry apple cider . . . usually, extra dry means harsh and bitter. Orchard Hill Extra Dry [is] very light and delicate. It is handmade from a blend of the more astringent Okanagan apples."

Modestly priced, the ciders are packaged both in 750 millilitre bottles and, like many competing ciders, in half bottles.

The ciders are crisp and refreshing.

OPENED 2006

3480 Fruitvale Way
Oliver, BC V0H 1T1

T   250.689.0240

W www.orchardhillcidery.com

WHEN TO VISIT
Open daily 8 am – 8 pm July to
August; and 8 am – 6 pm June,
September and October.

ORCHARD HILL RED ROOF CIDER

OROFINO VINEYARDS

John and Virginia Weber were novice farmers—he was a teacher, she still works as a nurse—when they moved from Saskatchewan in March, 2001, to take over a 1.8-hectare (4½-acre) vineyard near Cawston just as pruning began. "We spent the first year on a huge learning curve," John remembers. Within a decade, their success inspired other neighbours to plant vineyards for them as well.

A mural in Orofino's tasting room identifies the other five Similkameen growers now supplying the winery. Increasingly, John has focused on making single vineyard–wines, acknowledging each vineyard on the labels. Orofino's flagship white is Riesling, initially from the mature vines on the winery's Home Vineyard blended with purchased fruit. Since the 2012 vintage, John has made three Rieslings, showcasing the distinctive flavours of the Scout Vineyard and the Hendsbee Vineyard as well as his own vineyard.

Orofino's success with late-harvest wines from its 25-year-old Muscat block led a neighbour to plant more Muscat for John. Since the 2011 vintage, the fruit from these young vines has been dedicated to Moscato Frizzante, the winery's popular sparkling wine.

Small-lot wines create significant work for a winery in which John and one employee produce up to 5,000 cases a year. The winery's growth has been driven not just by sales but by John's penchant for making yet another varietal when he is offered well-grown grapes. "That's how we started making Sauvignon Blanc," he says. "I find exciting grapes and I want to see what I can do with them."

Orofino—which is Spanish for "fine gold," and the name of a nearby mountain—now relies almost exclusively on Similkameen grapes. The one exception is the Okanagan Merlot, which John has been buying since 2005 for the wine he calls Red Bridge. The grapes are from Chris Scott's two-hectare (five-acre) Oak Knoll Vineyard at Kaleden, a site renowned for quality Merlot.

The Orofino is a unique design. The two buildings—the winery itself and the smaller tasting room separated by a breezeway—are built with straw bales. The buildings look conventional except for thick energy-efficient walls, naturally cool in summer, which are finished attractively in dusty pink stucco. Solar panels added in 2012 provide much of the electrical energy.

MY PICKS

Everything, including the remarkable Rieslings, the Chardonnay, the Gamay, the Cabernet Sauvignon, the Pinot Noir, the Syrah and Red Bridge Merlot. The flagship red is a sophisticated Bordeaux blend called Beleza.

OPENED 2005

2152 Barcelo Road
Cawston. BC V0X 1C2

T   250.499.0068

W www.orofinovineyards.com

WHEN TO VISIT
Open daily 10 am – 5 pm during spring wine festival in early May; Friday to Monday mid-May through June; daily July to mid-October; and by appointment.

PICNIC AREA
Tables shaded by almond trees.

JOHN AND VIRGINIA WEBER
(COURTESY OF OROFINO VINEYARDS)

THE ORPHAN GRAPE

The genesis of this winery, operated by Anthony Lewis, is the devastating 2010 Haiti earthquake. At that time, Anthony was winemaker at The Vibrant Vine, the Kelowna winery his parents Wyn and Marion had opened earlier that year.

When the earthquake hit, Anthony's father-in-law, Rick Wilkerson, went to Haiti as a volunteer with Doctors Without Borders. He returned with harrowing tales and photographs of orphans and orphanages that profoundly moved every member of the Lewis family, including Anthony's three-year-old daughter, Madeleine. Asked what she wanted for her birthday, she replied: "Pyjamas for the children in grandpa's orphanage." Anthony held a charity tasting at The Vibrant Vine and collected 1,000 pairs of pyjamas. He followed that with another event that brought in 1,000 pairs of flip-flops. When his family began raising money to sponsor an orphanage, Anthony decided to set up his own winery, The Orphan Grape, to generate revenue for the Haiti orphanage.

The winery is also designed to help orphan grape growers in the Okanagan, so called because their vineyards are without winery contracts. Their relationship with Anthony includes profit sharing, while the winery sends $1 from each bottle sold to Haiti.

Anthony's business model is lean. "We don't own a wine tank; we don't own a wine press or a bottling line or anything," Anthony says. "We outsource every single thing." He uses other wineries to process the grapes, limiting his investment to tastings rooms on three vineyards initially and on more as the project develops. The wines will be sold exclusively through these tasting rooms.

The Orphan Grape is actually an umbrella company managing tasting rooms with labels and themes of their own. The subsidiary winery at Garner Road is called Frequency, reflecting Anthony's previous careers as a rock musician and music producer. Guests walking into the tasting room are greeted by a drum set hanging overhead like a chandelier.

ANTHONY LEWIS

"We give you the whole sonic experience of wine," he says. "It is designed to be fun. We are trying to provide memorable experiences for people who come to visit the Okanagan." Frequency, based on a five-hectare (12-acre) vineyard, is launching with Pinot Noir and Riesling. A second subsidiary winery called Bubbling Vine will open with sparkling wines.

PROPOSED OPENING 2014

2261 Garner Road
Kelowna, BC V1P 1E3

T   250.764.5450

MY PICKS

No wines available for tasting at press time.

OSOYOOS LAROSE ESTATE WINERY

At this time, Osoyoos Larose offers no public tours and is unlikely to do so, until a winery is built some time in the future on the vineyard. The 32-hectare (80-acre) vineyard is a few kilometres northwest of Osoyoos, on the western slope of the valley and near the Desert Interpretation Centre. It is worth looking through the fence, if only to see how the French grow grapes. The vines are crowded together more closely than is customary in the Okanagan, reducing their vigour and forcing them to produce really ripe, full-flavoured grapes.

Osoyoos Larose, which started in 1998 as a joint venture, is now owned entirely by the French partner, Groupe Taillan, the owner of the distinguished Château Gruaud-Larose and five other Bordeaux properties. The 1998 partnership was initiated by Vincor International, then Canada's largest wine company, in order to benefit from French know-how. Groupe Taillan picked the vineyard site, decided what to plant (Merlot, Cabernet Sauvignon and the other Bordeaux reds) and appointed a French winemaker. Constellation Brands, which acquired Vincor in 2006, sold its interest in the partnership in 2013.

The winemaking style is definitely French. The winemaker from 2001 through 2012 was Pascal Madevon, the grandson of a Burgundy wine grower and a graduate of Bordeaux's top winemaking school. When he left to join Culmina Family Estate Winery, he was succeeded by Mathieu Mercier. Born in Cognac, Mathieu grew up on a family vineyard and winery and also studied in Bordeaux, earning a master's degree in viticulture and enology. He had previously worked at several Groupe Taillan estates. Unlike Pascal, he also had prior New World experience, having made wine in Chile and in the Napa Valley.

There are only two wines at Osoyoos Larose. The flagship is Le Grand Vin, an age-worthy blend anchored by Merlot and fleshed out with four other Bordeaux reds. In the 2004 vintage, the winery launched its

MATHIEU MERCIER

second label, Pétales d'Osoyoos, a softer, earlier-drinking red blend.

MY PICKS

The quality of Le Grand Vin has risen steadily as the vines matured. No collector of Okanagan wines should be without this wine in the cellar, along with Pétales d'Osoyoos for more immediate pleasure.

OPENED 2004

(Jackson-Triggs Winery)
38691 Highway 97 North
Oliver, BC V0N 1T0

T   250.498.4981
W www.osoyooslarose.com

WHEN TO VISIT
No tasting room.

OVINO WINERY

Legend has it that Yankee Flats Road, not far west of Salmon Arm, was named for the Vietnam-era draft dodgers who once lived in this bucolic farm country between the Salmon River and the Fly Hills. John Koopmans considered it as a name for his winery but decided against it, concerned about attracting anti-American sentiment. He settled on OVINO, a name with an allusion to the farm's flock of sheep. He jokes that he will just hang an "N" in front of the name when he is sold out.

Born in Holland in 1956, he became interested in wine as a student at a Dutch agricultural college that organized several field trips to French vineyards. "My chemistry professor was fascinated with wine and used it a lot as examples," John remembers. "He had a bit of a club there, messing about with smaller batches of wine."

Discouraged by a perceived lack of opportunity to farm in Holland, he joined an uncle in Canada in 1977. A muscular, sturdily built man, John spent many years both in forestry and in dairy farming before he and Catherine, his wife, bought this 12.5-hectare (31-acre) Yankee Flats farm in 1992 for a dairy herd of their own. Fourteen years later, deciding it was time to do something new, he replaced the cows with the small herd of sheep. That gave him time to concentrate on the 1.6-hectare (four-acre) vineyard planted mostly in 2007. His winery is large enough to make about 1,000 cases a year. "We will stay small," he says. "I sell most of the wine from the shop. Local support is good but there are only so many wine drinkers."

While a consultant helped him with the 2009 vintage, John has taken over making the wines since. His preference is for dry wines but, recognizing that his customers are likely to prefer some off-dry wines, he adds a touch of sweet reserves to many of the white wines.

The domed vineyard has exposures to "all sides of the compass," he notes. He grows Pinot Gris, Gewürztraminer, Pinot Meunier and Maréchal Foch, along with a small block of Petite Milo (a Blattner white

JOHN KOOPMANS

hybrid). He is expanding the block of Regent, a winter-hardy red grape, and he has planted L'Acadie Blanc, an Ontario-developed white widely grown in Nova Scotia.

MY PICKS

Pinot Gris and Gewürztraminer are made in a crisp, fresh style. The two varieties also are blended in a pleasant off-dry wine called Pinot Tramino. Those who prefer more sweetness should try the four-grape white blend called Entice. The medium-bodied reds include Maréchal Foch and Black Riesling— the name John gives to his Pinot Meunier.

OPENED 2010

1577 Yankee Flats Road
Salmon Arm, BC V1E 3J4

T   250.832.8463

W www.ovinowinery.com

WHEN TO VISIT
11 am – 5 pm mid-May to mid-October; select weekends in December; and by appointment.

PAINTED ROCK ESTATE WINERY

Painted Rock's elegant tasting lounge, which opened in the summer of 2013, is the penultimate step in the making of a destination winery. The final step, still being planned, will be a luxurious country inn. That will cap a decade of development since 2004, when John Skinner bought this 24-hectare (60-acre) abandoned apricot orchard near the Skaha climbing bluffs.

John was setting out on a dramatic career change to coincide with his 50th birthday. A long-time Vancouver investment advisor, he was born in 1958 in Portage La Prairie. The son of a Canadian Forces pilot, he grew up on a succession of military bases. He was paying his way through university by working in a sawmill when the prosperity of a stockbroker friend persuaded John to take the investment business instead. Like many in that business, he developed an educated wine palate and then a passion to own a winery. He retired entirely from the investment business in 2009 to open Painted Rock with his wife, Trish.

The vineyard, a sculptured southwest-facing slope toward Skaha Lake, is planted with Bordeaux reds, Syrah and Chardonnay, all of which succeed on this site. John tapped the expertise of highly-regarded viticulturists and winemakers, most notably consultant Alain Sutre, one of Bordeaux's winemaking stars. Acclaim followed quickly. The winery won so many awards when it débuted at the 2009 Okanagan Fall Wine Festival that it was named the Best New BC Winery 2009. To date, four Painted Rock wines have won Lieutenant Governor's Awards of Excellence, among many other awards.

It did not take John long to realize Painted Rock's original tasting room, a renovated picker's cabin, did not fit the image of the wines. The new gleaming white tasting lounge, with windows offering a vineyard panorama, did not cost a million dollars but it looks like it did. In addition to welcoming tasting room visitors, it has been designed as a venue for weddings and vineyard dinners.

JOHN SKINNER

MY PICKS

Everything, including the polished Chardonnay, a full-bodied Merlot and elegant examples of Cabernet Sauvignon and Syrah. The flagship wine is a sophisticated Bordeaux blend called Red Icon—a must-have wine for collectors.

OPENED 2009

400 Smythe Drive
Penticton, BC V2A 8W6

T   250.493.6809

W www.paintedrock.ca

WHEN TO VISIT
Open daily 11 am – 5 pm mid-June to mid-October; weekends May to mid-June; and by appointment.

PELLER ESTATES WINERY

The Peller wines have been available in the Calona Wines boutique on Richter Street in Kelowna since 2005, when Andrew Peller Ltd. took over Calona and thus merged two of the Okanagan's oldest producers. More recently, the Wayne Gretzky Okanagan wine portfolio has been added.

Now a national company, Peller was launched in British Columbia in 1961 by Andrew Peller, a Hungarian-born brewer whose winery application had been thwarted in Ontario. Development-hungry British Columbia welcomed him with a low-priced winery site in the Vancouver suburb of Port Moody. Andrés, as it was then called, achieved national stature, in no small measure with the amazing success of its grapey Baby Duck sparkling wine that was created in Port Moody in 1971. Baby Duck still has a following, but the Port Moody winery closed at the end of 2005 when the business, now run by Andrew Peller's grandson, John, moved into the Calona winery.

Once a sponsor of the Inkameep Vineyard, Peller now is British Columbia's third largest grape grower. It owns the 28-hectare (70-acre) Rocky Ridge Vineyard in the Similkameen Valley, the 81-hectare (200-acre) Sandhill Vineyard and the recently-planted 121-hectare (298-acre) vineyard at Covert Farm near Oliver. It also buys the grapes from the 42.3-hectare (104½-acre) Vanessa Vineyard in the Similkameen, which grows only red varieties.

Peller's winemaker is Stephanie Stanley. Born in Kelowna, Stephanie joined Peller in 2005 on graduating as the top student at Brock University's enology and viticulture program. Her wines soon began piling up the awards, including two Lieutenant Governor's Awards of Excellence, testifying to her talent as well as to the quality of grapes being grown for Peller.

STEPHANIE STANLEY

MY PICKS

The Peller Family Series wines are good value-priced wines. I especially like the Sauvignon Blanc, the Pinot Gris, the Pinot Blanc, the Chardonnay, the Merlot and the Cabernet/Merlot. The Pinot Grigio, the Chardonnay, the Merlot and the Cabernet Sauvignon/Syrah are excellent value. The Wayne Gretzky Okanagan wines, first released in 2013, include an impressive Cabernet/Syrah blend.

OPENED 1961
(AS ANDRÉS WINES)

1125 Richter Street
Kelowna, BC V1Y 2K6

T 250.762.9144
   1.888.246.4472 (toll free)

W www.peller.com
   www.gretzkyestatewines.com

WHEN TO VISIT
Open daily 9 am – 6 pm mid-May to November; and 9 am – 5 pm November to mid-May.

PENTÂGE WINERY

Pentâge Winery opened its tasting room in 2011, eight years after opening the winery. The reason: it took Paul Gardner 11 years to plan and dig the massive 500-square-metre (5,500-square-foot) cave from the crown of hard rock commanding this vineyard's million-dollar view of Skaha Lake. Cool and spacious, this cave accommodates barrels and tanks of wine in a feat of engineering unlike anything else in the Okanagan, except perhaps the Mission Hill cellar. You can even appreciate the ambiance without a tour by peering through the gigantic glass doors at the front of the cave.

This was a derelict orchard when Paul and Julie Rennie, his wife, were so enchanted with the property in 1996 that they decided to change careers. Julie, the Scots-born daughter of a marine engineer, was executive assistant to a well-known Vancouver financier. Paul, born in Singapore in 1961, spent 20 years as a marine engineer before tiring of going to sea. "I got caught up in winemaking in the early 1990s," he says.

Now, he spends most of his time in the winery's two Skaha Bench vineyards, which total 6.5 hectares (16 acres), growing so many varieties—including even Zinfandel—that one vineyard is called the Dirty Dozen. "I would still rather make small lots of interesting wine than big tanks full of wine," he says. An example of an eccentric but delicious wine is the 2011 Cabernet Franc Appassimento Style where he mimicked Amarone by drying the grapes 58 days before crushing them.

The winery now produces about 5,000 cases a year, divided into a remarkable kaleidoscope of wines from entry level (under the label Hiatus) to premium. The winery's three-litre bag-in-the-box Pinot Gris is especially popular with restaurants. Julie's marketing savvy turned the winery's icewine into a steady seller by offering it in 200 ml bottles

JULIE RENNIE AND PAUL GARDNER

for $21.50 rather than in 375 ml bottles at $55. "There is still a profit in there," she says, "and consumers are buying it and consuming it, because it is not priced as a special occasion wine."

The winery name, a play on the Latin word for five, was chosen after Gardner planted five red varieties to make his flagship Pentâge red. The wine is built primarily with Merlot and Cabernet Sauvignon; small amounts of Cabernet Franc, Syrah and Gamay add complexity and personality.

OPENED 2003

4551 Valleyview Road
Penticton, BC V2A 8V8
T   250.493.4008
W www.pentage.com

WHEN TO VISIT
By appointment only.

MY PICKS

Everything including the Pentâge red, the Syrah, the Cabernet Franc, the Gamay, the Merlot and the Hiatus blends. Keep an eye peeled for Zinfandel, Malbec, Tempranillo and port. The white wines, including Gewürztraminer, Chenin Blanc, Sauvignon Blanc, Sémillon, Pinot Gris and Viognier, are good fruit-forward expressions of these varieties.

PERSEUS WINERY

This is a rare find: an urban winery in a 60-year-old house that is within walking distance of downtown Penticton. Perseus is so confident about its accessibility that it even installed a bike rack. And it takes pride in being the gateway winery to Naramata Bench, providing information about its competitors in its information centre.

The winery, which released its first wine in 2009 under the Synergy label, opened its wine shop in 2010 in a residential neighbourhood. It has been positioned as an urban winery, with a tasting room patio overlooking the city. There is a glimpse of the country, however: Perseus's Lower Bench Vineyard, a two-hectare (five-acre) Pinot Gris planting and one of its three vineyards, is just beyond the parking lot at the rear of the winery.

The winery was launched initially by three Penticton businessmen. Larry Lund is a hockey professional who trained young players at the Okanagan Hockey Camps and Academy from 1963 to 2004. Ron Bell, a developer and hotelier, planted the 2.6-hectare (6½-acre) Old Station Vineyard near Skaha Lake with Syrah and Sauvignon Blanc. In 2009, he and Larry planted 22.25 hectares (55 acres) of grapes at what they call the Blind Creek Vineyard near Cawston in the Similkameen Valley. Their third partner, Jim Morrison, owns a construction company.

In 2011, this trio sold the majority interest in Perseus to Terrabella Wineries, a company headed by Summerland chartered accountant Rob Ingram. Terrabella is structured to be a holding company for up to four British Columbia wineries, all in high traffic locations comparable to the site enjoyed by Perseus.

Perseus has a long-term contract for grapes with the Blind Creek Vineyard. "All the red wines from there are phenomenal," says Jean-Martin Bouchard, one of the consulting winemakers. The vineyard currently grows Syrah, Merlot, Cabernet Sauvignon, Malbec and Petit Verdot and has newer plantings of leading white varieties.

MY PICKS

The flagship wines are Invictus, a Bordeaux blend, and Tempus, a Syrah, and both are delicious. Merlot and Cabernet Shiraz are solid and good value. Sauvignon Blanc and Pinot Gris are crisp and appealing.

OPENED 2009
(AS SYNERGY)

134 Lower Bench Road
Penticton, BC V2A 1A8

T   250.490.8829
    1.888.880.6605 (toll free)

W www.perseuswinery.com

WHEN TO VISIT
Open daily 10 am – 7 pm April to October; Fridays and Saturdays 11 am – 5 pm in November and December; and by appointment.

ROB INGRAM

PLANET BEE HONEY FARM & MEADERY

Ed Nowek, who runs this busy farm and health store with his wife, Taosha, has been fascinated with bees since he was a teenager. Born in 1953 in Fairview, Alberta, a town 125 km north of Grand Prairie, Ed was still in high school when he took a summer job with a commercial beekeeper in Peace River country. "That is some of the best honey producing area in the world, because of the long days and short nights in the summertime," Ed says.

After a year in university, Ed went back into beekeeping for 10 years, spending the summers in northern Alberta and the winters in Mexico, California and for two years, in Australia. "Then I got restless," he remembers. "I got a chance to work in an oil company and got into management and marketing. So I had my sabbatical from bees. Then in 1997 I got back into beekeeping."

He opened the first Planet Bee in Armstrong, moving in 2003 to Vernon, a larger community with a more developed agri-tourism sector. The rambling Planet Bee facilities offer visitors everything from an education about bees to honey products ranging from therapeutic to edible—and mead, of course.

Ed began making mead in 2004 with an old friend, Martin Dournova, then the owner of a U-Brew, and now Ed's mead master. Martin is a chemist who has made wine for more than 35 years. "He told me he has never had to throw a batch out in this life," Ed says. In short order, Ed and Martin were winning awards. "We won this fancy mead 'mazer'," says Ed, referring to a drinking vessel with three handles. "You pass it around in a circle and everyone is always facing a handle." Success in competitions led to the addition of a meadery to Planet Bee.

The products are focused on melomels (fruit-flavoured meads) and traditional meads reflecting the flavours of the honey variety used (such as blueberry blossom or apricot blossom).

ED NOWEK

MY PICKS

Okanagan Delight is a floral, fruity mead with a dry finish. In Blueberry Bliss, the fruit is subtle and the honey flavours more pronounced. Apricot Elixir is off-dry, with the honey flavours delicately kissed by apricot. The Sour Cherry melomel has proved to be a bestseller.

OPENED 2011

5011 Bella Vista Road
Vernon, BC V1H 1A1
T   250.542.8088
    1.877.233.9675 (toll free)
W www.planetbee.com

WHEN TO VISIT
Open Monday to Saturday 8 am –
7 pm, and Sundays 9 am –
6 pm July and August; Monday
to Saturday 8:30 am – 5:30 pm,
and Sundays 9:30 am – 4:30 pm
September to June.

PLATINUM BENCH ESTATE WINERY

The seed for this winery, which opened in 2012, was planted a decade earlier when Murray Jones and Fiona Duncan took a cycling vacation through the vineyards of Bordeaux. "It was one of those 'ah ha' moments when we were out in the vineyards," Fiona remembers. "What an incredible reality that somebody has this as their lifestyle!" But they returned to their fast-paced business lives in Winnipeg. It took an Okanagan vacation seven or eight years later to germinate the seed.

Murray, who was born in Winnipeg in 1954 and graduated initially in zoology, became a chartered accountant to pursue a successful career in manufacturing (buses, garments, tents for the military). Fiona, who was born in 1962 and grew up in West Vancouver, met Murray after she went to Winnipeg in 1988. She spent a number of years as vice-president of production development for Nygård International, a major garment designer and manufacturer.

"We've always had a keen interest in wine," Fiona says. They absorbed knowledge from Murray's sister, Tina Jones, a wine educator and owner of a wine store called Banville & Jones. They supplemented that by both taking the first level of sommelier training. Many of the wines they purchased in Winnipeg were from California; Manitoba gets only a limited selection of British Columbia wines. They were astonished at the quality of wine in the South Okanagan when they vacationed there.

"We started talking to the people who owned the wineries," Fiona says. "Here were people who had taken this on as a second career. We started thinking maybe this could be our reality as well." They researched the wine business for a couple of years before buying a vineyard on Black Sage Road. After moving there early in 2011, both plunged into six months of viticulture and cellar management courses at Okanagan College to acquire the skills for their career changes. The 5.6-hectare (14-acre) vineyard, about 15 years old when they bought it,

FIONA DUNCAN AND MURRAY JONES

grows Chardonnay, Pinot Gris, Merlot, Cabernet Sauvignon and Merlot.

Fiona even honed an additional skill as a baker. She bakes at least 100 loaves of artisan bread daily for eager customers who often buy the loaves when they still are warm. The delicious breads also are matched with wines in the tasting room.

MY PICKS

Pinot Gris, Chardonnay and Gamay are delicious. The flagship wine here is a full-flavoured Bordeaux blend called Benchmark. The components—Merlot, Cabernet Franc and Cabernet Sauvignon—also are released as excellent single varietal wines.

OPENED 2012

4120 Black Sage Road
Oliver, BC V0H 1T1

T 250.535.1165

W www.platinumbench.com

WHEN TO VISIT
Open daily 10 am – 6 pm April to October; 11 am – 5 pm November and December; and by appointment.

FOOD SERVICES
Artisan bread, local cheeses and cold cuts.

POPLAR GROVE WINERY

The 882-square-metre (9,500-square-foot) winery that Poplar Grove opened in 2011 is king of the hill on the side of Munson Mountain, with breathtaking views of Penticton and its two lakes. The winery's understated architecture against the landscaped hillside has an elegance that visitors find irresistible. It is a far cry from founder Ian Sutherland's tiny original Poplar Grove winery, which was about the size of a pickers' cabin, or the homely metal-clad warehouse that replaced it when Poplar Grove needed the cabin for cheese making.

Poplar Grove was a boutique producer (about 2,000 cases a year) until 2007 when Tony Holler invested in the winery, giving it access to the 44.5 hectares (110 acres) of vineyard owned by Tony's wife, Barbara. Tony is a doctor who was born in Summerland in 1951 and who has run a succession of successful pharmaceutical companies. A Napa Valley vacation in 2004 spurred him to buy property on the Naramata Bench and to plant a vineyard just south of Poplar Grove. When Tony gets a passion about something, he thinks big. "I wasn't that interested in having a tiny boutique winery," he says.

A talented self-taught winemaker, Ian succeeded in a minimally-equipped winery. "What if we had the proper infrastructure," Tony asked, "a winery with the right cooling systems, with the right tanks and the right barrels, what can this winery really become? This valley can produce world-class wines. That's what got me excited about going into the wine business."

Now equipped with modern technology, Poplar Grove has increased to 15,000 cases, with a target of 25,000 cases, all from estate-grown grapes. Ian is now executive winemaker. Stefan Arnason became winemaker in 2008 and was joined in 2011 by Nadine Allandar as assistant winemaker. And Tony delights in surprising his international business colleagues with some of the Okanagan's best wines.

TONY HOLLER

Everything, including the $50 Legacy, a Merlot-anchored Bordeaux blend; the CSM, a blend of Cabernet Sauvignon, Syrah and Merlot; the Cabernet Franc, Merlot, Syrah, Pinot Gris, Viognier and Chardonnay.

OPENED 1997

425 Middle Bench Road North
Penticton, BC V2A 8S5

T 250.493.9463

W www.poplargrove.ca

WHEN TO VISIT
Open daily 10 am – 6 pm April
to October; weekends 10 am –
5 pm November to March.

RESTAURANT
Vanilla Pod Restaurant
T 250.494.8222
Open for lunch and dinner
February to December.

PRIVATO VINEYARD & WINERY

John and Debbie Woodward know that their vineyard is marginal, even with its sunbathed slope facing southeast, toward the North Thompson River. The property, a half hour drive north of Kamloops, is one of the more northerly vineyards in British Columbia planted to vinifera (Pinot Noir and Chardonnay).

"Debbie has always wanted a vineyard," says John, who was born in Kamloops in 1954. A professional forester, he and Debbie, a certified general accountant, met when they worked for the same forestry company. Preferring to work independently, they bought their 32-hectare (80-acre) farm in 1987. Here, they established a tree nursery now growing 30,000 Christmas trees and deciduous trees for landscaping needs.

Early in his forestry career, John began making wine at home from kits. He liked the wine until he moved it to storage that was too hot over summer and the wine fell apart. That ended his winemaking until he and Debbie vacationed among Italian wineries during crush several years ago. Seeing tiny wineries harvesting and processing grapes inspired them. "It was just the fuel we needed to get going," Debbie says.

They figured there was nothing holding them back: they had land for vines and farm buildings readily convertible to winemaking. And they had finished putting their children through school. "Before, we were running a business with the purpose of supporting the family," Debbie says. "Now we are doing it because we are passionate to make a really good glass of wine."

In 2010, they planted 1.2 hectares (three acres) of vines—Pinot Noir, Chardonnay and one row of Maréchal Foch. John is open to changing the varieties if these do not make it through the Kamloops winters. "We'll end up growing what will actually grow here,"

JOHN AND DEBBIE WOODWARD

he says. He also reacquainted himself with winemaking by making two barrels of wine in 2010 with consultant Gustav Allander of Foxtrot Vineyards. The first commercial vintage in 2011 comprised about 600 cases of Pinot Noir, Chardonnay and Cabernet Franc. In 2013, when Gustav stopped consulting, the Woodwards turned to New Zealand–trained Jacqueline Kemp for guidance on sourcing Okanagan grapes and making wine.

The Woodwards sell their wines through restaurants and directly to consumers. Initially, they did not plan to open a tasting room, considering their farm too far "off the beaten path." They changed their minds in 2013, no doubt to the delight of Kamloops area wine lovers.

MY PICKS

Both the Chardonnay and the Pinot Noir are elegantly polished wines.

SALES BEGAN 2012

5505 Westsyde Road
Kamloops, BC V2B 8N5

T 250.319.0919

W www.privato.ca

WHEN TO VISIT
Thursday to Sunday 11 am – 5 pm
June to mid-October; 12 am – 5 pm
weekends late October; daily
10 am – 4 pm in the three weeks
preceding Christmas, when the
farm also sells trees.

QUAILS' GATE ESTATE WINERY

The Stewart family, which operates Quails' Gate Estate Winery, credits their father, Richard, for planting the first successful Pinot Noir in 1975. The Stewarts, who are from Irish stock that settled in the Okanagan in 1911, are pioneering horticulturists. Part of the 50-hectare (125-acre) Quails' Gate vineyard was planted in 1956. Later, it was one of the earliest vineyards to convert to premium European varieties. Today Quails' Gate is the Okanagan's largest producer of Pinot Noir, with eight clones on 16 hectares (40 acres) in its vineyard on the slope of Mount Boucherie. Pinot Noir comprises one-fifth of the winery's total production, now about 60,000 cases per year.

Credit Grant Stanley for establishing the elegant style of Quails' Gate Pinot Noirs in his 10 years as the winemaker. Born in Vancouver in 1967, he became a winemaker in New Zealand where he made six vintages with Ata Rangi, a leading Pinot Noir producer. Grant left Quails' Gate in the summer of 2013 to become a partner in 50th Parallel Estate.

Nikki Callaway moved down the slopes of Mount Boucherie from Mission Hill to succeed Grant. She also brought a sure touch for Pinot Noir. At Mission Hill, her responsibilities included making the premium Martin's Lane wines. At the 2013 Decanter Wine Awards in Britain, the 2011 Martin's Lane Pinot Noir was judged best among a huge class of Pinot Noirs from around the world.

Born in Calgary in 1982, Nikki lived 10 years in Saudi Arabia where her father was a doctor. She came back to Canada for a bachelor's degree in microbiology at the University of Victoria. "Dad talked me out of medicine," she says. "He thought I would have more fun drinking wine." She graduated in 2007 with a Diplôme National d'Oenologue from the University of Bordeaux and worked in France and South Africa before joining Mission Hill in 2009.

TONY STEWART

NIKKI CALLAWAY

MY PICKS

Everything. Top-tier wines are released as Stewart Family Reserve; Chardonnay and Pinot Noir are especially fine. The regular Quails' Gate tier includes excellent Chenin Blanc, Dry Riesling, Gewürztraminer, Chardonnay, a popular Chasselas/Pinot Blanc/ Pinot Gris blend; rosé, Pinot Noir, Merlot and the Old Vines Foch. The Botrytis Affected Optima is a superb dessert wine.

OPENED 1989

3303 Boucherie Road
Kelowna, BC V1Z 2H3
T   250.769.2501
     1.800.420.9463 (toll free)
W www.quailsgate.com

WHEN TO VISIT
Open daily 9:30 am – 7 pm July
to early September; 10 am – 7 pm
in May, June and September; and
10 am – 6 pm October through
April. Check website for extensive
tour schedule.

RESTAURANT
Old Vines
T   250.769.2500
Open daily at 11:30 am for lunch
and dinner; Sunday brunch
10:30 am – 2:30 pm.

QUINTA FERREIRA ESTATE WINERY

John Ferreira jokes that he got his first taste of cork when he was five and growing up in Portugal, where he was born in 1954. It was his chore to have the family's wine flask refilled at a nearby shop. Barely tall enough to see over the cork-surfaced counter, he sometimes chewed on it while he was waiting. Today, his Black Sage Road winery, on a ridge overlooking Oliver, fulfills the imperative of his heritage. "I believe every man on earth would either like to have a vineyard or a winery," he maintains. "I have always wanted to have a vineyard."

John grew up fast. His parents came to Oliver from Portugal in 1960, working as hardscrabble farm labour. John was driving the tractor when he was seven. Later, he (and his sisters) often missed the first few weeks of school because the family was picking apples. Hard work enabled the Ferreiras to lease, and then buy, this farm, a mere stone's throw from town. Here, they carved an orchard from raw sagebrush. In 1979, John and his wife, Maria, bought the orchard. To meet mortgage payments, they had to sell fruit privately. When that got them expelled from the packing house co-operative, the Ferreiras opened their own independent packing house. That packing house, grandly renovated, is now their sandy-hued Mediterranean-style winery.

Beginning in 1999, John replaced his fruit trees with eight hectares (20 acres) of grapes. "I didn't know the first thing about growing grapes when we put the first one in," John admits. "I was just tired of the fruit business." He opened a winery after seeing his grapes—Merlot, Syrah, Malbec, Zinfandel, Petit Verdot, Chardonnay, Viognier and Pinot Blanc—being turned into prize-winning wines at other wineries.

The Ferreiras also celebrate their Portuguese heritage with proprietary wine names. The blends are called Mistura Branca (white) and Mistura Tinto (red). The dessert wine is Vinho du Sól. The flagship

JOHN FERREIRA

red blend is Obra-Prima, Portuguese for masterpiece. Most of the reds age two years in barrel and one year in bottle and are released in their prime. Of course, every bottle is closed with natural cork.

MY PICKS

The Obra-Prima lives up to its name. Other delicious wines here include Malbec, Syrah, Zinfandel, Viognier, Chardonnay Pinot Gris, Sauvignon Blanc and rosé, as well as a Chardonnay dessert wine called Vinho du Sól.

OPENED 2007

6094 Black Sage Road
Oliver, BC V0H 1T8

T 250.498.4756

W www.quintaferreira.com

WHEN TO VISIT
Open daily 10 am – 6 pm.

RECLINE RIDGE VINEYARDS & WINERY

Until Celista vineyards opened in 2010, Recline Ridge was British Columbia's northern-most winery, 14 kilometres (nine miles) west of Salmon Arm, in the pastoral Tappen Valley, just off the Trans-Canada Highway. The quiet countryside appealed to Graydon and Maureen Ratzlaff when they bought the winery in 2010 from founder Michael Smith. They had lived 25 years in Greater Vancouver where Graydon had a series of senior positions with food processing firms. "We were looking for a lifestyle improvement," he says. "We view the wine industry as a happy industry."

Born in New Westminster in 1952, Graydon grew up in Summerland. After graduating from the University of British Columbia's food sciences program, he began his career with Kelowna's SunRype Products. In 1985 he and Maureen, a retail specialist, moved to Vancouver to experience big-city living. Graydon became a specialist in setting up and managing processing plants. He worked at various times with snack food manufacturers, producers of food for aquaculture, a poultry processor and, ultimately, for Vincor Canada's RJ Spagnols division. A home winemaker himself, Graydon set up a plant to make kits and other supplies for home vintners. Here, he discovered that the wine industry was "a community of folks that just love the products." By taking over Recline Ridge, he and Maureen joined that community.

The business plans call for making about 3,000 cases of wine a year. Niagara-born Jesse Steinley, who joined Recline Ridge several years ago as a vineyard worker, has emerged as one of the Shuswap's most accomplished winemakers. Recline Ridge's three-hectare (7½-acre) vineyard grows Maréchal Foch, Siegerrebe, Optima, Madeleine Sylvaner, Madeleine Angevine and Ortega. The winery also buys grapes from other Shuswap growers, having largely stopped buying grapes from the Okanagan.

MAUREEN AND GRAYDON RATZLAFF

"I would prefer it that we still exploit those varietals that are grown locally," Graydon says. "If I bring in a Merlot or a Cabernet Sauvignon, I am competing with 175 other wineries down south that can do it better from their own grapes. I think there is room grow with the varieties that are here."

MY PICKS

The Siegerrebe is my favourite mouthful here (it is pronounced *zeeg-er-ay-beh*). The winery also has a crisp and refreshing Ortega and a zesty Bacchus. Maréchal Foch, the big red, is well-made.

OPENED 1999

2640 Skimikin Road
Tappen. BC V0E 2X0

T 250.835.2212

W www.recline-ridge.bc.ca

WHEN TO VISIT
Open daily 10 am – 5 pm July and August; 11 am – 5 pm June; noon – 5 pm May, September, October; and by appointment and on-site pager in winter.

RED ROOSTER WINERY

As a former winemaker said once, the challenge here is to make wines that "fit the building." Both the spacious wine shop and the separate winery itself are the most baronial of architect Robert Mackenzie's Okanagan winery designs.

This is a far cry from Red Rooster's original modest winery on a side street near the Naramata fire hall. In 2004, founders Beat and Prudence Mahrer relocated Red Rooster to this "you can't miss it" location right on Naramata Road. Being art lovers, the Mahrers turned the wine shop's second floor into a gallery for local artists. They also found space in the tasting room for Frank the Baggage Handler, the controversial nude sculpture that suffered strategic vandalism when it was first displayed in a traffic circle in nearby Penticton. Andrew Peller Ltd. bought Red Rooster in 2005 but, appreciating the attraction of lively irreverence, kept Frank in the rambling tasting room. In fact, a second statue was erected outside the winery!

The winery has come up with several effective ways for attracting and keeping its customer base, including a wine club with many benefits, including discounts on wines. The winery's "adopt a row" program enables Red Rooster customers to adopt their own rows in the winery vineyard. There is a waiting list.

Winemaker Karen Gillis has proven herself by making wines as grand as the architecture. Born in Vancouver, she grew up in a family of chefs. She initially had the same career in mind when she completed a diploma in food technology at the British Columbia Institute of Technology in 1996. But after three years developing food products, she zeroed in on wine and joined Andrés (as Andrew Peller Ltd. was then called) to become a winemaker. She has been at Red Rooster since 2007, crafting cellar-worthy reserve wines and ready-to-drink regular wines whose fresh flavours are captured under screw cap. When that

KAREN GILLIS

closure was unveiled to the "adopt-a-row" club, the members gave Karen a standing ovation.

MY PICKS

The array of refreshing whites includes Pinot Gris, Pinot Blanc, Riesling, Gewürztraminer, Chardonnay and Viognier. Reserve versions of several whites show even more intense flavours. Bantam is an aromatic easy-drinking white blend of five or six varieties. The Meritage, the Merlot, the Pinot Noir and the Syrah, along with the Reserve Malbec, are excellent. The icon red is called The Golden Egg, currently a blend of Mourvedre, Syrah and Grenache.

OPENED 1997

891 Naramata Road
Penticton, BC V2A 8T5

T   250.492.2424

W www.redroosterwinery.com

WHEN TO VISIT
Open daily 10 am – 6 pm April to October; 11 am – 5 pm November to March.

RESTAURANT
The Pecking Room Patio Grill Open daily for lunch and snacks from noon – 5 pm mid-May to mid-October.

RIVER STONE ESTATE WINERY

Like any serious wine lover, Ted Kane would like to taste Cheval Blanc, a legendary Bordeaux red with an astronomic price tag. The difference between Ted and the rest of us is that he has the grapes to make a wine in that style. Cheval Blanc is primarily a blend of Cabernet Franc and Merlot, which Ted grows along with Cabernet Sauvignon, Malbec and Petit Verdot. "This site is great with Cabernet Franc," he says of his vineyard. "At some point, I am going to make a Cabernet Franc Merlot blend, just to see what it can do. I like that Cheval Blanc idea."

He worried—needlessly, as it turned out—that there might be no more good vineyard sites available before he and his wife, Lorraine, then a medical student, bought this riverside property in Oliver in 2001. Born in Edmonton in 1962, Ted was so focused on wine growing that he grew grapes in a greenhouse there just to learn how. They moved to Oliver in 2002, planting a three-hectare (seven-acre) vineyard while Lorraine, now the mother of three, began a family medicine practice.

River Stone's well-drained property has ideal slopes to the south, the southeast and the southwest. The vineyard is planted in the French tradition, in the proportions Ted wanted for Corner Stone, the Merlot-dominant flagship blend that the winery launched with the 2009 vintage. "My Bordeaux blend is transitioning a bit," he says after experience gained in subsequent vintages. "My blend is still Merlot driven but Cabernet Franc is equal to or greater than the Cabernet Sauvignon in the blend. Cabernet Franc does better on my property than Cabernet Sauvignon." Recently, he grafted Petit Verdot onto a small block of Cabernet Sauvignon, not so much for viticultural issues but to grow all five Bordeaux reds for the 450 or so cases of Corner Stone made every year.

River Stone's wines, which Ted makes with the help of New

LORRAINE AND TED KANE

Zealand–trained consultant Jacqueline Kemp, all are estate-grown, with the minor exception of Splash, the refreshing summer white that includes Viognier from a neighbour. "The vineyard is where it starts out and what carries us from season to season," he says. "The best grapes make the best wines. I wanted to see where that was going to take us."

OPENED 2011

143 Buchanan Road
Oliver, BC V0H 1T2

T   250.498.7798

W www.riverstoneestatewinery.ca

WHEN TO VISIT
Open 11 am – 6 pm Easter weekend; Thursday to Sunday May to June; daily July to mid-October; and by appointment.

MY PICKS

Everything from Splash and the Pinot Gris to the intense Malbec rosé, the brambly Cabernet Franc, the elegant Merlot and the complex Corner Stone.

ROAD 13 VINEYARDS

In 2012, to resolve a brand conflict with an Ontario winery, Road 13 changed the name of Rockpile, a popular red blend, to Seventy-Four K. Mick Luckhurst, who owns the winery with Pam, his wife, calculated that he has to walk 74 kilometres to patrol all of Road 13's vineyard rows. That speaks to the physically challenging but satisfying lifestyle that the couple chose when they bought this winery in 2003. Mick once said, while gazing over his vines, that he certainly would not have the same passion if those were potato plants.

Mick, who was born in Port Alberni in 1950, was a lumber broker, a real estate developer and a building-supply owner. Manchester-born Pam, a former flight attendant, has long been Mick's business partner. Attracted to the winery lifestyle after a summer-long Okanagan sabbatical, they purchased Golden Mile Cellars, a winery that resembled a draughty 17th-century Bavarian castle. The winery had only been making an anemic 1,000 cases a year, held back by a name that did not distinguish it from the Golden Mile viticultural area. In 2008, when the Luckhursts changed the name to Road 13 (the winery is at the end of that road), their sales exploded. Today, Road 13 produces about 25,000 cases a year. In 2014, Joe Luckhurst, their son, was named Road 13's general manager.

Excellent winemakers have helped craft this success. California-trained Lawrence Herder, who had his own Similkameen winery, was there in the first year the Luckhursts owned the winery. He was succeeded by Michael Bartier. When Michael left in 2010 to join Okanagan Crush Pad, he turned the cellar over to Jean-Martin Bouchard, a Sherbrook native. J-M, as he calls himself, studied hotel management but, when restaurant jobs fostered a love of wine, he went to Australia in 1998 to study wine science at Charles Sturt University. He then made wine in Australia, Alsace and Germany before returning to Canada and, as winemaker, turning Ontario's Hidden Bench winery into a rising star before coming to Road 13. Shauna White, a Niagara Collage

PAM AND MICK LUCKHURST

J-M BOUCHARD

graduate and a niece of winemaker Ann Sperling, joined Road 13 in 2013 as associate winemaker.

Michael preferred to make large-volume blends. J-M has not sacrificed that even as he expanded Road 13's portfolio dramatically. Five blends—the three Honest John wines, Seventy-Four K and Stemwinder—account for half the winery's production. The 20 or so other wines in the portfolio are interesting small-lot wines of varietals that show off terroir and capable viticulture.

MY PICKS

OPENED 1998
(AS GOLDEN MILE CELLARS)

799 Ponderosa Road, Road 13
Oliver, BC V0H 1T1

T   250.498.8330
     1.866.498.8330

W www.road13vineyards.com

WHEN TO VISIT
Open daily 10 am – 5:30 pm April to October; Monday to Saturdays (except holidays) 11 am – 4 pm November to March.

FOOD SERVICE
Lounge open daily noon – 5 pm May to October.

Everything, especially sparkling Chenin Blanc, Old Vines Chenin Blanc, Fifth Element, Seventy-Four K, Stemwinder and the moderately-priced Honest John wines (a red, a white and a rosé). Small-lot standouts include Jackpot Riesling and Jackpot Viognier Roussanne Marsanne.

ROBIN RIDGE WINERY

The Robin Ridge wine shop very near the Similkameen Valley's well-known summer attraction, the Grist Mill and Gardens on Upper Bench Road just outside Keremeos. Yet in 2012 Tim and Caroline Cottrill, the owners of Robin Ridge, bought a second vineyard property on Highway 3, with a long-range plan to move the tasting room to this higher traffic location on the Similkameen wine route.

Tim also needs more of his own grapes to support Robin Ridge's success. The winery's production has doubled in recent years to more than 2,000 cases. He has been planting about one hectare of new vineyard a year. Cabernet Sauvignon, Cabernet Franc and Petit Verdot were planted initially to blend with the winery's Merlot for Big Bird, a Meritage now made with purchased grapes. In the second year of planting, Tim added Riesling and Gamay, a variety with which Robin Ridge excels.

The son of a carpenter, Tim was born in Kelowna in 1966 and grew up in Summerland, where he helped his father build houses. When they tired of the construction industry's boom and bust cycles, Tim and Caroline (who grew up on a peach orchard) switched to grapes. In 1996, they purchased a four-hectare (10-acre) hayfield near the Grist Mill. It took them a full season during 1998 to clear enough of the stones to plant vines. While Tim studied winemaking and viticulture at Okanagan College, they started by planting a 1.2-hectare (three-acre) block of Chardonnay in 1998, adding Gamay in 1999, Merlot in 2001 and Pinot Noir in 2004. As well, there are small plots of Gewürztraminer, Cabernet Sauvignon, St. Laurent and Rougeon (a rustic French hybrid since replaced with Cabernet Franc), along with half a hectare of Sovereign Coronation table grapes.

In the 2011 vintage, Tim let his son, Charles, who was 15 at the time, make 26 cases of a grapey aperitif wine called Flamingo. Although playing soccer takes precedence in Charles's schedule, Robin Ridge continues to make this wine and, in 2013, added Sparkling Finch, a bubbly made from Chardonnay and Pinot Noir.

MY PICKS

The excellent Chardonnay has a touch of oak supporting the citrus flavours. The Gewürztraminer is fresh and spicy. I have always been a big fan of the robust Gamay and would also recommend the elegant Pinot Noir, the full-bodied Merlot and a red blend called Robin's Return.

OPENED 2008

2686 Middle Bench Road
Keremeos. BC V0X 1N2

T 250.499.5504

W www.robinridgewinery.com

WHEN TO VISIT
Open daily 11 am – 5:30 pm
May to October 14; and by
appointment.

CAROLINE AND TIM COTTRILL

ROLLINGDALE WINERY

In 2013 Rollingdale announced it had become the first winery in North American to accept Bitcoin, the controversial digital currency that was launched in 2009. Time will tell whether that gives the winery an edge—but it tells you something about proprietor Steve Dale's penchant for thinking outside the box.

Rollingdale was the first Okanagan winery to win organic certification. Steve is so committed to organic practices that he has used chickens (until the coyotes got them) for insect control and livestock for weed control in his two-hectare (five-acre) vineyard. Steve is categorically against inorganic products in vineyards. "I don't want to be responsible for poisoning the land, the air, the water, or the inhabitants thereof," he vows. "Systemic fungicides, pesticides, chemical fertilizers, and herbicides are ugly. I won't handle them and I won't pay someone else to. There is always an organic solution to every problem encountered."

Steve and Kirsty, his wife, come to wine by way of an organic gardening store they once had in Port Moody. Although Steve, born in Ontario in 1971, has a degree in English literature, he became a horticultural consultant based in Switzerland. The Dales took advantage of that locale to explore Italian and French wine regions, nurturing their desire to be in the wine business. In 2003, they returned to Canada and Steve enrolled in the winery assistant course at Okanagan University College. To get practical experience at the end of the course, he went to prune vines in this vineyard, then being managed by the Hainle winery. By the end of his first day, he had struck a deal to take over the lease. In 2005, he bought the property, launching a winery the following year.

A functional metal building serves for what Steve calls a "garagiste" winery. The tasting bar is among the tanks and barrels, where Steve and his enthusiastic staff often can be viewed working as hard as they play.

STEVE DALE

MY PICKS

The wines here at times have been eclectic, like the aromatic white blend whimsically called Riewurztrafelseron, and at times as serious as any in the Okanagan. Try the pair of distinguished barrel-aged reds, Merlot La Droite and Cabernet Sauvignon La Gauche and the Pinot Noir. The Estate Red is a good barbecue wine made chiefly with Maréchal Foch. The icewines are a specialty of the house.

OPENED 2006

2306 Hayman Road
West Kelowna, BC V1Z 1Z5

T   250.769.9224

W www.rollingdale.ca

WHEN TO VISIT
Open daily 10 am – 6 pm May
to October; 10 am – 5 pm
November to April.

PICNIC AREA

RUBY BLUES WINERY

Prudence Mahrer is an effervescent personality who grew up with the music and culture of the 1960s. That included a Rolling Stones song, "Ruby Tuesday", about a free-spirited young woman following her dream. That inspired the name of the winery when, following her dream, she convinced her husband, Beat, to launch their second Naramata winery in 2009. Unfortunately, an American restaurant chain with 900 locations, Ruby Tuesday, has been around since the 1970s (with a single Canadian location in Niagara Falls). When they objected, Prudence renamed the winery Ruby Blues in an apparent allusion to a Beatles song. "Some of the songs from the sixties have so much meaning to them," she believes.

Red Rooster Winery, which opened in 1997, was their first. They sold the chateau-styled winery in 2005 to Andrew Peller Ltd., intending to retire. They travelled in winter and piloted their float planes in summer. Prudence, who also spent the summers running their 5.6 hectares (14 acres) of vineyard, soon discovered how much she missed the winery and meeting the public. Had there been a support group for ex-winery owners, she says, she would have joined it. That is why at 55 (she was born in Switzerland in 1953), she persuaded her husband to start Ruby Blues. "That's the reason why I wanted to start again," she says. "I can easily do another 10 to 15 years." Believe it: she and Beat are remarkably athletic, having run fitness centres in Switzerland.

Ruby Blues, with an annual production between 2,000 and 3,000 cases (all from Naramata Bench fruit), never will be as large as Red Rooster (16,000 to 20,000 cases). Prudence found that there had been far too much administration and not enough contact with clients. "I want to do what I really loved the most—producing wine, quality wine, of course—and then selling it myself to customers," she says. Winemaker Lyndsay O'Rourke, who trained in New Zealand, is a rising star among Okanagan winemakers, and also operates her own winery, called Tightrope.

The tasting room at Ruby Blues sparkles with Prudence's personality.

PRUDENCE MAHRER

The tasting fee? "The cost for a tasting is a smile," has become the winery's slogan. If you are not smiling, she will tease one out of you, perhaps by trying to sell you a pair of shoes. The wine labels have always included the red stiletto shoes that Ruby Tuesday might have kicked off to chase her dream. In 2011 Prudence ordered 170 pairs of ladies' shoes from a cobbler in Vietnam.

"They are very high-heeled, very feminine, probably nothing to walk in the vineyard with," Prudence laughs. "They are meant to walk from home to the car and to the restaurant and then back. They look extremely fancy."

OPENED 2009
(AS RUBY TUESDAY WINERY)

917 Naramata Road
Penticton, BC V2A 8V1
T 250.276.5311
W www.rubyblueswinery.com

WHEN TO VISIT
Open daily 11 am – 5 pm April
to October.

MY PICKS

The wines are solid across the range, including a juicy Pinot Gris, a full-flavoured Gewürztraminer and a Viognier-based blend called White Stiletto. The tasty reds include Merlot, Syrah, Cabernet Sauvignon and a juicy blend called Red Stiletto.

RUSTIC ROOTS WINERY

"It was one of our goals to make wines that would surprise people," winemaker Sara Harker says. She challenged the perception that fruit wines are sweet by producing wines that range from dry to sweet to sparkling. She also builds complexity into the wines with blending and with creative winemaking. For example, she blends about 30 percent Santa Rosa plum wine with 70 percent Fameuse apple wine to create a lively pink sparkling wine. Fameuse, also called Snow Apple, is a heritage variety produced by a tree planted on this farm in 1916. All the wine labels include an image of the immensely-rooted Snow Apple tree.

The Rustic Roots winery, making about 1,200 cases a year, is incorporated into the highway-side organic fruit stand operated since the late 1950s by the Harker family, which has very deep roots in the Similkameen Valley. The current head of the family, Bruce Harker, has farmed here since 1975. His maternal great-grandfather was Sam Manery, the fourth settler baby born in the valley after Sam's parents came there in 1888. The photo gallery on the winery's website once included an image of Sam, a crusty-looking cowboy on a spirited horse.

Bruce and Kathy, his wife, developed a flourishing business with organic fruit. As they reached their 60s, they were thinking of retirement when sons Jason and Troy (now assistant winemaker) returned to the farm and the business. This brought a fifth generation into Harker Organics, with a sixth in the wings. That was the incentive to develop the winery with winemaking by daughter-in-law Sara, Troy's wife.

Born in Oliver in 1982, Sara is a member of a family that emigrated from Hungary in 1956. She comes to wine through the restaurant business. After studying science for a year at Langara and then business administration at Okanagan University College, she spent eight years working at various positions at the Fairview Mountain Golf Club. Sara equipped herself for the winery by taking OUC's winery assistant program and mentoring with consultant Christine Leroux.

SARA HARKER

MY PICKS

Start with the refreshing
dry Peach Nectarine wine
or the spicy Apple Pear,
made with five varieties of
apples and three varieties
of pear, or the apple and
plum sparkling wine,
Fameuse frizzante. The
Cherry wine, fermented
deliberately on the pits, is
dry with a nutty undertone.
The Apricot wine is tangy.
Dessert wines include a
delicious Santa Rosa plum
wine, the delicate Iced
Orin apple wine and the
rich Mulberry Pear wine.

OPENED 2008

2238 Agar Road (Highway 3)
Cawston, BC V0X 1C2

T   250.499.2754

W www.rusticrootswinery.com

WHEN TO VISIT
Open daily 10 am – 5 pm
spring and fall; 10 am – 8 pm
August and September; and by
appointment January to March.

RUSTICO FARM & CELLARS

When Bruce Fuller capped a long career in marketing by getting into wine, he first tried to recreate an Italian village in the southern Okanagan. He was reliving memories of a time long ago in the village of Asolo near Venice. Wines for the D'Asolo label, made for Bruce by other wineries, were in the market for a few years until his partners backed out of the project.

However, Bruce hit paydirt in 2007 when, with new silent partners, he took over a vineyard that included the Okanagan's most eccentric log cabin. "I don't think there is any winery that has the story to tell like this one does," Bruce asserts. The Italian village has been transformed into a frontier trading post and what Bruce calls Canada's "most romantic" winery.

The 3.6-hectare (nine-acre) vineyard was begun in 1968 by a debonair Hungarian named John Tokias who came to British Columbia in 1951. He purchased this property, then raw Crown land, in 1963. He worked for about 17 years at the silver mines near Beaverdell. As mines started to close, he acquired a log cabin bunkhouse. He relocated it log by log to his Okanagan property, apparently using his Volkswagen truck and a trailer to transport the logs gingerly around mountain highway curves. When he put the cabin back together, he added a massive sod roof. The sod roof, whose rustic appearance inspired the winery name, is ornamented with flowering cactuses and other seasonal plants.

Wearing a 10-gallon hat, Bruce presides theatrically in the tasting room, serving wine from pitchers into tumblers. Most guests are enrolled in the Wine Posse and invested with a deputy wine marshal's star. There is no pay for deputies but, as the certificate states, every Wine Posse member is "considered quite a big shot and square shooter . . .." Not only that: there are discounts on wine purchases.

The varietals in the vineyard include Gewürztraminer, Merlot and

BRUCE FULLER

Zinfandel. The long surviving block of Chancellor, one of the remaining original varietals here, is being replaced with Cabernet Franc. The wine in which Chancellor was blended was called Last Chance, appropriate because this likely is the last chance to taste this vanishing variety.

MY PICKS

The attraction here includes the creative names of the tasty wines: Farmer's Daughter Gewürztraminer, Isabella's Poke Pinot Gris, Mother Lode Merlot, Bonanza Zinfandel and Doc's Buggy Pinot Noir. The latter is inspired by the vintage doctor's buggy parked in front of the wine shop.

OPENED 2009

4444 Golden Mile Drive
Oliver, BC V0H 1T1

T 250.498.3276

W www.rusticowinery.com

WHEN TO VISIT
Open daily 10 am – 6 pm May to October; 1 pm – 5 pm November to April.

PICNIC PATIO

SADDLE RIDGE VINEYARDS

Saddle Ridge's initial wines are being released under the Rafter F label, with the historic Rafter F cattle brand cut into each label. The brand belongs to Bill and Darlene Freding who produce Okanagan's Finest Angus Beef from animals that are finished with a litre of wine daily for 90 days. However, they did not start this winery just to supply the feedlot.

Saddle Ridge Vineyard, now 19 hectares (47 acres), was begun in 1998. "I wanted a vineyard," Darlene says. "That was going to be my future and my business. Mission Hill advised what varietals to plant—Cabernet Sauvignon, Syrah and Cabernet Franc are dominant—and veteran vineyard manager Richard Cleave, one of their neighbours, became their viticulturist. The grapes were sold first to Mission Hill and subsequently to other wineries. In 2011, the Fredings, having seen others make award-winning wines with their grapes, decided to have wines made under their own Rafter F label by Okanagan Crush Pad Winery.

Rafter F has been the Freding brand for a long time. Bill, who has a master's in agriculture, is a fourth-generation rancher. His great-grandfather, John Allison, was the first settler and rancher near Princeton where Bill was born in 1943. He and Darlene, a Nova Scotian, ran four different Cariboo ranches before buying the Oliver feedlot in 1988 where they now grow exquisite beef and exquisite wines.

The modest Saddle Ridge winery was established in 2014 by modifying an existing building on the property. The decision to repatriate wine production was taken after their daughter, Kerri, and son-in-law Ken Hinsberg, who had been Charolais breeders in Manitoba for 15 years—decided to join what has now become a family winery. "Kerri is taking her winery assistant course and applying for a land-based winery license," Darlene explained just before the 2013 vintage. "There is no

BILL FREDING

DARLENE FREDING

point of her dad and I doing it. I am 64 and he is going to be 70. It is nice to pass it on to the next generation."

The first vintage was made here with the help of a consulting winemaker. When a tasting room opens, it will be a plank on two barrels in the winery, suiting this family's salt of the earth informality.

SALES BEGAN IN 2012

487 Sibco Landfill
Oliver, BC V0H 1T1

T 250.498.3077

W www.rafterfwines.com

WHEN TO VISIT
No tasting room.

KERRI HINSBERG

MY PICKS

The debut Pinot Gris and Chardonnay wines were fresh but light. The reds—Cabernet Sauvignon, Cabernet Franc and Syrah—are bigger and more satisfying, just the thing with good wine-fed Angus beef.

SAGE BUSH WINERY

Tucked away in the corner of Gerry's Fruit and Vegetable Stand, Sage Bush is the second winery on this high-traffic location on Highway 3 in Keremeos. The first winery here was the ill-fated K Mountain Vineyards, named for the mountain looming above Keremeos with its prominent K-shaped debris slides.

The K Mountain winery was opened in 2008 by Naramata winery operator Keith Holman who had purchased the fruit stand and planted some vines. The bankruptcy of Holman's seven wineries in 2010 led to the closure of the Keremeos winery. Then in 2011, a fire that broke out very early on May 8 completely destroyed both the winery and the fruit stand. A winery came back to life here when the property was purchased after the fire by Sunny and Jasminder Lasser. Since 1990, they had operated their own fruit stand, Lasser's Produce, on the other side of the highway, competing directly with Gerry's.

Sunny, who left school at 14 to become a farmer, came from India to Keremeos about 1980 to join a brother. His wife, Jasminder, came five years later, turning down a job as a school principal in India where, as a student, she had been at the top of her class.

They proved to be a power couple among the South Asian immigrants in the area. Sunny started as a farm worked at Cawston and then gained experience working in one of the major fruit stands lining the highway before opening Lasser's. In 1995, they began buying orchards to supply Lasser's. Today, they own 56.6 hectares (140 acres) of fruit and vegetable farms, operate a packing house and sell to export markets as well as locally.

Gerry's was rebuilt, complete with a winery whose name comes from the sage plants that grow all over the hills. Beginning in the 2011 vintage, the Lassers retained Megan Mutch, the winemaker for nearby Cerelia Winery, to make the Sage Bush wines. The winery opened with

SUNNY AND JASMINDER LASSER

about 600 cases of wine. It is unlikely to stay small under the energetic hands of the Lasser family.

MY PICKS

Lovers of pink wine will like Vin Gris, a blush wine from Pinot Noir, and the rosé which incorporates five varietals (Gewürztraminer, Pinot Gris, Orange Muscat, Cabernet Sauvignon and Syrah). The big red blend here is called Red Fusion.

OPENED 2013

3045 Highway 3
Keremeos, BC V0X 1N1
T 250.499.0095
W www.sagebushwinery.ca

WHEN TO VISIT
Open daily 9 am – 6 pm.

SAGE HILLS ESTATE VINEYARD & WINERY

For Rick Thrussell, the dream of the winery lifestyle was planted during an Okanagan camping vacation in the early 1980s when he and his friends spent an afternoon at Uniacke Estate Winery. The predecessor to CedarCreek Estate Winery, Uniacke had opened in 1980 and was one of the Okanagan's earliest cottage wineries.

Rick has a vivid memory of that afternoon. "It was one of those quintessential Okanagan days," he remembers. "It was warm and I was in my shorts. I looked out over this vineyard and thought what an enjoyable way to live—to get up every day and look at this." The dream was set aside until 2006, while he pursued other careers.

Born in Vancouver in 1959, Rick majored in geography, political science and communications at Simon Fraser University. He spent the 1980s in government-related jobs, managing communications around major infrastructure projects. After a 1991 change of the provincial government, he became a home builder and was so successful that, by 2006, he could afford to move to the Okanagan and revive the winery dream. "Building homes was something that I liked," he says. "But I can't bend nails until I am 80."

He bought a 4.5-hectare (11-acre) orchard on a Summerland bench with breathtaking lake views and, in 2007, began planting an organic vineyard with Pinot Gris, Gewürztraminer and Pinot Noir. Now the unromantic side of viticulture caught up, with unusually cold winters setting the vineyard back so that it wasn't until 2012 that enough grapes could be produced for Sage Hills's debut vintage of 800 cases. The wines were made by consultant Tom DiBello at nearby Okanagan Crush Pad Winery. The 2013 vintage was made on Rick's property by South African–born winemaker Danny Hattingh. Rick's ultimate target is to make 4,000 cases a year.

The Sage Hills vineyard has an exceptional view of Okanagan Lake

RICK THRUSSELL

to the east and of the mountains that border the lake. The planned Sage Hills tasting room will make the most of that view. It will also share the modernist lines of Rick's clifftop home, a design inspired by his admiration for the work of the legendary architect, Frank Lloyd Wright. The home and the planned winery have geothermal heating and cooling. It is an extension of Rick's insistence on growing grapes organically without herbicides, even when it means weeding by hand. Indeed, Rick calls himself the "head weed picker."

MY PICKS

The winery launched with excellent Gewürztraminer, Pinot Gris, Syrah rosé and Pinot Noir.

SALES BEGAN 2013

18555 Matsu Drive
Summerland. BC V0H 1Z6

T 250.276.4344

W www.sagehillswine.com

WHEN TO VISIT
Tastings by appointment.

ST. HUBERTUS ESTATE WINERY

In the spring of 2012, Leo and Andy Gebert, owners of this winery, more than doubled their Chasselas plantings. The four hectares (10 acres) of Chasselas in this winery's 24.7-hectare (61-acre) vineyard almost certainly is the largest block of that white variety in Canada. It speaks to their heritage. Chasselas, which yields a soft, easy wine, is the leading white in the vineyards of Switzerland where the brothers grew up.

Born in 1958 in the wine growing town of Rapperswil, Leo is a banker by training but a farmer at heart. He came to the Okanagan in 1984 and bought the historic Beau Séjour vineyard that has grown grapes since 1928. His younger brother, Andy, who had skippered yachts in the Caribbean, joined Leo in 1990 in developing this family winery. Their wives, who are sisters, are involved in the business. Leo's son, Reto, is working in New Zealand after graduating from Niagara College's winery program.

The varieties grown here have changed several times with new owners and new consumer tastes. Chasselas is a sentimental favourite but the most important white variety here is Riesling, including a good-sized block planted in 1978 from which Dominic McCosker, the winemaker here in the 2012 and 2013 vintages (before moving to La Frenz winery), persuaded the owners that an Old Vines Riesling should be added to the portfolio. He made 100 cases in 2013.

Dominic's passion for Riesling and Pinot Noir has influenced the Gebert brothers to make these the signature varieties here, even without taking away from the qualities of the other varieties in this historic vineyard. Aerial tours of the vineyard are offered on the winery's website, photographed from flying enthusiast Andy Gebert's model aircraft.

ANDY AND LEO GEBERT (PHOTO BY SUZANNE GEBERT)

MY PICKS

St. Hubertus has crisp and fruity whites, notably Riesling, Gewürztraminer, Pinot Blanc and Chasselas. The winery's top reds include Maréchal Foch, Chambourcin, Gamay Noir and Pinot Noir.

OPENED 1992

5225 Lakeshore Road
Kelowna, BC V1W 4J1

T 250.764.7888
   1.800.989.WINE (toll free)

W www.st-hubertus.bc.ca

WHEN TO VISIT
Open daily 10 am – 5:30 pm May
to October; Monday to Saturday
noon – 4 pm November through
April.

LICENSED PICNIC AREA

ST. LASZLO VINEYARDS ESTATE WINERY

St. Laszlo is a winery marching to an entirely different drummer. It grows, among other varieties, Clinton and Interlaken, two American labrusca hybrids found at no other winery in British Columbia. When he planted this vineyard in 1976, Slovenian-born Joe Ritlop worried about vine survival in cold winters and chose many hardy hybrids. However, his test plots also included vinifera such as Chardonnay, Riesling and Gewürztraminer.

His son, Joe Ritlop Jr., who manages the winery now, has added Merlot, Gamay, Pinot Noir and Pinot Gris to the vineyard. As if that were not a broad enough selection in the tasting room, Joe Jr. claims he resurrected fruit wine production in British Columbia. The most exotic is the occasionally produced rose petal wine—when he can get petals. The winemaking, which eschews sulphur, is unadorned and traditional. "We are from the old school of thought," Joe Jr. has said.

The generous family usually has most wines available for sampling, sometimes even the red and white icewine. If you want to touch a moderately sore point, ask who made the first commercially available icewine in Canada. Credit usually goes to the late Walter Hainle, the German-born textile salesman who started Hainle Vineyards at Peachland. As a hobbyist, he made icewine in 1973 and continued to do so for years. His first vintage that was available commercially was 1978—but it was not on sale until 1988 when the Hainle winery opened. The elder Ritlop did not make icewine as early as Hainle but he did have one available in his wine shop in 1985. He had taken advantage of a snap frost in his vineyard to crush frozen grapes. While he entered it in a Vancouver wine competition that fall, he got no recognition because there was no icewine category.

JOE RITLOP JR.

St. Laszlo's sulphur-free wines—"one of our selling points," Joe Jr. says—are a boon for consumers with sulphur allergies. Unsulphured grape wines may maderize if not consumed young. This sherry-like character is rather tasty in St. Laszlo's apricot and plum wines.

OPENED 1984

2605 Highway 3 East
Keremeos, BC V0X 1N0
T   250.499.2856.

WHEN TO VISIT
Open daily 9 am – 5 pm, and
later if you knock.

SANDHILL WINES

On the Sandhill Estate Vineyard on the Black Sage Bench (next door to Burrowing Owl Winery), two plots have been left free of vines. In the end, however, the dedicated Sandhill winery opened in 2014, adjacent to Calona Vineyards in Kelowna.

Sandhill's first vintage in 1997, and every vintage since, has been made in sprawling Calona winery in downtown Kelowna. Sandhill initially was launched as Calona's premium label. But winemaker Howard Soon stamped such individuality on the wines that it seemed imperative for Sandhill to have its own winery. The project was delayed largely because Andrew Peller Ltd., which bought Sandhill and Calona in 2005, first invested heavily in additional vineyards for the entire Peller group.

Sandhill wines stand apart because Howard makes single-vineyard wines only: wines that display the terroir where the grapes are grown. Each vineyard delivers its own flavours. For example, the Phantom Creek Vineyard Syrah is rich, soft and full-bodied. Yet the Syrah from the Sandhill Vineyard literally on the other side of Black Sage Road has a firmer structure. The six vineyards that supply Sandhill are named on the labels, each with its own symbol. No wine is made by blending several of the vineyards, since that would obscure the terroir.

Planted on Black Sage sand in the 1990s, the Sandhill Vineyard, at 79 hectares (174 acres), is the largest. The other Black Sage vineyards on the Sandhill labels are Phantom Creek (2.8 hectares or 7 acres) and Osprey Ridge (4.8 hectares or 12 acres). The winery gets Pinot Gris from the 17.4-hectare (43-acre) King Family Vineyard near Penticton. It gets Pinot Gris, Chardonnay and Sauvignon Blanc from the 119-hectare (294-acre) Hidden Terrace Vineyard at Covert Farm, near Oliver. Recently, the winery has begun making a Cabernet Merlot blend from the 42.3-hectare (104½-acre) Vanessa Vineyard in the Similkameen Valley.

HOWARD SOON

The very best blocks and some of the rare varietals (like Sangiovese and Barbera) are reserved for Sandhill's "small lots" program. These wines, made in volumes ranging from 100 cases to 500 cases, are super premium in quality—not that any Sandhill wine ever disappoints.

OPENED 1999

1125 Richter Street
Kelowna, BC V1Y 2K6

T   250.762.9144
     1.888.246.4472 (toll free)

W   www.sandhillwines.ca

WHEN TO VISIT
See Calona Vineyards.

MY PICKS

I admire all Sandhill wines, especially those in the Small Lots program. *Sandhill one* and *Sandhill two* are among the Okanagan's best Meritage reds while *Sandhill three*, a blend incorporating Sangiovese and Barbera, recalls a fine super-Tuscan red. Syrah, Petit Verdot and Malbec are real treats. The Sandhill Cabernet Merlot—with grapes from both the Sandhill and the Vanessa Vineyards— are very good budget-priced red blends.

SAXON ESTATE WINERY

Paul Graydon changed careers in 2011 when with his wife, Jayne, he bought Hollywood & Wine Winery in Summerland. "I come from this dog-eat-dog software industry," he says. "It is refreshing to come to the wine industry where watching your back is not the first issue. It sounds like there is room for everybody to play."

Born in London in 1960, Paul pursued a high-flying sales career, first with Xerox, then as vice president with a software company called Emtex and with Pitney Bowes, which bought Emtex in 2006. That was three years after he had moved from London to Calgary to accelerate the Emtex business in North America. In the summer of 2010, he and Pitney Bowes parted company and he decided he'd had enough of that life.

"I said to Jayne that I could go back into the software industry and earn the big dollars, but I was fed up with looking at airport ceilings and travelling all over the United States and Canada. I wanted something that we can both do together, without having to report to our boss every day." So they set up a wine agency called Great Wines of the World and looked for an Okanagan winery.

"We had always been wine people," Paul says. "I had been drinking the best wines in the world, having travelled all over Europe and the United States on expenses." Jayne had also spent several years selling Piper-Heidsieck Champagne in Britain. It is not surprising, then, that they quickly launched a sparkling brut at Saxon. "We love Champagne," Paul says. "Every case we sell is one less case for us to drink."

Hollywood & Wine (one of the owners was a trucker for movie productions) had been making just 1,000 cases a year. With Saxon Estate Winery the Graydons have doubled production, with a target to get to 5,000 cases by 2017. They have kept such popular labels as Cranky Old Man, a red blend that, paradoxically, appeals to women. An unoaked

JAYNE AND PAUL GRAYDON

Merlot became a hot seller when some customers discovered they could drink it without headaches. "We hadn't realized how many people are allergic to oak," Paul says.

MY PICKS

The star of the organic vineyard here is Léon Millot, a French hybrid made both into a full-bodied red and a delightful rosé. Also good are the winery's Pinot Gris, Gewürztraminer, Pinot Noir and sparkling brut. Don't miss the tongue-in-cheek wines—Cranky Old Man and Four Play (a white blend).

OPENED 2007
(AS HOLLYWOOD & WINE)

9819 Lumsden Avenue
Summerland, BC V0H 1Z8

T 250.494.0311

W www.saxonwinery.com

WHEN TO VISIT
11 am – 5 pm May to October,
and by appointment.

SCORCHED EARTH WINERY

This winery and its hillside vineyard are surrounded by Okanagan Mountain Park. The landscape is still bleak with dead blackened trees from the 2003 fires that destroyed most of the homes and the forests in this area. That prompted the name for the winery that Anita and Peter Pazdernik are opening on the five-hectare (12-acre) property which they bought in 2004.

The previous owner had planted a vineyard in 1989, primarily growing table grapes with a little Auxerrois. The vineyard, along with the lakeshore home, escaped destruction because fire retardants and water were dumped liberally on the property. However, this damaged the vines and they had to be pulled out.

"We rebuilt the vineyard from the ground up," Peter says. "When we removed the table grapes, we ripped out the trellis system and the irrigation system. We then re-sculpted the land to gain better exposure. Then we put in over 400 dump truck loads of compost to re-nourish the soil. The previous owners were conventional farmers, not organic. And we let the land lie fallow for a year." Beginning in 2009, Peter and Anita, together with son Shae and daughter Kiana, planted about 7,000 vines, all Pinot Noir grown organically.

They come by their love of wine from Peter's European heritage. Peter was born in Prague, growing up there and in Toronto when his parents immigrated to Canada in 1976. He has a commerce degree from the University of Toronto and has had careers in sales and marketing. Anita is a Winnipeg native who grew up in the Okanagan, which is why she and Peter moved back to the valley after a brief business stint in Calgary. "We have friends who own wineries in different places around the world," Anita says, explaining their decision to develop one. "Everyone said it is a great opportunity."

In 2011, with help from consultants, they made their first barrel of Pinot Noir, a trial so successful that friends and family had consumed it all within months of bottling the wine. The first commercial release is three barrels of Pinot Noir from the 2012 vintage. Because the wine is from young vines, it is being released under the PASK label, created from the first letters of each family member's name. "Once our vines are mature enough," Peter says, "we will switch to the Scorched Earth label."

MY PICKS

The first releases included a fruity wine called Bearly Pinot Noir because bears ate most of the grapes in 2012.

PROPOSED OPENING 2014

6006 Lakeshore Road
Kelowna. BC V1W 4J5

T 250.764.9199

W www.scorchedearthwinery.ca

WHEN TO VISIT
No tasting room.

PETER AND ANITA PAZDERNIK
(COURTESY OF SCORCHED
EARTH WINERY)

SEE YA LATER RANCH AT HAWTHORNE MOUNTAIN VINEYARDS

This is a dog lover's winery with a wonderful story, reflected both in its name and in that of several wines—Belle, Nelly, Ping, Rover, Hunny and Jimmy My Pal, formerly the names of dogs. This picturesque property on a mountainside above the vineyards of Okanagan Falls was owned for about 45 years by Major Hugh Fraser. Over that time he owned Nelly, Ping and numerous other dogs. When they died, each was buried under a headstone. In recent years, they have been placed at the base of a tree near the vintage home (circa 1902) now serving as the charming tasting room.

According to one legend, the Major brought an English bride with him when he moved to this farm after service in World War I. She could not handle the isolation and returned to England, leaving a note signed "See Ya Later." The real explanation, or so it is said, is that the major, a prolific correspondent, scrawled "See Ya Later" at the end of his letters.

This is the third name for this winery. An entrepreneur named Albert LeComte launched the winery in 1986 under his own name. It became Hawthorne Mountain Vineyards when Sumac Ridge founder Harry McWatters bought it in 1995. A few years after Vincor (now Constellation) purchased the winery in 2000, it was rechristened to take advantage of the history and the canine legacy. The winery honours that legacy by welcoming visitors with dogs and by contributing to the major's favourite charity, the Society for the Prevention of Cruelty to Animals.

This 40.5-hectare (100-acre) property is the highest elevation vineyard in the South Okanagan, rising to 536 metres (1,759 feet) and sloping to the northeast, an unusual exposure for the northern hemisphere. However, this cool location makes it one of the Okanagan's best sites for Gewürztraminer, Pinot Gris and Ehrenfelser. Its Gewürztraminer block,

at 26 hectares (65 acres), is believed to be the single largest planting of this aromatic variety in North America. The other grapes for See Ya Later wines come from Constellation's extensive plantings in the South Okanagan.

If you make the short but steep drive to this winery from Okanagan Falls, consider continuing south to Oliver by Green Lake Road. This quiet back road cuts through a landscape of ranches that retain the feeling of remoteness so unappealing to the major's wife (if he really had a wife).

MY PICKS

The entire range of See Ya Later Ranch wines is appealing—notably Ping (a red Meritage), Riesling, Gewürztraminer, Pinot Gris and Pinot 3 (a white blend based on three Pinot varieties). The Ehrenfelser icewine has lovely ripe pineapple flavours. See Ya Later Ranch Brut is as good a bubbly as anyone makes in British Columbia.

OPENED 1986
(AS LECOMTE ESTATE WINERY)

2575 Green Lake Road
Okanagan Falls, BC V0H 1R0

T   250.497.8267

W www.sylranch.com

WHEN TO VISIT
Open daily 10 am – 5 pm March to October; daily 9:30 am – 6 pm July and August; Friday to Sunday 11 am – 4 pm mid-November to Christmas and in February (closed January).

RESTAURANT
Open daily (weather permitting) 11:30 am – 4 pm mid-May to mid-August; Wednesday to Sunday 11:30 am – 3:30 pm mid-August to mid-October, with limited menu on Monday and Tuesday.

SERENDIPITY WINERY

Judy Kingston found it daunting to show her wines to restaurateurs and consumers when the winery opened in 2011. "For me, it was like I was in the bottle," she says. "It was because I planted the grapes. I have seen them all the way through and then helped put them in the bottle. It was a funny experience to sit there and watch others taste."

You have to appreciate that, in her previous career, she spent 25 years practising computer law in Toronto. "I have never sold anything in my life because I've been a lawyer," she explains. "I never had to."

An automobile accident triggered her decision to do something completely different. Passionate about food, she thought about running a bed and breakfast. In the fall of 2005, during an Okanagan vacation, she was charmed by Naramata and, on a whim, bought an apple and cherry orchard next to Therapy Vineyards. By 2007, the property had been contoured and the fruit trees were replaced with 4.2 hectares (10½ acres) of vines.

Embracing her new project with enthusiasm, Judy enrolled in both the viticulture and winemaking programs at Okanagan College. In 2009 she went to New Zealand to work the crush with Palliser Estate Winery, a four-week crash course that left her with special appreciation for Sauvignon Blanc and Pinot Noir, two of the varieties grown here. The other varieties here are Merlot, Cabernet Franc, Malbec, Syrah and Viognier. The first harvest was 2009.

The winery, which is built into the side of a hill, has the capacity to house 350 barrels in a U-shaped barrel room. There is room as well for the tasting room and the lengthy table that is set from time to time so that Judy, now comfortable in her new career, can host wine dinners. She has been joined at the winery by Katie O'Kell, her daughter, who decided against law school to study winemaking.

JUDY KINGSTON AND KATIE O'KELL

OPENED 2011

MY PICKS

Start with Devil's Advocate, a red blend, and then proceed through the private reserve red varietals and end with Serenata, an elegant Bordeaux blend. I also like the Sauvignon Blanc, the Viognier and White Lie, a blend.

990 Debeck Road
RR 1, Site 2, Comp 50
Naramata, BC V0H 1N0

T   250.496.5299

W www.serendipitywinery.com

WHEN TO VISIT
Open daily 10 am – 5 pm.

SEVEN STONES WINERY

George Hanson likes to keep his wines so close at hand that a short tunnel runs from the basement of his house to the underground cellar that he built alongside the house in 2013. At 279 square metres (3,000 square feet), the cellar accommodates 300 barrels, a small waterfall (for good humidity), a commercial kitchen and a special events table with seating for more than 30. Visitors, of course, need not use George's tunnel. There is a spiral staircase from the winery's tasting room.

The man who once described himself as the Yukon's best amateur winemaker has come a long way since leaving his telephone company job there to plant an eight-hectare (20-acre) vineyard in the Similkameen Valley in 2001. "The reason I planted this vineyard was to make a Meritage blend," he says. That's why he grows Cabernet Sauvignon, Cabernet Franc, Merlot, Petit Verdot and Malbec, along with a little Pinot Noir and Syrah. Acknowledging a demand for white wine, he also planted one hectare (2½ acres) of Chardonnay.

"The Legend is my top priority," George says of his iconic red blend of Bordeaux varietals. The Legend—only 100 cases are made each year—crowns the winery's entire production, now 3,000 cases a year and rising to more than 4,000. George selects his favourite barrels for The Legend, then makes another selection for his Meritage blend. The remaining wines are released as single varietals. That requires George to grow everything to the quality than can produce The Legend. "This is an exceptional place to grow grapes," George says.

The vineyard is called Harmony One. George considered that name for the winery as well until his wife, Vivianne, dipped into the Similkameen's aboriginal history. The winery is named for seven massive rocks that are freighted with aboriginal history. Speaking Rock, for example, was a First Nations meeting place, while Standing Rock—Highway 3 jogs around it—is associated with a tale of a woman who

GEORGE HANSON

rode her horse to the top. These and other stories are celebrated on the wine labels and in the tasting room mural. Vivianne, a vivacious Quebecer who once operated a Prince George health foods store, died in 2012. The Seven Stones Pinot Noir from that vintage has a tribute label for her.

Besides building the barrel cellar in 2013, George also launched the first Seven Stones Wine Club, hoping to enrol about 50 members that year. To his surprise, the club had 52 members by the end of its first month. "What I learned from that," he says, "is that our brand has some traction."

OPENED 2007

1143 Highway 3
Cawston, BC V0X 1C3

T 250.499.2144

W www.sevenstones.ca

WHEN TO VISIT
Open daily 10:30 am – 5:30 pm
May to October, and by
appointment.

MY PICKS

Everything, including the Chardonnay, the rosé, the Pinot Noir, the Cabernet Franc, the Meritage, the Syrah and the Row 128 Merlot. Of course, The Legend is the wine for your bucket list.

SILKSCARF WINERY

Roie Manoff spent 20 years flying combat jets for the Israeli air force, hence the name of the winery the Manoff family opened in Summerland in 2005. Roie's son, Idan, draws a parallel between aviation and wine. Both involve "meticulous work, day in and day out."

Roie Manoff, who was born in Argentina in 1951 but grew up in Israel, has had a long love for wine. He began technical wine studies somewhere between his pilot's career and subsequent ownership of a Tel Aviv software firm. "My dream when I became a winemaker was to make a good Cabernet Sauvignon," he says. The Silkscarf portfolio is now much longer that that, including a Malbec, the signature Argentinean variety.

When the family decided to leave Israel, a study of wine growing regions brought them in 2003 to the Okanagan and the quiet beauty of a Summerland orchard, most of which has been converted to 3.4 hectares (8½ acres) of vines. While Roie was settling business affairs in Israel, Idan was sent ahead to start the vineyard. Born in 1976, Idan is a computer science and business graduate. His more relevant experience for Silkscarf includes growing fruit crops in Israel and working in the Margalit Winery, one of Israel's finest boutique wineries. "The farming part here is not different from what I know," Idan says of the Gartrell Road orchard.

The varieties planted include Pinot Gris and Gewürztraminer. Almost a third of the vineyard has been planted to Shiraz. In 2011, Roie removed the last of the cherry trees and planted Cabernet Franc. He confesses that he did not like the variety until he began tasting the vibrant Okanagan Cabernet Francs. "It is just the perfect grape to grow here," he maintains.

IDAN AND ROIE MANOFF

MY PICKS

The winery's fruity whites include Viognier, a Riesling Muscat blend and an Alsace-inspired white blend called Ensemble Blanc. Among the reds, I particularly like the Shiraz Reserve, the Merlot Reserve, the Malbec and the Bordeaux blend, called Ensemble Red.

OPENED 2005

4917 Gartrell Road
Summerland, BC V0H 1Z4

T 250.494.7455

W www.silkw.net

WHEN TO VISIT
Open weekends 10 am – 5:30 pm in April and May; daily June to October.

SILVER SAGE WINERY

The choices in Silver Sage's baronial tasting room range eclectically from intensely flavoured fruit wines to original table wines. Among the latter is Sage Grand Reserve. This is a Gewürztraminer turbocharged by fermenting the wine with sage that grows in the South Okanagan, resulting in a unique white with the herbal aroma and flavour of rosemary.

Another singular offering is The Flame, a dessert wine made with Gewürztraminer, peach and apricot, with a red pepper tingling in each bottle. Such unusual wines sprang from the imagination of Victor Manola. Both he and Anna, his wife, had managed vineyards and made wine in Romania before coming to Canada about 1980. After successful business careers, the couple returned to their roots in 1996, purchasing a 10-hectare (25-acre) property beautifully situated beside a meandering valley-bottom river. The winery stands peacefully amid vineyards with the aplomb of a French château, a testament to Victor's skills as a builder. Victor died in a winery accident in 2002 as the building neared completion.

Anna, a former mathematics teacher with a sure touch with fruit wines, operates the winery and is often behind the tasting room bar, helped by her sister, Elena. On occasion, the sorrow of her loss has been expressed in the wines. She takes particular pains with Silver Sage's Pinot Noir, leaving the fruit on the vines long into the autumn to develop ripe flavours, then focusing all her winemaking skills on it. The result is a supple red called "The Passion." The original label was deep clerical mauve, the colour of a widow's garb in Romania.

The winery's banquet room and its garden-like setting—the winery is on the banks of the Okanagan River—have made Silver Sage a favourite wedding venue in the South Okanagan.

ANNA MANOLA

MY PICKS

The Pinot Noir and the Pinot Blanc are tasty. Sage Grand Reserve (perhaps like Retsina) must be tried with Greek cuisine to be enjoyed ideally. Then go to the fruit wines, all with room-filling aromas and intense flavours, and to the blends of grape and fruit wines. The peach and apricot–flavoured Pinot Blanc dessert wine is a particular delight.

OPENED 2001

4852 Ryegrass Rd RR1
Oliver, BC V0H 1T0
T 250.498.0310
W www.silversagewinery.com

WHEN TO VISIT
Open daily 10 am – 6 pm.

ACCOMMODATION
Three guest suites and a
banquet room in the winery.

SKIMMERHORN WINERY & VINEYARD

Until Skimmerhorn opened, wine tourists just whipped through Creston on their way to the Okanagan (unless they paused to tour the Columbia Brewery). Now, Creston, with three wineries, could call itself the wine capital of the Kootenays. Skimmerhorn started this development.

Skimmerhorn's owners, Al and Marleen Hoag, grew tree fruits here from 1984 until selling their orchard in 2005. Al first considered opening a cidery but decided they were more likely to succeed with a mainstream beverage like wine. Beginning in 2003, they planted 5.6 hectares (14 acres) of vines on a sunny slope at the south edge of Creston, intelligently choosing varieties that will ripen here (Pinot Gris, Gewürztraminer, Ortega, Pinot Noir and Maréchal Foch).

Knowing it would be difficult to attract Okanagan expertise to Creston, the Hoags went to New Zealand to find a winemaker willing to spend his off-season in the Northern Hemisphere. They knocked on winery doors across New Zealand's South Island until they found Geisenheim-trained Mark Rattray, who has owned or made wine for numerous wineries there in a 40-vintage career. For many years, he has come to Creston in September, bottled the red wines from the previous year and made the current vintage before going home where he mentors Al from a distance. Eventually, that relationship will end. In 2013 the Hoags began testing the real estate market by listing the winery for $2.9 million.

Al made his first solo wine in the summer of 2009 after a sudden rainfall rendered some cherries unfit for the fresh fruit market but not for winemaking. When one orchard offered Al cherries for the cost of picking them, he made Skimmerhorn's first cherry wine. "We don't know if there is any market for fruit wine," he admitted as he dumped juicy cherries into the crusher. The result was an off-dry crowd-pleaser,

AL AND MARLEEN HOAG

Cherry Twist. When that sold out, he made an equally popular fortified wine, Old Coot, blending cherry wine and Maréchal Foch.

MY PICKS

The whites—Pinot Gris, Ortega, Gewürztraminer—and the rosé are packed with fruit flavours. Autumn Tryst is a white blend aimed for consumers who prefer a touch of sweetness. The Maréchal Foch is a bold, rich red, a counterpoint to the lighter Pinot Noir. Devil's Chair is a rare blend of Foch and Pinot Noir.

OPENED 2006

1218 27th Avenue South
Creston, BC V0B 1G1

T 250.428.4911

W www.skimmerhorn.ca

WHEN TO VISIT
Open daily 11 am – 5 pm July to Labour Day; Wednesday to Sunday 11 am – 5 pm April to June and Labour Day to December 24.

RESTAURANT
Bistro open Wednesday to Sunday 11 am – 3 pm mid-June to September.

SLEEPING GIANT FRUIT WINERY

Thousands visit Summerland Sweets each year, attracted by the fruit products and, in summer, by the generous ice cream parlour. The fruit winery, which opened here in 2008, was a logical addition to the business started in 1962 by the legendary Dr. Ted Atkinson.

He was one of the Okanagan's leading scientists, head of food processing at what was then called the Summerland research station. When he was near retirement, he created a line of fruit candies for a Rotary Club fundraiser. Frustrated that no company would take on the product, he set up Summerland Sweets to commercialize a range of fruit-based products that has grown to include syrups and jams for domestic and export markets.

Ted Atkinson's family still operate Summerland Sweets. His granddaughter's husband, Len Filek, was a young commerce graduate when he joined the company in 1984. Today, he is the general manager. He spearheaded the addition of a fruit winery with a tasting room inside the Summerland Sweets store. "It's been a thought in the family for quite a while," he says. "With the other projects we had, we just kept putting it off." The winery went ahead after Sumac Ridge founder Harry McWatters urged Len to give the stream of visitors to Summerland Sweets another reason to visit.

Len retained Ron Taylor, a veteran winemaker already working with numerous fruit wineries in British Columbia. "My dad was a home winemaker but I am not interested in making wine," Len admits frankly. "I am interested in wine and I am interested in a good product. That's why we have someone making it for us."

LEN FILEK

MY PICKS

Almost two dozen fruit wines are available here, including dry examples from pear and apple to delicious off-dry wines from cherry and raspberry. Recent additions (there's a waiting list for them) are pumpkin table wine and "pumpkin pie" dessert wine. All wines are remarkable for aromas and flavours that could be fresh from the tree.

OPENED 2008

6206 Canyon View Road
Summerland, BC V0H 1Z7
T   250.494.0377
    1.800.577.1277 (toll free)
W www.sleepinggiantfruitwinery.ca

WHEN TO VISIT
Open daily 10 am – 6 pm year-round, except 10 am – 4 pm in winter.

SOAHC ESTATE WINES

Let's clear up the name first: it is nothing more than "chaos" spelled backwards. Proprietor Jamie Fochuk explains that it is an allusion to the biodynamic viticultural practices in his vineyard.

Born in Edmonton in 1973, Jamie grew up in a farming family. After a post–high school stint on the ski hills at Lake Louise, he decided to get "a real job," and moved to Ontario wine country (his father was living in St. Catherines). When a basic viticulture course at the University of Guelph revealed an aptitude for grape growing, Jamie found a job in 1996 with Klaus Reif, a leading Niagara vintner.

Eventually, Jamie was torn between a desire to continue studies at Brock University, where he was doing well, or moving to the Okanagan. The practical-minded Klaus advised that "you will learn more behind a press than at school" and recommended him to Harry McWatters. Jamie immersed himself in viticulture at a succession of Okanagan wineries including Hawthorne Mountain Vineyards, Stag's Hollow Winery and Black Hills Estate Winery.

He began his search for suitable vineyard land with several years of climate study. A property near Fairview Cellars was appealing but too expensive. Then his research lead him to the Columbia Valley southeast of Trail. The Columbia Valley Vineyards had opened here in 2001, giving credibility to growing grapes in the valley. In 2006, Jamie and his partner, Kim McLaughlin, bought a nearby hillside property with excellent climate and soil properties. Detailed soil analysis revealed, as Jamie expected, no negative impact from the Trail refinery. "I know that giant molecules of heavy metals can't float in the air," he says. "We are a long way away. The one question would be the Columbia River, but our water comes off the mountains."

In 2010, after clearing the trees and making biodynamic amendments to the soil, Jamie planted Chardonnay and Riesling on the

vineyard's 2.7-hectare (6½-acre) lower terrace. He followed that by planting Pinot Noir, Gamay and Siegerrebe on the 4.85-hectare (12-acre) middle terrace. A three hectare upper terrace remains to be planted. For his planting decisions, he has taken advice from Alain Sutre, the Bordeaux consultant who works with leading Okanagan wineries.

With no farm building yet converted to a winery, Jamie began making his wines at the Synchromesh winery in Okanagan Falls, producing about 30 cases in 2012 and 400 cases in 2013. When a winery opens here, Jamie says the tasting room likely will resemble the original Black Hills wine shop—a plank across two barrels.

PROPOSED OPENING 2014–15

(Mailing Address)
P.O. Box 242, Fruitvale P.O.
Fruitvale, BC V0G 1L0

T   250.367.7594

W www.soahc.com

WHEN TO VISIT
Tasting room not yet open.

MY PICKS

No wines available for tasting at press time.

SONORAN ESTATE WINERY

As this book was being completed, Arjan and Ada Smits, the retirement-age owners of Sonoran, had the winery for sale. After emigrating from Holland in 1982, the Smits grew flowers both in Ontario and in British Columbia's Fraser Valley before moving to the Okanagan in 2000. They planted a small vineyard and, while waiting for the vines to produce, operated their Windmill Bed and Breakfast, for many years a landmark beside Highway 97 north of Summerland.

In 2006 the Smits moved the two-year-old winery to a Summerland vineyard that they had acquired and planted the year before. This proved to be a better location because it is at the beginning of Bottleneck Drive, Summerland's popular wine route.

Their son, Adrian, born in 1979, became the winemaker after taking the assistant winemaker's program at Okanagan College and mentoring with consultants. He previously worked with a company providing computer technical support, an office job that lost its appeal once his parents involved him in the winery. Because the pending sale of Sonoran created uncertainty for his future, in 2013 Adrian became a cellar master at nearby Dirty Laundry Vineyards.

Throughout its first decade, Sonoran single-handedly championed an obscure German white variety called Oraniensteiner. It was developed in 1985 at Geisenheim University by crossing Riesling and Sylvaner. Not authorized for quality wine production in Germany, it has a niche in the Okanagan. Sonoran has turned the variety, which has citrus flavours and bracing acidity, into table wine and, even more successfully, into intense icewine.

Sonoran also has championed the work of Summerland artist Will Enns. His energetic images of musicians serve as memorable labels for Sonoran's Jazz Series wine. The wines are as fine as the art.

ARJAN AND ADRIAN SMITS

MY PICKS

Look for the Jazz Series, including Riesling, Ehrenfelser, rosé, Merlot and, of course, Oraniensteiner. The Jazz Series Cabernet Sauvignon is as bold as the brassy saxophone on the bottle.

OPENED 2004

5716 Gartrell Road
Summerland, BC V0H 1Z7
T 250.494.9323
W www.sonoranestate.com

WHEN TO VISIT
Open Monday to Saturday
10 am – 6 pm and Sundays
11 am – 6 pm May to October;
and by appointment.

RESTAURANT
Full Moon Bistro
Open daily 11:30 am – 2:30 pm
May to October.

SPERLING VINEYARDS

The history of North Okanagan grape growing and winemaking lives here. This winery was launched in 2009 by the Sperling family whose Casorso ancestors planted Kelowna's first vineyard in 1925 and were among the original investors in what is now Calona Vineyards.

The story began when Giovanni Casorso came from Italy in 1883 to work at Father Pandosy's mission before striking out on his own (he was once the Okanagan's largest tobacco grower). His sons planted several vineyards. Formerly known as Pioneer Ranch, the 18.2-hectare (45-acre) Sperling Vineyards was planted initially in 1931 with grapes and apples by Louis and Pete Casorso. When Pete retired in 1960, Bert Sperling, his son-in-law, switched the entire property to vines, both wine grapes and table grapes. The grapes here include a 50-year-old (in 2014) planting of Maréchal Foch, a 37-year-old planting of Riesling and a planting of indefinite age of Perle of Csaba, a Muscat variety once grown widely in the Okanagan. Recent plantings include Gewürztraminer, Pinot Gris, Pinot Noir and Chardonnay.

Undoubtedly, the Sperling family has been thinking about a winery of its own ever since Bert's daughter, Ann, who was born in 1962, began her winemaking career in 1984, first with Andrés Wines and then with CedarCreek Estate Winery. She moved to Ontario in 1995 where she helped launch such several stellar wineries. She and Peter Gamble, her husband, consult internationally and own a premium boutique winery in Argentina which produces under the Versado brand.

As busy as her career has been, one thing had been missing in Ann's life. "I have always wanted to make wine with my parents' vineyard," she says. "I got to make wine with some of the grapes when I was at CedarCreek, but not anything extensive." The Casorso story came full circle with this premium winery in 2013 when a production facility with a 10,000-case capacity was completed in the middle of the vineyard. The new winery is licensed as Magpie Cellars, named for a flock

ANN SPERLING

(or murder) of magpies that have lived here a long time. "They have watched over us and criticized our work for generations," Ann says. "It seemed fitting to acknowledge their role." The site is not convenient for wine touring. The tasting room remains in Pioneer Country Market, the popular restaurant and delicatessen operated by Ann's mother, Velma.

OPENED 2009

1405 Pioneer Road
Kelowna, BC V1W 4M6

T 778.478.0260

W www.sperlingvineyards.ca

WHEN TO VISIT
Open daily 10 am – 6 pm.

MY PICKS

Everything, including the Old Vines Riesling, the Chardonnay, the Pinot Noir, the Old Vines Foch, the Pinot Gris, the Gewürztraminer, the affordable Riesling icewine and a sparkling brut based on Pinot Blanc. One of the most popular wines here is the aromatic Market White.

SPIERHEAD WINERY

This winery's switchback driveway twists tightly among McIntosh apple trees, remnants of the 8.25-hectare (20½-acre) orchard that preceded what is now called the Gentleman Farmer Vineyard. Planted in 2008, the vineyard is so named because the partners all have city backgrounds. William (Bill) Knutson is a Vancouver lawyer and Bruce Hirtle is a semi-retired investment dealer with Okanagan roots. Brian Sprout, who initiated the winery idea, is a Kelowna native. He established his photography practice there in 1998 and became a leading winery photographer. He sold his interest in the winery in 2013 to concentrate again on photography.

Brian has been a regular visitor to the Napa Valley since 1979. "I had that passion for wine," he says. "The romance of the grape had a real hold on me. For a couple of years, I was thinking that I wanted to buy some property in the South Okanagan and plant a vineyard and get a winery going." However, the partners decided to establish the winery in Kelowna to be near a year-round market for the wines.

The location also determined SpierHead's emergence as a Pinot Noir specialist. The 2.8-hectare (seven-acre) Gentleman Farmer Vineyard was planted primarily with Pinot Noir (with small blocks of Riesling and Chardonnay). SpierHead's debut 2010 Pinot Noir won a major national wine award. "On the strength of that, we decided to try and create a niche role for ourselves with Pinot Noir," Bill says. In 2014, the vineyard was doubled by planting multiple clones of Pinot Noir.

For the 2013 vintage, Bill secured Pinot Noir grapes from several nearby vineyards. "I would also like to develop some vineyard-designated Pinot Noirs," he says. That started with selecting the four best barrels of 2012 Pinot Noir from Gentleman Farmer. Premium wine from the other vineyards will also be bottled specially. "I want to have a portfolio of a few different high quality vineyard-designated wines, always including our own," Bill says.

The current portfolio includes two solid Bordeaux reds, called Vanguard and Pursuit, with grapes purchased from Harry McWatters's Sundial Vineyard on Black Sage Road. SpierHead does not have a long-term contract for the grapes, which Harry may eventually need for his own Time Estate Winery.

"We don't have any plans to change at the moment, but increasingly we will be Pinot Noir dominant," Bill says. "We have to keep an eye on the question of how diversified a small winery should be." SpierHead produces 2,000 cases and intends to grow to 5,000 cases a year.

MY PICKS

Everything. The Pinot Noir, Pinot Noir rosé, Riesling and Chardonnay display the vibrant flavours of the cool-climate vineyard. The Bordeaux reds, Vanguard and Pursuit, are full-bodied and elegant.

OPENED 2010

3950 Spiers Road
Kelowna, BC V1W 4B3

T   250.763.7777

W www.spierheadwinery.com

WHEN TO VISIT
Open weekends 11 am – 5:30 pm
May to June; daily 11 am – 5:30 pm
July to October; and by
appointment.

BILL KNUTSON

SQUEEZED WINES

You might think that Michael Ferreira already has his plate pretty full as the winemaker at Quinta Ferreira, the winery his parents launched in 2007. He makes terrific wines there: the 2009 Syrah was the Canadian red wine of the year in one national competition. Yet with his sisters, Christina and Nicole, he launched Squeezed Wines, producing 1,000 cases annually of easy drinking wines—a red blend, a white blend and a rosé. Squeezed wines are deliberately different from the wines Michael makes at Quinta Ferreira, notably the big reds.

"We are going for the entry-level consumer," he says. "The reason for Squeezed is to get people to start liking wines."

Those consumers would fit into Michael's demographic. He was born in 1984 and was 15 when his parents, John and Maria, converted their orchard to grapes and turned the packing house into a winery. He had a different career planned. "I started my degree in computer science," he says. "Halfway through, I decided I did not want to be sitting in an office all day." He switched to viticulture and enology and will have that degree when he has time to complete a final year at Brock University. "Here, I get to work outside and work with my hands a lot."

Squeezed Wines is based on Michael's two-hectare (five-acre) vineyard, conveniently just a short drive north of Quinta Ferreira where Michael began his winemaking career in 2005. On his property, a former cherry orchard, he has planted Tempranillo, Sangiovese and Carmenère, among other varietals. "I was told they can't grow here, so I wanted to try for myself," Michael says.

If they succeed, they will be crafted as small-lot wines for Quinta Ferreira. "I will use some of those grapes in a blend at Squeezed," he says. "Squeezed is just going to be three wines, three blends. We are just trying to keep it really simple. They are all fruit-forward wines."

MICHAEL FERREIRA

MY PICKS

These affordable wines, all $20 or less, are exactly as described—accessible and easy to drink.

OPENED 2012

7229 Tucelnuit Drive
Oliver, BC V0H 1T0

T 250.485.4309

W www.squeezedwines.com

WHEN TO VISIT
No tasting room.

STAG'S HOLLOW WINERY

Larry Gerelus and Linda Pruegger showed a pioneering spirit when they left big city professional careers for the Okanagan. In 1995, Stag's Hollow Winery was the Okanagan's first winery to install energy-saving geothermal technology for heating and cooling. In the 1999 vintage, the winery began selling futures. In 2006, it was one of the first in the Okanagan to plant Tempranillo, Spain's major red varietal. In 2011, it was the first in the Okanagan to plant Dolcetto, a red wine grape from northwest Italy's Piedmont region. In 2013, the winery released the Okanagan's first Grenache table wine, with grapes from contract growers.

Born in Winnipeg in 1952, Larry trained as an insurance actuary. He was an independent pension and benefits consultant in Calgary while Linda, a Calgary native, worked in banking and then in marketing with an oil company. When Larry prepared for a career change, counselling suggested he was better suited either to running a ski resort or a winery. In 1992, he bought a four-hectare (10-acre) Okanagan Falls vineyard growing Chasselas and Vidal; two years later, most of the Vidal was grafted over to Chardonnay and all of the Chasselas was grafted to Merlot and Pinot Noir. These were all sound choices. However, Linda and Larry inadvertently created a cult wine by labelling their dwindling supply of Vidal as Tragically Vidal. They had to remove the Chardonnay grafts and restore the Vidal to meet demand for the wine. A second Vidal block was planted in a new vineyard in 2012.

Stag's Hollow has worked with several of the Okanagan's best winemakers. Dwight Sick, the winemaker since 2008, persuaded Larry and Linda to augment their solid portfolio with Rhône varietals and small-lot blends that have added to the buzz at Stag's Hollow. Born in Edson, Alberta, Dwight developed an interest in wine during 19 years as a flight attendant. After accepting an Air Canada retirement package, he came into the Okanagan wine industry in 2004 as a cellar hand

LARRY GERELUS AND DWIGHT SICK

at Township 7 Vineyards & Winery, quickly developing into one of the valley's most accomplished winemakers.

Stag's Hollow is among the few Okanagan wineries to offer futures. This is a historic Bordeaux concept where producers sell a portion of each vintage at a discount months before the wine is released. The winery inaugurated its futures program by offering a limited number of cases of its 1999 Estate Merlot at $17 ($3 a bottle under the subsequent release price), and its Estate Reserve Merlot at $21.25 ($3.75 under the subsequent release price). The winery now offers futures in Renaissance Merlot, as the Estate Reserve Tier came to be known, and in Renaissance Pinot Noir.

OPENED 1996

2237 Sun Valley Way
Okanagan Falls, BC V0H 1R2

T 250.497.6162
   1.877.746.5569 (toll free)
W www.stagshollowwinery.com

WHEN TO VISIT
Open daily 11 am – 5 pm May to October; and by appointment.

MY PICKS

Everything. The Renaissance range, notably the buttery Chardonnay, the deep and brooding Merlot and the Pinot Noir, are always impressive. Heritage Block 1 is a fine Bordeaux blend. The Estate Merlot is good value. The recently-added Syrah, Viognier and the Cachet series of wines are excellent. Do not leave without savouring the juicy flavours of Tragically Vidal.

STONEBOAT VINEYARDS

In 2013, Stoneboat Vineyards launched Piano Brut, its first sparkling wine, with the help of a $125,000 grant from the federal government. The grant paid for researching and acquiring Charmat sparkling wine technology that had not been used in the Okanagan for a generation.

There is no one better to revive winemaking history than Lanny Martiniuk, who operates this family winery with his wife, Julie, and two of their three sons (the third is a commercial pilot). Lanny began growing grapes here in 1983 and he continues to nurture varieties after they are out of favour with wineries. "They come around again," he says. Currently, he is expanding his block of Müller-Thurgau because its fruity flavours are essential to Chorus, the winery's delicious white blend.

The Charmat process takes its name from a French scientist, Eugène Charmat, who in 1907 perfected a method of fermenting wines in bulk that initially had been invented in Italy and is still used in Prosecco production. Stoneboat chose this method because they wanted to make a fresh and fruity sparkling wine, competing in flavour and price with Prosecco. The purpose of government grants is precisely to support Canadian competitiveness.

Lanny, who was born in Vancouver in 1949, has pursued numerous careers (electrician, stone mason, prospector, nuclear medicine technician). He is a farmer by avocation and has learned that farmers always need to adapt to compete. The Martiniuks launched Stoneboat to secure a market for some of the grapes grown on their 20 hectares (49 acres) of vineyard. Son, Jay, has trained as the winemaker, working with winemaker Alison Moyes. Tim, Jay's twin, handles the marketing. They both can play the grand piano in the wine shop, the inspiration for the name of the sparkling wine.

Stoneboat has a 2.8-hectare (seven-acre) block of Pinotage, the

THE MARTINIUKS: LANNY, TIM, JAY, JULIE, CHRIS

South African red, and is championing its future in the Okanagan. This
is another instance of Lanny looking
for a competitive edge. He was propagating the vine in the 1990s for Lake
Breeze Vineyards, was impressed with
the variety and propagated it for his
own vineyard, enabling Stoneboat to
become one of four Okanagan wineries
making Pinotage.

OPENED 2007

356 Orchard Grove Lane
Oliver, BC V0H 1T1

T 250.498.2226
   1.888.598.2226 (toll free)

W www.stoneboatvineyards.com

WHEN TO VISIT
Open daily 10 am – 5:30 pm
April to December.

MY PICKS

The winery won awards of excellence in
the Lieutenant Governor's wine competition
with Pinot Noir and then with Pinotage.
The winery also has excellent Pinot Gris
and Pinot Blanc and Chorus is downright
delicious. The dessert wines also impress.
Verglas is icewine by another name and Pinot
Blanc VLH tastes like a fine Sauternes.

SUMAC RIDGE ESTATE WINERY

The oldest continually operating estate winery in the Okanagan, Sumac Ridge has given rise to three independent brands under Constellation Brands, the winery's owner since 2005 (and the world's largest wine company). All can still be found in the Sumac Ridge wine shop.

One brand is Steller's Jay Brut for the traditionally-made sparkling wine originated by Sumac Ridge in 1987. A bestselling Canadian competitor to Champagne, the wine—named for British Columbia's official bird—was given its own brand identity in 2012. The marketers at Constellation believe this positions it more like Champagne. All Champagne comes from wineries specialized only in sparkling wines.

The passion for Steller's Jay began with Harry McWatters, who founded the winery in 1979 with Lloyd Schmidt. Harry quips that sparkling wine is what he drinks while deciding what wine to have for dinner. A bit of a showman, Harry also learned the French trick of cracking open a bottle with a sharp sabre tap on the neck. Harry retired to his own consulting company in 2008, leaving the sparkling wine culture to be carried on by winemaker Jason James. Jason would like to break consumers of the practice of drinking sparkling wines only on celebratory occasions. "We'd like them to drink it at least once every two weeks," he says.

The second brand is Black Sage Road Vineyard, named for the original 46.5-hectare (115-acre) vineyard on Black Sage Road planted by Harry in 1993. When the vineyard was divided several years ago, Harry's half was renamed Sundial while Constellation's half kept the original name. The primary releases have been Cabernet Sauvignon, Merlot and Cabernet Franc. The latter is one of Jason's favourite varietals. "It is one of the stars of British Columbia."

The third brand is Sumac Ridge with a slimmed down portfolio of value-priced wines. Gewürztraminer remains a core white wine;

Sumac Ridge's Private Reserve often is the largest selling brand of that varietal in Canada—between 6,500 cases and 9,000 cases a year, depending on the vintage.

MY PICKS

Steller's Jay Brut does stand on its own as a top-quality sparkling wine, along with its partner, Pinnacle Brut. The Black Sage Vineyard reds, along with the fortified Pipe, show the power of that mature vineyard.

OPENED 1980

17403 Highway 97
PO Box 307
Summerland, BC V0H 1Z0
T 250.494.0451
W www.sumacridge.com

WHEN TO VISIT
Open daily 9:30 am – 6 pm July and August; 10 am – 5 pm in spring and fall; 11 am – 4 pm mid-November to February.

JASON JAMES

SUMMERGATE WINERY

Mike and Gillian Wohler, the owners of SummerGate, are wine growers with a strong green sensibility. That ranges from growing grapes organically to asking consumers to return wine bottles for recycling. "We have a young family of five," Mike says. They made their decision to be organic as soon as they bought their vineyard in 2007. "We did not want the chemicals around for practical reasons."

Born in Ontario in 1972, Mike was managing a Vancouver call centre and Gillian, trained in accounting, was working there when they decided in 2003 to move to the Okanagan for a different lifestyle. "We realized, as some people do, when you are climbing up the corporate ladder, sometimes it is leaning against the wrong wall," Mike says. "We were young enough to make a change."

They bought the property near Summerland where winemaker Eric von Krosigk had already planted about 3.6 hectares (nine acres) of grapes for a winery before shelving the project and selling the vineyard. Half of the vineyard is planted to Muscat Ottonel. The remainder of the vineyard is planted to Riesling and to Kerner. A neighbour has planted Pinot Noir for them.

"I love Kerner," says Mike. While at a German wine industry trade show a few years ago, he and Gillian researched the origins of the grape. It is a 1929 cross of Riesling and Trollinger, named for some obscure reason after a poet called Justinus Kerner. Mike has planted more Kerner because the variety is well-suited to his comparatively cool site. Mike, who also works as a real estate agent, is a disciplined grower. "We crop down to one or two tons an acre," he says.

Gillian—she pronounces her name with a hard G—is the winemaker, having taken Okanagan College winemaking courses while mentoring with a consultant. Her small batch winemaking involves cool fermentation and the liberal use of dry ice to protect the delicately

GILLIAN AND MIKE WOHLER

aromatic wines from air. This reductive winemaking yields fresh, clean and focused wines. The winery made about 450 cases in 2009, growing to 1,100 cases in 2012. "It is all about careful growth," Mike says. "Being big is not part of our plan. We're happy doing what we are doing."

MY PICKS

The wines are well-made, usually as dry table wines. The Muscat shows the classic rose petal spice. The Kerner has tropical fruit flavours and the Riesling is a refreshing display of tangy lime and apple flavours.

OPENED 2011

11612 Morrow Avenue
Summerland, BC V0H 1Z8

T 250.583.9973

W www.summergate.ca

WHEN TO VISIT
Open daily noon – 6 pm May to October; weekends noon – 6 pm the rest of the year; and by appointment.

SUMMERHILL PYRAMID WINERY

Summerhill owner Stephen Cipes is an idealist and a mystic, and that is reflected in this winery, one of the most interesting stops on the wine tour. Before you enter the tasting room, you should linger at the World Peace Park in front of the winery. Towering over a globe encircled with flowers is Summerhill's Peace Pole. Inscriptions exhort: "May peace prevail on Earth" in 16 languages.

Stephen's spiritual side is represented by the gleaming white pyramid that dramatically dominates the grounds here, and is employed to age wines. He believes that the pyramid's rejuvenating energy improves both good wine and the spirit and well-being of those who spend time inside. The memorable tours of the pyramid often include brief periods when visitors are invited to sit in contemplative silence. When does that happen in today's frantic world?

Stephen, an engagingly mercurial personality, was born in New York in 1944 and succeeded in real estate before moving to the Okanagan in 1986 in search of a more environmentally positive lifestyle for himself and his family. Sons Ezra, the chief executive, and Ari, share those values. Summerhill grows grapes organically in its 20-hectare (50-acre) vineyard and has been adopting biodynamic practices. Most of the winery's 14 contract growers also have been converted to organic production. Since 2007, the winery itself has been certified to make wine organically.

"Our goal is the least amount of manipulation to get the wine from the field to the bottle," winemaker Eric von Krosigk says. "We want to let the grapes speak for themselves. Our ultimate goal here is that if there was ever an ingredients list on a bottle of wine, it would say 'just grapes'."

The extensive portfolio is notable for sparkling wines and for Rieslings. Summerhill also champions French hybrids like Baco Noir

ERIC VON KROSIGK AND EZRA CIPES

and Maréchal Foch. "I like to position them as the heritage of this region," Eric says. "These are now old vines, grown organically and producing moderate amounts of grapes. They are not being overcropped like they used to be. They make respectable wines.

MY PICKS

The winery built its reputation with sparkling wines like Cipes Gabriel and Cipes Brut. Riesling stars in a table wine range that also includes Ehrenfelser, Gewürztraminer, Pinot Gris, Pinot Noir and Merlot. Good red and white blends are released under the Alive label. Riesling Icewine is excellent.

OPENED 1992

4870 Chute Lake Road
Kelowna, BC V1W 4M3

T 250.764.8000
   1.800.667.3538 (toll free)
W www.summerhill.bc.ca

WHEN TO VISIT
Open Fridays and Saturdays
10 am – 7 pm; and Sunday to
Thursday 10 am – 6 pm.

RESTAURANT
Sunset Bistro open daily
11 am – 9 pm for lunch, tapas
and dinner.

SUMMERLAND HERITAGE CIDER COMPANY

The avuncular trio who launched this cidery are veteran apple growers who dabbled, naturally, in making their own cider. In fact, it was Tom Kinvig's skills with the cider press that was at the heart of it. Born on a ranch in Merritt in 1956, he grew up in Summerland after his family moved there in 1963. After working for his father for several years, he bought his own orchard in 1979 and soon began making cider with apples that couldn't be sold.

It was rustic cider but his apple-growing friends, Bob Thompson and Ron Vollo, enjoyed it well-chilled on hot days. They developed a tradition of getting together after work on Tuesday afternoons over glasses of cider, which all had begun to make. That tradition inspired the name, Tuesday's Original, for the debut product after the friends navigated the "steep learning curve" of cider making courses to begin making a commercial cider.

Bob Thompson was born in Manitoba in 1960 and was a banker before moving to the Okanagan in 1988. "I sort of fell into orcharding," he says. He and Ron, a Kamloops native, farm 16 hectares (40 acres) of Summerland orchards (Tom farms 8 hectares). The cidery has been set up on Ron's property. While the building currently is too small to house a tasting room, this is where the partners plan to erect a purpose-built cidery because the location is just off the highway near Trout Creek.

While their original home ciders were made with dessert apples, the trio realized that they needed cider apples to achieve the complexity of European ciders. About a decade ago, Tom started grafting some of his Spartan apple trees to cider varieties. He now has about a hectare.

"We don't have enough yet but we don't want a huge influx of apples at one time," Bob says. The only market for cider varieties is other cideries. While the number of cideries is growing, these three savvy

TOM KINVIG, BOB THOMPSON AND RON VOLLO
(COURTESY OF SUMMERLAND HERITAGE CIDER)

growers don't want to get ahead of the demand for the apples.

They have been equally measured with the production of Summerland Heritage Cider, starting with 500 cases in 2012 and only doubling by 2014. They are also working on additional ciders. "If we are ever going to have a tasting room, we are going to have more than Tuesday's Original for people to try," Bob says. "For one thing, we'd like to have something that was drier."

SALES BEGAN 2012

T 250.488.9703
W www.summerlandcider.com

WHEN TO VISIT
No tasting room.

MY PICKS

Tuesday's Original is a delicious, richly-flavoured sparkling cider.

SUNNYBRAE VINEYARDS & WINERY

The large framed photograph in the tasting room of Sunnybrae Vineyards & Winery—a picture of a muscular farmer with his team of Belgian draft horses—conveys heritage. The man is the late Mac Turner, the father of Barry Turner who, with his wife, Nancy, and their family, operates this winery beside Shuswap Lake. A stylized Mac Turner and his team appear on Sunnybrae wine labels.

Barry's family has farmed in the Sunnybrae district for five generations. The winery's three-hectare (7½-acre) vineyard is part of an eight-hectare (20-acre) property that once belonged to a Turner ancestor, a Major Mobley, said to have been one of the first non-native settlers in the area. Barry says that his ancestor sold the land in 1907. In 2000 Barry reacquired the land for his family. "It's a beautiful field if you did something with it," Barry says. "Everybody told me it was an ideal spot for grapes. It has gravel soil, probably eight inches of top soil, with a south slope of up to 6 percent."

Barry's career as a heavy equipment operator and a road builder often has taken him away from home and family. "My plan was, later in life, to phase out of that and get into this full-time," he said when he began planting the vineyard in 2006. "I didn't even grow grapes for a hobby before," Barry added. "She's quite a learning curve." On the recommendation of James Wright, who operates the nearby Ashby Point Vineyard, Barry planted one hectare (2½ acres) of Maréchal Foch, half a hectare (1½ acres) of Siegerrebe and just under half a hectare (one acre) each of Ortega, Kerner and Schönburger. "He is one of these guys, he's doing it by the book," James said of Barry in a 2006 interview. "I wish my rows were as straight as his."

Barry just continued to do things by the book when it came to winemaking. The winery's first vintage, 2010, was started with consultant Hans Nevrkla, the former owner of Larch Hills Winery (the Shuswap's original winery). Jesse Steinley, who is also the winemaker at the

NANCY AND BARRY TURNER

nearby Recline Ridge Winery, took over with consulting support from Mark Wendenburg, the former long-time Sumac Ridge winemaker. Sunnybrae made 2,100 cases in 2012.

MY PICKS

Siegerrebe, exotically tropical, is especially tasty. Ortega's apple and melon flavours are fresh. Even though the vineyard grows just one red, Maréchal Foch, the grape is in four distinctive wines, including a rosé. There is a barrel-aged Foch and two easy-drinking wines, Bastion Mountain Red and Redneck Red. The latter, a bestseller, has what the winery calls "a glorious absence of sophistication."

OPENED 2011

3849 Sunnybrae Canoe Point Road
PO Box 22
Tappen, BC V0E 2X0

T 250.835.8373

W www.sunnybraewinery.com

WHEN TO VISIT
Open daily 10 am – 5:30 pm mid-May to mid-October; weekends 11 am – 5 pm in December; and by appointment.

PICNIC PATIO LOUNGE

SYNCHROMESH WINES

Anyone who follows road racing knows that Le Tertre Rouge is a very high-speed corner at the Le Mans, the racetrack in France that has staged an annual 24-hour sports car race since 1923. The Dickinson family which owns this winery has a long interest in motor racing; John Dickinson once raced sports cars. That is why the family named the winery Synchromesh, referring to the technology that allows the smooth shifting of manual transmissions. That is also why the flagship red blend here is called Tertre Rouge.

Alan Dickinson, John's son, brought both his classic MG sports car and his knowledge of wine to the Okanagan. Born in Vancouver in 1982 and trained in marketing and entrepreneurship, he was a founder of Vancouver Wine Vaults, which stores private wine collections. In March 2010, he and his wife, Amy, moved from Vancouver after buying a two-hectare (five-acre) vineyard that previously had been planted by Wild Goose Vineyards. The anchor variety was Riesling. Alan added more Riesling and some Pinot Noir.

Initially, the winery was licensed as Alto Wine Group, primarily providing winemaking services for clients and for Alan's winemaking partners. In 2012, several partners left, either to license their own wineries or work elsewhere. Alan and his parents restructured the business by transferring the license to Synchromesh (previously a brand).

Alan was attracted to the Storm Haven Vineyard, as he christened it, by the Riesling vines. "I am a fan of German Rieslings," he says. The first wine released by Synchromesh from the 2010 vintage was actually labelled *kabinett halbtrocken* because he made it to those German standards. He increased the Riesling to two-thirds of the vineyard, replacing the Merlot, Malbec and Muscat that had been planted there. The remainder is Pinot Noir, with a small block of Gewürztraminer. Synchromesh also buys Pinot Noir from an East Kelowna vineyard,

ALAN DICKINSON

Riesling from one Naramata grower and Cabernet Franc and Merlot for Tertre Rouge from another Naramata grower.

Alan's minimalist winemaking style begins with using indigenous yeast so that the wines, especially racy Riesling, express Storm Haven's terroir. "It builds complexity," he says. "I certainly have noticed some distinctive characteristics."

OPENED 2011
(AS ALTO WINE GROUP)

4220 McLean Creek Road
Okanagan Falls, BC V0H 1R0

T   250.535.1558

W www.synchromeshwines.ca

WHEN TO VISIT
Open Thursday to Sunday
noon – 5 pm June to harvest;
appointments recommended.

MY PICKS

Production is small but the top-flight Rieslings and the Tertre Rouge are worth seeking out and the Pinot Noir is very promising.

TANTALUS VINEYARDS

You might assume that this winery is named for the Tantalus mountain range near Vancouver. Eric Savics, the investment dealer who owns the winery, says that was not the only inspiration.

"Do you know the background of Tantalus in mythology?" he asks. "Zeus was quite angry with Tantalus [his son], who had been behaving terribly, to the point that Zeus finally sentences Tantalus to live forever in purgatory. There is water up to his knees, and hanging above him are big fat delicious grapes. When Tantalus, being thirsty, reaches for the water, the water recedes. Being hungry, he reaches for the grapes and the grapes recede. So he is being tantalized."

That is a metaphor for the winery's tantalizing Old Vines Riesling, a limited-production wine made from a small Riesling block planted in 1978. However, the sentence is not life in wine purgatory for those who can't find it. Eric has planted a lot more Riesling since buying the property in 2004. On this site, even the young vines yield impressive Riesling.

"It is a good piece of dirt," says Eric. This is one of the Kelowna area's most historic vineyards, planted in 1927 by pioneering grower J. W. Hughes. His foreman, Martin Dulik, bought it in 1948 and it remained in the Dulik family for 56 years. In 1997 Martin's granddaughter, Sue, opened a winery that she called Pinot Reach Cellars. She had already turned heads with Old Vines Riesling when the family sold the vineyard and winery to Eric.

Since then, Eric has almost doubled the site, buying contiguous properties with similar soils and similar southwestern aspects. In addition to Riesling, the new plantings have also included Pinot Noir and Chardonnay. That enables this winery to focus on three varietal wines along with sparkling wine and icewine. At 30 hectares (75 acres), the vineyard will grow enough grapes to produce a targeted 8,500 cases a

ERIC SAVICS

DAVID PATTERSON

year, all of it with a terroir-driven sense of place. "It is all estate wine," Eric says. "It is going to stay that way."

MY PICKS

Everything. The Tantalus Old Vines Riesling and the regular Riesling share the same laser beam brightness of aromas, tangy flavours and mineral backbone. The fresh, racy Riesling icewine is intense in its taste, as fine as any top German Eiswein. The silky Pinot Noir is also headed to the front ranks of Okanagan Pinot Noir and the Chardonnay has a Chablis-like crispness.

OPENED 1997
(AS PINOT REACH CELLARS)

1670 Dehart Road
Kelowna, BC V1W 4N6

T 1.877.764.0078

W www.tantalus.ca

WHEN TO VISIT
Open daily 10 am – 6 pm June
to mid-October; Tuesday to
Saturday 11 am – 5 pm mid-
October to May.

TERRAVISTA VINEYARDS

If there were a winery hall of fame, Bob and Senka Tennant would be in it for the creation of Nota Bene, one of the Okanagan's great icon red wines. They were one of the two couples that founded Black Hills Estate Winery, where Nota Bene is the flagship red. Senka made the first nine vintages before the founders sold Black Hills in late 2007, when their partners, Peter and Susan McCarrell, were ready to retire.

After taking a few years off, the Tennants returned to wine growing in 2009 with Terravista Vineyards and a completely fresh approach. Their 1.6-hectare (four-acre) vineyard high on the Naramata Bench grows only Albariño and Verdejo, two Spanish white varieties never grown before in the Okanagan. "If you are doing this again, you might as well go for it," Senka says of this choice. "I felt we couldn't plant Merlot clone 181." She is referring to the most widely planted varietal in the Okanagan. "That would have been rather redundant."

It was not easy to get even the small quantities of vines they needed. The University of California had just released disease-free stock; nurseries were scrambling to build up stocks of vines to meet the strong demand for these somewhat exotic varieties. The Tennants received just enough vines in 2009 to plant a quarter of the vineyard and some of those vines were killed in a freeze that fall. It was not until 2011, with their new winery under construction, that they got enough vines to finish planting Terravista.

The 600-square-metre (2,000-square-foot) vineyard, set into a hillside and partly below ground, is designed exclusively for producing small volumes of white wine. "We just like focusing," Senka says. "We always have." In 2010, she made the Terravista wines in a nearby winery, using Rhône variety whites (Roussanne, Marsanne and Viognier) purchased from Black Sage Road. The resulting 220-case blend was released under the label Figaro. The blend of the Spanish varieties is

SENKA AND BOB TENNANT

called Fandango.

Both wines are dry, reflecting Bob and Senka's preferences. "For me, that's my palate," she says, drawing a parallel to cooking. "Those recipes that you make occasionally to try them, but you really don't like to eat them, never turn out very well. You have to cook what you like and it really tastes good."

OPENED 2011

1853 Sutherland Road
Penticton, BC V2A 8T8

T 778.476.6011

W www.terravistavineyards.com

WHEN TO VISIT
Open daily 11 am – 5 pm
mid-April to October.

MY PICKS

There are just two wines and both are excellent whites. Figaro is a blend of Roussanne, Viognier and Marsanne. Fandango is a blend of Albariño and Verdejo.

THERAPY VINEYARDS

Therapy Vineyards might seem overly cute as a winery name until you experience the therapy of sipping Pinot Gris here while watching the sun set over the vineyards of Naramata. The property was the original Red Rooster winery. When Red Rooster moved to its Naramata Road location in 2004, a group of wine-loving investors relaunched the property as Therapy Vineyards.

The winery's name inspired a series of clever labels. Many of the wines are labelled provocatively with what resemble Rorschach ink blots, a psychoanalytical tool. Before you start psychoanalyzing yourself with a bottle of Therapy wine, remember that authentic Rorschach blots (there are only 10) are guarded carefully by the professionals who use them. Take these colourful labels for the fun they are meant to be.

Perhaps the most famous name in the history of psychoanalysis is Sigmund Freud. The winery has appropriated his name for the labels of such wines as Super Ego and Freud's Ego (two red blends), Alter Ego (a white blend), Freudian Sip (a blend of Riesling, Kerner and Pinot Gris) and Pink Freud (obviously a rosé). These names add to the fun of visiting Therapy's tasting room without taking anything from the fact that these are very well-made wines.

Therapy's initial winemaker, Marcus Ansems, put the stamp of his native Australia on the wine styles, notably the winery's full-bodied, peppery Shiraz. He was succeeded in late 2008 by Steve Latchford. Born in Ontario's Prince Edward County in 1982, Steve once worked on a dairy farm and believes the transition to a winery is not a big leap. "I worked with pumps in the dairy barn, too," he says laughing. A 2004 graduate from Niagara College's wine program, he started his winery career at the Jackson-Triggs winery in Ontario.

At Therapy, Steve took over a superbly-equipped winery. Completed in 2009, it has an underground cellar now housing about 500 barrels,

STEVE LATCHFORD

with room for twice as many. Therapy makes about 10,000 cases a year and plans to reach 15,000 cases.

MY PICKS

Therapy wines are excellent across the range, notably the Shiraz, the Merlot, the Chardonnay, the Pinot Gris, the rosé and the Freudian Sip. Freud's Ego is an affordable red blend for drinking now while you cellar the bold Super Ego blend, which is mostly Cabernet Sauvignon filled out with Merlot, Petit Verdot, Cabernet Franc and Shiraz.

OPENED 2005

940 Debeck Road
RR 1, Site 2, Comp 47
Naramata, BC V0H 1N0
T   250.496.5217
W www.therapyvineyards.com

WHEN TO VISIT
Open daily 10 am – 6 pm May to October, and by appointment.

ACCOMMODATION
Guesthouse with four bed and breakfast units.

THORNHAVEN ESTATES WINERY

With its Santa Fe architecture, the Thornhaven winery is an Okanagan jewel. Tucked away behind Giant's Head Mountain near Summerland, the adobe-hued winery is at the top of a slope covered with about 3.2 hectares (eight acres) of vines. The patio affords postcard views, but the best view is from the bottom of the undulating vineyard, preferably when the late afternoon sun paints a golden tint on the winery and the hillside behind it.

The vineyard was planted by Dennis Fraser, a former grain farmer from Dawson Creek who sold his farm of almost 1,000 hectares (2,500 acres) in 1989 and then began converting a Summerland orchard to vines (Pinot Noir, Chardonnay and Gewürztraminer, with a bit of Sauvignon Blanc and Pinot Meunier). Winemaking began here in 1999, with Fraser planning a modest tasting room in the basement of his home. Then, a farmer's habit of thinking big took over and he built a picturesque winery.

The winery was purchased in 2005 by Dennis's cousin, Jack Fraser, who was changing careers after 24 years working in overseas oil fields (mostly in Libya). Thornhaven is now managed by Jack and his wife Jan, a lively tasting room personality. Son Jason, who mentored with consultant Christine Leroux, is the winemaker.

Now making about 5,500 cases a year, Thornhaven has a portfolio of 13 to 15 wines. The Gewürztraminer is a flagship wine and this is one of the few Okanagan wineries with a varietal Pinot Meunier. The winery also offers an unusual Sauvignon Blanc/Chardonnay blend because the varieties are interplanted in the vineyard. The grapes are picked and fermented together, yielding a delicious wine tasting of peaches and citrus. Jack Fraser has a simple explanation for the consistency of the award-winning wines: "The main thing is that the grapes come from nearby vineyards."

JACK AND JAN FRASER

JASON FRASER

MY PICKS

Thornhaven has made its reputation with award-winning Gewürztraminer, supported with Pinot Gris and Sauvignon Blanc/ Chardonnay, both full of tropical fruit flavours. The Pinot Meunier has jammy strawberry flavours and a lovely silken texture. The rosé combines Pinot Noir and Merlot in a tangy wine with character. There is always an interesting dessert wine in the portfolio: in the vintage of 2012, the winery made a late-harvest Gamay Noir called Decadence.

OPENED 2001

6816 Andrew Avenue
RR2 Site 68 Comp 15
Summerland, BC V0H 1Z7

T 250.494.7778

W www.thornhaven.com

WHEN TO VISIT
Open daily 10 am – 5 pm
May to mid-October, and by
appointment.

RESTAURANT
Patio offers wine by the glass
and deli food. Picnics welcome.

3 CRU WINES

3 Cru is the brand that is launching an ambitious Similkameen organic vineyard and winery near the historic Mariposa Organic Farm. The farm was started in 1962 by the late Bob McFadyen and his wife, Lee. They considered starting a winery but, frustrated by regulatory barriers, concentrated on organic farming. Now in her 70s, Lee is one of the Similkameen's leading authorities on organic agriculture.

The winery and vineyard project came about while learning consultant Jacques LeCavalier was working with Lee to develop online courses in organic farming and discovered she had raw land for sale. Jacques, a Quebec-born agriculture engineer, talked about this opportunity with a friend, Kelowna physician Thomas Kinahan, who has a small vineyard in East Kelowna. The friends recognized that they needed an expert in organic grape growing and asked Karnail Singh Sidhu, the owner of Kalala Organic Estate Winery, to look at the McFadyen property. "He said he did not know if he would be involved in our project," Jacques says, "but whatever we did, we should not let this land go."

Eventually, Karnail became the third partner in what they called Mariposa Vineyard Limited Partnership. There is a strong dedication to organic practices in the Similkameen, and Karnail was eager to apply his grape growing expertise there. In the spring of 2011, the Partnership planted about eight hectares (20 acres) of vines and prepared about another two hectares on the sun-drenched site. Most of the vineyard is planted with mainstream varietals: Merlot, Cabernet Franc, Cabernet Sauvignon, Malbec, Pinot Noir, Chardonnay, Riesling and Gewürztraminer. A quarter of the vineyard is experimental plantings of varieties such as Italy's Teroldego, Austria's Lagrein and Argentina's Torrontés. "We are going to try them out and see how it goes," Jacques says. "We will make some blends and we will take out the varieties that do not succeed."

JACQUES LECAVALIER

The Partnership is planning an energy-efficient winery, with the design intended to complement the vineyard's organic ethos. Meanwhile, the wines are being produced and sold by Kalala, Karnail's winery in West Kelowna. The strategy has been to launch the 3 Cru brand early in the venture to establish the brand. The Similkameen vineyard started producing fruit in 2013.

OPENED 2011

330 Highway 3
Cawston, BC V0X 1Cs

T 250.878.0406

W www.3cru.com

WHEN TO VISIT
No tasting room at this time.
Tastings available at Kalala
Organic Estate Winery.

MY PICKS

The 3 Cru wines have all won awards. Wanderlust is an unconventional blend of unoaked Chardonnay, Sauvignon Blanc and Pinot Gris. Nomad is a crisp and fruity white (85 percent Gewürztraminer with Riesling and Pinot Gris) and Traveller is a full-bodied red (75 percent Merlot with Cabernet Sauvignon and a dash of Petit Verdot).

3 MILE ESTATE WINERY

Colleen Gunther and Gayle Rahn, the sisters who run this family winery, have deliberately limited the number of wines they offer. "It is nice not to have too big a portfolio, so you can really focus on perfecting the wines," says Colleen, who does most of the winemaking under the tutelage of Kelly Symonds, their consultant, while Gayle handles sales. "Maybe someday we'll introduce something else, but I would like to get known for what we do."

The winery project began in 2004 when Colleen and Jake, her husband, acquired three adjoining Naramata properties as part of a lifestyle decision to move to the Okanagan from Abbotsford. At the time, Colleen operated a successful spa and Jake raised pigeons for sale to restaurants and consumers. The Naramata properties included a producing vineyard. The Gunthers planted more vines until they had 5.6 hectares (14 acres) of grapes, including Gewürztraminer, Pinot Gris, Viognier, Merlot, Cabernet Franc, Cabernet Sauvignon, Syrah, Pinot Noir and Gamay. Dennis Cenerini, Colleen and Gayle's retired Italian-born father, pitched in enthusiastically to help Jake with the vineyard.

For several years, they sold grapes to Hillside Winery on the other side of Naramata Road. In 2010, when Hillside did not need the grapes, Colleen and Jake enlisted Gayle and Gayle's husband, Darryl, to partner in developing a winery. Darryl, a BC Hydro manager, effectively serves as 3 Mile's controller. "We would never have bought an operating winery," Colleen says. "We had to learn to walk before doing a winery." The learning curve was tougher than it should have been because they started with 2010, one of the Okanagan's most challenging vintages. When the much riper 2012 grapes arrived in the cellar, they exulted that the vintage was a "bonanza."

Colleen learned winemaking from Kelly, a former winemaker at Hillside, who established the 3 Mile style of crisp, clean whites and

GAYLE RAHN AND COLLEEN GUNTHER

quite credible reds. "I am really passionate about the winemaking and I am also really particular," Colleen says. "I have to get to that wine constantly or I can't sleep. If I haven't been to the barrels in a couple of weeks, I will start thinking about it when I go to sleep and that is what I will think about when I wake up. I taste and I smell constantly."

The passion involves several generations. Gayle's son, Taylor Ballantyne, has done several crushes in New Zealand and is expected to get formal enology training. "It will be good to have a chemist in the family," Colleen says.

MY PICKS

The Gewürztraminer is crisp while the Pinot Gris/ Viognier blend is rich and full of fruit. The winery also offers a good Syrah, a Cabernet Merlot blend and a blend of three Bordeaux varieties called Trio.

OPENED 2011

1465 Naramata Road
Penticton, BC V2A 8X2

T 778.476.5918

W www.3milewinery.com

WHEN TO VISIT
Open daily 11 am – 6 pm June to October.

ACCOMMODATION
Three guest rooms.

TH WINES

Tyler Harlton's passion for wine was cemented during a law school semester in Paris in 2007, when he spent his weekends in French wine regions helping pick grapes. "Seeing the vines in France really connected with me," says Tyler, who was born in Saskatchewan in 1976 and grew up on a wheat farm. "I had that in my background. The wine industry is sophisticated and popular but at the same time it has an agricultural tradition."

After he graduated from McGill law school in 2008, Tyler articled with a Penticton law firm to be near the Okanagan's wine industry. In short order, Tyler decided against a career in law, becoming first a picker, then a cellar hand, at Osoyoos Larose Estate Winery. He moved to the cellar at Le Vieux Pin in 2009 and to Dirty Laundry Vineyards in 2010, while also planning a holistic agricultural lifestyle for himself, including opening a winery.

"I rent land and grow ground crops and I sell at farmers' markets and to local restaurants," he says. "My idea is to have a sustainable lifestyle where I get to grow food and make wine. My idea is to be working with vines at the same time as I am growing food. The farming season slows down in September and that is when the grape picking starts. I would like to live an old-fashioned lifestyle doing the things that I love—growing food and making wine."

He crafted a strategy allowing him to open a winery with limited capital. For a processing facility, he leases about 139 square metres (1,500 square feet) in an industrial building next to Ripley Stainless, the major supplier of tanks for the wine industry. He has handshake agreements with growers in the South Okanagan for top quality grapes, and operates the winery under a commercial licence that, unlike a land-based winery licence, does not require him to be based on his own vineyard.

TYLER HARLTON

Tyler and his winemaker, William Adams, launched about 500 cases (Pinot Gris, Viognier, Cabernet Franc rosé, Pinot Noir and a Merlot/Cabernet Franc blend) in 2012, and because there were plenty of apples available, they made a initial 100-case lot of cider as well. "Cider for me is another agricultural product," Tyler says. "There is a really good cider tradition that has died off."

OPENED 2012

1 – 9576 Cedar Avenue
Summerland, BC V0H 1Z2

T 250.494.8334

W www.thwines.com

WHEN TO VISIT
Open Wednesday to Sunday
10:30 am – 5:30 pm May to
September.

MY PICKS

The flagship red is an excellent Cabernet Merlot blend. The Pinot Noir, the rosé, the Viognier/Pinot Gris blend and the apple wine are all well-made.

TIGHTROPE WINERY

The seed for Tightrope Winery was planted in the decade that Lyndsay and Graham O'Rourke spent working in bars and restaurants at the Whistler ski resort. The jobs supported their skiing, Graham's fly fishing and shared meals in fine restaurants.

"The thing about Whistler is that you get spoiled because there are so many fine dining restaurants for such a small town," Lyndsay says. "You get a lot of chances to go out and try nice wines with good food." Graham agrees. "My wine experience all started with really good wine," he says. "I did not grow up drinking Baby Duck and the box wines."

Both were born in 1971. Lyndsay, whose geologist father, Grenville Thomas, is a diamond explorer who is in the Canadian Mining Hall of Fame, has a University of Windsor business degree. Graham, the son of an accountant, grew up near Sarnia and learned to fish during summers in a family cottage on the river. His love of the outdoors led to a University of British Columbia degree in wildlife management.

They moved to the Okanagan in 2003. Immediately drawn to the vineyard lifestyle, they both took Okanagan College courses in grape growing and winemaking. To further improve their skills, they both went to Lincoln University in New Zealand for honours degrees in those disciplines. The studies paid off quickly. When they returned, Graham joined Mission Hill for six years as a vineyard manager before, with a partner, setting up his own vineyard consulting firm. Lyndsay became the winemaker for Ruby Blues Winery in 2009.

In 2007, the couple bought a four-hectare (10-acre) Naramata Bench property with a million dollar view over the lake. They planted about three hectares (seven acres) of grapes—Pinot Gris, Riesling, Viognier, Pinot Noir and Merlot, with small blocks of Cabernet Franc and Barbera. They made the first 900 cases of Tightrope wines in 2012,

LYNDSAY AND GRAHAM O'ROURKE

using the Ruby Blues winery until they built their own winery in 2014.

They avoided place names and animal names for their winery, coming up with Tightrope, an evocative term for them. "It represents the balancing act you go through when you make wine, from decisions in the vineyard, depending on the season, to decisions in the winery and winemaking," Lyndsay explains. "All of those variables have to be balanced."

SALES BEGAN 2013

1050 Fleet Rd
Penticton, BC V2A 8T7

W www.tightropewinery.ca

WHEN TO VISIT
Wine shop expected to open
September 2014.

MY PICKS

All of Tightrope's debut releases won awards in the first competitions the winery entered. The portfolio includes Riesling, Pinot Gris, Viognier, Pinot Noir and Pinot Noir rosé.

TIME ESTATE WINERY

By the 2014 crush, the elegant curves of the newly built Time Estate Winery will be a gleaming white beacon among the vineyards of Black Sage Road. It also sums up the legacy of Harry McWatters who founded Sumac Ridge Estate Winery in 1980 and then 33 years later, at the age of 68, launched Time, a 30,000-case family winery.

Harry has been a force in British Columbia wines since 1968, starting as a salesman with Casabello Wines in Penticton. (Casabello later was folded into the Jackson-Triggs winery.) As one of the first estate wineries, Sumac Ridge played a lead role in elevating the quality of Okanagan wine. The key was Harry's 1992 decision to buy a 46.5-hectare (115-acre) vineyard property on Black Sage Road that formerly grew mediocre hybrid grapes. Harry gambled in replanting it almost entirely with Bordeaux varieties, primarily Merlot. His wines, starting with a national award for the first Black Sage Merlot, triggered the planting of these varieties throughout the South Okanagan and laid the foundation for the modern wine industry.

Harry sold Sumac Ridge in 2000 to Vincor (now Constellation Brands) but he retained half of the vineyard. Renamed as the Sundial Vineyard, Harry edged back into wine production by launching a McWatters Collection brand 2007 red Meritage, followed with a Chardonnay, made from the grapes that had produced the best Sumac Ridge wines. The wines were so well-received that he hired architect Nick Buvanda (whose father had been a Casabello grape grower) to design the Time winery. It is expected that Harry's children, Christa-Lee and Darren, will join him in running the new winery.

The first wines under the Time label were a Chardonnay, a white Meritage and a red Meritage. The Meritage term was developed in California when wineries stopped using Bordeaux place names on labels. Harry negotiated the right for Canadian wineries to use Meritage in 1993. When the new owners of Sumac Ridge discontinued its Meritage wines, Harry filled the vacuum with Time's Meritage wines.

Currently, Harry's iconic new winery plans to offer tastings but no public tours. The winery is set at the vineyard's highest point, with the barrel cellar tucked into a gully. The view south from the tasting room's floor-to-ceiling windows takes in the more than 400 hectares (1,000 acres) of vineyards planted on the Black Sage after Harry showed the way.

MY PICKS

Both the McWatters Collection and the Time Estate wines are superb. The special treat is the White Meritage, a blend of Sauvignon Blanc and Sémillon, in the same rich style that won many awards for Sumac Ridge.

OPENED 2013

30861 Black Sage Road
Oliver. BC V0H 1T0

(Office)
7 – 7519 Prairie Valley Road
Summerland. BC V0H 1Z4

T   250.494.8828

W www.timewinery.com

WHEN TO VISIT
By appointment only.

HARRY MCWATTERS

TINHORN CREEK VINEYARDS

Cabernet Franc has long had a friend in Tinhorn Creek president Sandra Oldfield. She even resisted when some of her partners wanted to replace the winery's 8.5-hectare (21-acre) block with the better known Cabernet Sauvignon. Eventually, some Cabernet Sauvignon was planted but Cabernet Franc, which ripens earlier and more reliably, retained primacy in Tinhorn Creek's vineyards. And Sandra's advocacy has been vindicated. The varietal is Tinhorn Creek's bestselling red and the 2008 vintage got a rave review and 92 points from American wine critic James Suckling.

Sandra, then working on her master's degree in enology in California, had significant input in the 1993 decision to focus just on six varietals: Cabernet Franc, Merlot, Pinot Noir, Chardonnay, Pinot Gris and Gewürztraminer, grown in the winery's Diamondback Vineyard on Black Sage Road and in the older Fischer Vineyard at the winery. The development in 2004 of a reserve tier of wines, now called the Oldfield Series, led to the planting of Syrah, Cabernet Sauvignon, Sémillon, Viognier, Sauvignon Blanc and Muscat. Tinhorn Creek is still focused—just on a larger portfolio of reliable wines.

The winery draws its name from the Tinhorn Quartz Mining Company, in operation from 1896 to 1910. The remains of the stamp mill are a brisk hike up the mountain behind the winery's Gewürztraminer vineyard. A map to the Golden Mile hiking trail is provided in the wine shop. Famished hikers are welcome at the Miradoro Restaurant which opened in 2011 next to the winery. The views of the valley, whether from the winery, the restaurant or the trail, are spectacular.

Tinhorn Creek has often set trends. In 2004, it was one of the first Okanagan wineries to start bottling its wines under screw cap. Since 2006 all of the wines, including the reserve wines and now the icewine, have screw caps. Besides eliminating cork taint, these closures better

SANDRA OLDFIELD

retain freshness, so Tinhorn Creek has begun to age reds longer in bottle before release. This means the wines are ready to enjoy when purchased.

Since 2009, the winery has embraced sustainability with a wide range of practices to reduce Tinhorn Creek's impact on the environment. These include recycling, the use of lightweight bottles, drip irrigation in the vineyards and biodiesel in farm machinery. In order to reduce employee travel, Sandra does "virtual" wine tastings with the trade. The ultimate target is a 100 percent carbon-neutral winery, showing that you can do good and also make good wines.

OPENED 1995

537 Tinhorn Creek Road
Box 2010
Oliver, BC V0H 1T0

T 250.498.3743
    1.888.484.6467 (toll free)
W www.tinhorn.com

WHEN TO VISIT
Open daily 10 am – 6 pm May to October; 10 am – 5 pm November to April.

RESTAURANT
Miradoro Restaurant
T 250.498.3742
Open daily for lunch, afternoon tapas and dinner.

MY PICKS

Everything. The whites—Gewürztraminer, Pinot Gris, Chardonnay and 2Bench White—are refreshingly fruit-forward. Among the reds, Merlot is the flagship while the spicy Cabernet Franc is the winemaker's favourite. The Oldfield Series wines show well-crafted elegance— notably the Syrah, the Merlot, the Cabernet Franc, the Pinot Noir and the 2Bench Red.

TOPSHELF WINERY

With the reference to a goalie's net and with labels like goalie masks, this winery is quintessentially Canadian because the owners, Leonard and Myra Kwiatkowski, are hockey parents.

They are both Saskatchewan natives, where Leonard was born in 1948. "Out on the Prairies, that was all you had—hockey or curling," he says. "The winters are long." During Leonard's career as an agricultural representative with the Saskatchewan Wheat Pool, they lived for nine years in Fort Qu'Appelle. Every winter, they turned their backyard into a popular outdoor rink where the neighbourhood boys, including their two sons, played hockey far into the evening.

It rubbed off on their sons. Jason was a minor league defenceman for six years; a back problem ended a brief switch to roller hockey in 1996, and he became an airline pilot in the United States. Joel, his younger brother, also a defenceman, started in the Western Hockey League in 1994. Subsequently, he played for five National Hockey League teams, beginning with the Ottawa Senators, during seven seasons; he then spent two seasons playing in Russia before ending his playing career in Switzerland.

"We chose the Topshelf name because our boys are really involved in hockey," Myra says. "Most hockey players and sports people love beer. We thought, hey, maybe they would like a good bottle of wine."

This is the third career for Leonard and Myra. In 2000, he retired early from the Pool and the couple bought a fishing lodge on a secluded inlet near Sechelt, British Columbia. They loved fishing and still have their own boat but running the lodge tied them down much of the year. They sold it in 2008, buying a Kaleden property large enough for a 1.4-hectare (3½-acre) vineyard of Pinot Gris, Chardonnay and Merlot.

They are not deterred by taking on a venture entirely new to them. "I am the type of person who gets bored to death if I don't have a

LEONARD AND MYRA KWIATKOWSKI

challenge," Leonard says. Myra, who cooked professionally in Saskatchewan hospitals, took the Okanagan College winemaking course and with the help of a consultant made her first vintage in 2010. "I love to cook, so I thought I should be able to make wine," she says.

OPENED 2011

236 Linden Avenue
Kaleden, BC V0H 1K0

T 778.515.0099

W www.topshelfwine.ca

WHEN TO VISIT
Open daily 11 am – 6 pm May
long weekend to mid-October.

MY PICKS

The wine names alone— Point Shot Pinot Gris, Slapshot Chardonnay and Over the Top Merlot— are worth the visit.

TOWNSHIP 7 VINEYARDS & WINERY

Township 7 has two locations under the same name. The original Township 7 opened in 2001 on a heritage farm in the Township of Langley. The second Township 7 opened in 2004 at the beginning of Naramata Road. They attract an equal number of visitors, with the Langley winery getting more visitors in winter. That was why founders Gwen and Corey Coleman opened their initial winery in the Vancouver suburb.

They sold Township 7 in 2006 to a group headed by Mike Raffan, an amiable restaurateur. Born in North Vancouver in 1954, he is a former owner of both Keg and Milestones restaurants. Already a fan of Township 7 wines, he has found his new career in wine as captivating as his former life in restaurants. "I love it," he says. "When I was young, the restaurant business was very much that way—I just couldn't get enough of it." He made substantial enhancements to the Penticton winery, some as simple as a paved parking lot, to enhance the visitor experience. In 2014, the winery was acquired by a silent investor. Mike continues to manage it.

The winemaker is Bradley Cooper, who began making wine in 1997 at Hawthorne Mountain Vineyards with Michael Bartier, Township 7's initial winemaker. Born in New Westminster in 1958, Brad is a journalism graduate who spent several years as a writer and photographer with community newspapers before switching to restaurants and then to winemaking. He packed in experience in New Zealand, Washington State and Ontario before joining Township 7 in the summer of 2005.

The tightly focused portfolio currently includes 14 wines. Several reds are anchored with Merlot, including a single varietal, a blend with Cabernet Sauvignon and a complex Meritage called Reserve 7. "It's our flagship on the red side," Brad says of Merlot. The variety, along with other Bordeaux reds, even makes an appearance in Black Dog, a

MIKE RAFFAN

limited-production oak-aged red named for Brad's dog. The wine is offered exclusively to the members of Club 7, the wine club Township 7 launched in 2013.

MY PICKS

There is something for everyone here: an oaked Chardonnay and an unoaked Chardonnay; a crisp, herbal Sauvignon Blanc; occasionally, one of the Okanagan's rare Sémillon wines; and a rosé. The reds in addition to Merlot include Cabernet Sauvignon and Syrah. From its Langley vineyard, Township 7 makes a crisp sparkling wine called Seven Stars.

OPENED 2004

1450 McMillan Avenue
Penticton, BC V2A 8T4

T   250.770.1743

W www.township7.com

WHEN TO VISIT
Open daily 11 am – 6 pm,
weekends and holidays 10 am
– 7 pm April to October; and by
appointment.

UPPER BENCH ESTATE WINERY

There is a divine symmetry at Upper Bench. Gavin Miller currently has eight wines in the portfolio while Shana, his wife, has eight cheeses in her portfolio. Both are available in the tasting room.

The winery has undergone a profound transformation since 2011 when Gavin, backed by a silent partner, businessman Wayne Nystrom, acquired what was then known as Stonehill Estate Winery in a bankruptcy court auction of the winery and its three-hectare (seven-acre) vineyard. The partners started almost from scratch, including a new name, turning the page on the struggles of previous owners. The vineyard was planted in 1998 by German brewmaster Klaus Stadler. He launched Benchland Winery three years later to such a lukewarm reception that he stopped making wine after the 2002 vintage and returned to Germany, selling the winery in 2004 to orchardist Keith Holman. Renamed Stonehill, it specialized in port-style wines before slipping into bankruptcy in 2010 with the other six Holman wineries.

Rebranding the winery, which is within Penticton's city limits, has enabled Gavin and Shana to make a new beginning with high-quality wines and cheeses. "I am really pleased we got this winery," Gavin says. "I always thought it had good bones, this place. It was never used to its potential."

Born in Britain in 1965, Gavin was a sales manager in London when he came to Penticton on vacation in 1995 and met Shana. They lived in London for a year before returning to the Okanagan in 1997. Drawn to wine after a year as a sign maker, Gavin took Okanagan College courses. That launched him on a career that began in the vineyard at Lake Breeze, the cellars at Hawthorne Mountain Vineyards, the tasting room at Sumac Ridge and then winemaking, first at Poplar Grove and then at Painted Rock, where he made award-winning wines before leaving after the 2010 vintage.

GAVIN AND SHANA MILLER

Shana, a Nova Scotian, was working in Montreal when, on a whim, she decided to move to the Okanagan. "I was 25 at the time and had a pretty stressful accounting job, which I hated," she recalls. Travelling with four cats, she needed to stay on a farm. Ian and Gitta Sutherland, who were just planting the vineyard for Poplar Grove Winery, welcomed her. When Poplar Grove subsequently added a cheese plant, Shana acquired the art of cheese-making. "Cheese is like wine," she says. "It is all made the same way."

MY PICKS

Everything, including the Pinot Gris, Cabernet Sauvignon, Zweigelt and Pinot Noir, especially when paired with King Cole, Upper Bench's semi-soft blue cheese.

OPENED 2001
(AS BENCHLAND WINERY)

170 Upper Bench Road South
Penticton, BC V2A 8T1

T 250.770.1733

W www.upperbench.ca

WHEN TO VISIT
Open daily 10 am – 6 pm April to October; 10 am – 5 pm November to March. Check for holiday closures.

FOOD SERVICE
Cheeses for sale.

VAN WESTEN VINEYARDS

Every wine that Robert Van Westen releases has a name that begins with V—sometimes with a hilarious result. The winery's first Cabernet Franc was released in 2010 as Vrankenstein because the variety is usually harvested on Halloween. The icewine was called Vicicle. But even though the wine labels are light-hearted, the wines are serious.

Rob, his father and brother (both named Jake) are some of the best farmers on the Naramata Bench. The family, now with 21 hectares (52 acres) of cherries, apples and grapes, has farmed on the Naramata Bench ever since Jake Van Westen Sr. emigrated from Holland in 1951 after graduating from agriculture school. Rob, tall enough to tower over his vines, was born in 1966. He left school after the 10th grade and worked in construction in Vancouver until 1999, when he returned to help with the family's newly planted vineyard. He embraced viticulture with a passion, studying at Okanagan University College and, when he began making wine, spending nearly four months at wineries in Australia and New Zealand.

CedarCreek Estate Winery began buying Van Westen grapes. Impressed with the quality of the fruit, CedarCreek's winemaker at the time, Tom DiBello, encouraged Rob to make wine. Rob launched the winery in 2005. Since then, he has moved winemaking into a hulking apple packing plant on one of the family's properties. In 2009 he installed an informal tasting room here as well. When it is open, Rob presides over lively informal tastings. The spirit of the wine shop is mirrored aptly by the name that Rob has assigned to a new Merlot: Vivre la Vie.

The Van Westens have five hectares (12 acres) of vineyards, with another hectare or two slated for planting. They grow Merlot, Cabernet Franc, Pinot Gris and Pinot Blanc and plan to add Pinot Noir and Cabernet Sauvignon—but no Chardonnay. "I've never been

ROBERT VAN WESTEN

a Chardonnay drinker," Rob admits. Conveniently considering the winery's "V" theme, he does grow Viognier.

MY PICKS

The wines, like the delicious Viognier, all have names beginning with V. Vino Grigio is a tasty Pinot Gris; Vivacious is a crisp and remarkably complex Pinot Blanc; Voluptuous is a chewy, age-worthy Bordeaux blend. Vrankenstein and Vivre la Vie are both full-bodied reds. Also look for VD, the Pinot Noir made in collaboration with Tom DiBello.

OPENED 2005

2800A Aikins Loop
Naramata, BC V0H 1N0

(Mailing address)
850 Boothe Road
Naramata, BC V0H 1N0

T 250.496.0067

W www.vanwestenvineyards.com

WHEN TO VISIT
Tuesdays and Saturdays by appointment.

THE VIBRANT VINE / OKANAGAN VILLA ESTATE WINERY

Since its second season, The Vibrant Vine has had rave reviews on www.tripadvisor.ca as one of Kelowna's most entertaining wineries. The fun begins when your host hands you a pair of 3-D glasses and the huge mural in the tasting room immerses you in psychedelic colours and images. The same 3-D mural wraps around most of the wine bottles. The fun continues with live music on the lawn every Saturday afternoon in summer and with tours of the luxuriant gardens, perhaps with a glass of wine in hand. It is not surprising that this is also one of Kelowna's favourite wedding venues.

Formally known as Okanagan Villa Estate Winery, the winery is operated by two natives of Wales, Wyn Lewis and his wife, Marion. They came to Canada in 1975 after graduating from Cambridge (engineering and botany, respectively). Shortly after, they went to California where Wyn joined the Wells Fargo Bank. He was the bank's director of international operations, retiring in 2000, and also developed software for automated teller machines. They were on the way to settle in Victoria in 2003 when they first saw the Okanagan Valley. Almost on impulse—they were captivated by the region's beauty—they bought an apple orchard in East Kelowna on a plateau with a dramatic view over the city and the valley. They turned the house on the crown of the plateau into a Mediterranean villa surrounded by gardens and incorporated the winery. The apple trees were replaced with vines, including Riesling, Gewürztraminer, Pinot Gris, and Chardonnay and a heritage cottage became a wine shop.

They enlisted their sons in the winery. Phil, an artist with work displayed in the wine shop, created the mural and the labels. Anthony, a rock musician who formerly ran a recording studio in Denver, became the winemaker under the mentorship of consultants. He compares winemaking to sound mixing. Sometimes he uses his knowledge of

WYN LEWIS

music to open doors when he needs to pick the brains of wine professionals at, for example, the research station in Geneva, New York. "I always talk about music first," he says and laughs. "Everybody likes to talk about music. Then after talking about drums, why don't we also talk about pH?"

Phil's 3-D art is reproduced on plastic sleeves. These become wraparound labels by being slipped onto thousands of empty bottles which are immersed into boiling water by hand, one at a time. Whoops?, the winery's blend of five white varietals, resulted from an error when the image on about 4,000 sleeves was printed upside down. Wyn embraced it as an opportunity. "This by far has become our number one selling wine," he said at the end of summer in 2013.

OPENED 2010

3240 Pooley Road
Kelowna. BC V1W 4G7

T 778.478.4153

W www.thevibrantvine.com

WHEN TO VISIT
Open daily 11 am – 5 pm.

PICNIC AREA AND GARDENS

MY PICKS

The white wines, including the Pinot Grigio, the Gewürztraminer, the Chardonnay Muscat and the Reserve Chardonnay, are appealing for their crispness and intense cool-climate flavours.

THE VIEW WINERY

One wonders if it has occurred to Jennifer Molgat that she might call The View Winery the oldest winery in the Okanagan even though it only opened in 2008. The winery and the tasting room are in a packing house built in 1922 by George Ward, her grandfather. Wards Hard Apple Cider, which The View added to its portfolio in 2012, honours the five generations of growing apples here.

Chris Turton, Jennifer's father, began replacing some apple trees with vines in 1994. At the same time, he began producing a bulk cider for Alberta's Big Rock Brewery. This is still the engine driving the business here, with about a million litres of cider produced annually. When the winery was launched, The View's first winemaker, a German, was offended at having to ferment apples and returned to Germany. Subsequent winemakers have embraced what the orchard offers. In addition to the hard cider, The View also offers Temptation Frizzante, an effervescent beverage made with European cider apples.

The 19.4-hectare (48-acre) vineyard grows Riesling, Gewürztraminer, Ehrenfelser, Optima, Baco Noir and 3.4 hectares (8½ acres) of Pinotage, the largest block of that South African red in the Okanagan. Pinotage anchors the portfolio with a varietal wine, several blends incorporating Pinotage, and the best-selling Distraction Rosé, made entirely from that grape.

Since 2012, The View has produced a 7.5 percent sparkling Gewürztraminer in a single-serving sized can. Called Bling, the wine has been embraced by consumers. The product also helped The View recover from a violent 15-minute hailstorm in the summer of 2013. The hail damaged two-thirds of the grapes and compromised the ability of the vines to ripen other grapes fully. However, those grapes still made excellent Bling.

Because of the hail damage, The View purchased grapes for the first

JENNIFER MOLGAT

time from other growers. Jennifer prefers, however, to stick to estate-grown wines. "We make wine from what we grow, and we grow what does well in our area," she says.

MY PICKS

The Pinotage is dark, rich and spicy. The Gewürztraminer, the Riesling and Distraction Rosé are full of flavour. Red Shoe White is an off-dry blend of Optima, Riesling and Gewürztraminer. Don't overlook Fossil Fuel, a quaffable Pinotage with 5 percent Baco Noir. Stiletto, the port-style cherry wine, is what I would have with a cigar.

OPENED 2008

1 – 2287 Ward Road
Kelowna, BC V1W 4R5

T 250.860.0742

W www.theviewwinery.com

WHEN THE VISIT
Open daily 11:30 am – 5:30 pm
April to October; Monday to
Friday noon – 5 pm November
to March.

VINDICATION CELLARS

Jeff Del Nin is one of the best-educated winemakers in the Okanagan, but home winemaking has been critical to his career. In Thunder Bay, where he was born to an Italian father, almost everyone Jeff knew made wine from imported California grapes. The indifferent quality of those wines did not turn on Jeff's winemaking gene: he got an honours degree in chemistry and satisfied wanderlust by going to Australia in 1996 where he found work in the plastics industry.

He also found bold wines when he spent his weekends touring wineries. In 2000, he joined an Adelaide producer of synthetic wine closures in order to be closer to the wine industry. Two years later, he signed up for an amateur winemaking course and discovered how much his chemistry helped. So after working for Barossa Valley Estate winery, he enrolled in the University of Adelaide's winemaking program, graduating with ease in 2006.

Looking to broaden his winemaking experience, Jeff returned to North America that summer. He tasted wine in the Okanagan for the first time and found that Burrowing Owl also made bold reds like the Australian wines he liked. By coincidence, Burrowing Owl needed a winemaker that fall. Jeff stayed there for three years and then moved to nearby Church & State Winery.

Vindication Cellars was born after Jeff made a few barrels of Cabernet Sauvignon in 2007 for personal consumption. The wine caused a sensation when he started giving it to his friends. "We made a Syrah in 2008 and the same thing happened," Jeff says. Following a 2009 decision to make commercial quantities (about 500 cases a year), Jeff contracted grapes for a 2010 Meritage and bought property on the east side of Skaha Lake where 1.2 hectares (three acres) of grapes were planted in 2012.

To honour his Italian heritage, most of the vineyard is planted with Italian clones of Pinot Noir and with Teroldego, an Italian red from the

JEFF DEL NIN

Friuli region where his father grew up. "I don't want to be doing the same kind of thing that everyone else is doing in British Columbia," Jeff says. "I would like to differentiate and distinguish myself."

The three wines that Jeff released to restaurants in 2013 all have purple labels. It was the favourite colour of Pamela, his Australian-born wife who died in 2012. They gave the winery its name because they believed it vindicates their decision to sink their savings into making Okanagan wine.

SALES BEGAN 2012

PO Box 24
Oliver, BC V0H 1T0
T 250.408.9506

WHEN TO VISIT
No tasting room.

MY PICKS

Everything, including a fine dry Muscat, a tasty Cabernet Franc rosé and a Meritage called Blind Tiger, the name of a famous tavern in the Australian outback.

VINEGLASS RENEWAL RESORT

Try to find a hillside viewing point above the VineGlass resort to see the unusual vineyard feature: the vines have been planted in a way that leaves the shape of a huge wineglass exposed among the plants. The idea is drawn from the corn mazes that horticulturist Jyl Chegwin, one of the owners here, once managed on a family farm in the Fraser Valley.

Jyl's partner, Roger Hol, is a veteran Similkameen grape grower despite his professional training as a marine engineer. A farmer by avocation, he was formerly a partner with Andrew Peller Ltd. in operating the 28-hectare (70-acre) Rocky Ridge Vineyard. It was planted in 1998 and Roger looked after the 70,000 vines until 2008, when Peller exercised its option to acquire his interest.

His current farm, which he purchased on the heel of the Peller transaction, is a spiritually serene property beside the Similkameen River, not far from where it crosses into the United States. The resort that Roger and Jyl have begun—the first 3 of a planned 10 guest suites opened in 2013—is meant for those seeking renewal in the peaceful ambiance.

The scale is a tenth of Rocky Ridge. Roger planted about 7,000 vines in 2010. When Jyl mused about a corn maze, Roger jumped in to say: "Let's plant a wineglass. All the effort of my farming is going to be appreciated in a glass. So we decided we would plant the largest wineglass on earth. If you see our farm from Google Earth, you see a wineglass."

The vineyard was planted to support a red blend with Cabernet Franc, Merlot and Cabernet Sauvignon. It is modelled on wine that Roger admires: Trius, a blend made at Peller's Hillebrand Estates winery in Ontario. For a white, he has a small block of Viognier.

"That's all we will do here, and only from our farm," Roger says. "Our business is really about bringing experiential tourism on an

ROGER HOL AND JYL CHEGWIN
(COURTESY OF VINEGLASS RESORT)

intimate basis. You can come here, stay with us. Help us tend the vines. At the end of the day, you will go home with a whole new appreciation for what is in that bottle of wine."

MY PICKS

While no red wines were available yet for tasting, the Viognier is appealing.

OPENED 2013

306 Sumac Road
Cawston, BC V0X 1C3

T 1.888.694.6996

W www.vineglass.ca

WHEN TO VISIT
By appointment only.

ACCOMMODATION
Three suites.

VOLCANIC HILLS ESTATE WINERY

Here is the chance to discover how the professionals pair wine with South Asian food. Blue Saffron Bistro, the restaurant that chef Colin Rayner opened at Volcanic Hills, serves South Asian (and other) cuisine and you can bet it will be paired with the flagship wines here, including the Gewürztraminers and the rosé.

The cuisine reflects the heritage of the proprietors, Sarwan Gidda and his son, Bobby. Born in India in 1953, Sarwan came to Canada with his family as a child. His father insisted that he and his two brothers all get educated before being allowed to farm tree fruits and grapes. Sarwan studied accounting.

The brothers then became leading grape growers in the Okanagan and the Similkameen. In 2000, they built the Mt. Boucherie Estate Winery as an outlet for their best grapes. Sarwan left that partnership in 2008 and now, with the 1,400-square-metre (15,000-square-foot) Volcanic Hills winery, competes directly with his brothers. In fact, every visitor to Mt. Boucherie's cozy tasting room first passes Volcanic Hills. It is right on Boucherie Road, has a larger tasting room and now a restaurant. "I built where the business is," Sarwan says. "You need to be on that road to sell wine."

His son, Bobby, who was born in 1985, graduated in business administration at Okanagan College and worked in the finance department there while taking the college's winery assistant and winery sales courses. As part of the coursework, Bobby, who also previously worked in the Mt. Boucherie cellar, designed Volcanic Hills, a $2.3 million winery with geothermal heating and cooling. The expansive wine shop is above the processing cellars, with a view of Okanagan Lake.

Sarwan's 30.3 hectares (75 acres) of vineyard, primarily around Westbank, will support substantial production. The winery produced 7,000 cases in 2012 and is aiming to reach 10,000 cases a year. The sales growth is driven not just by a location you can't miss but also by

BOBBY GIDDA

DANIEL BONTORIN

award-winning wines. The winery's 2010 rosé garnered a Lieutenant Governor's Award of Excellence. The rosé style is a particular interest of Daniel Bontorin, the Volcanic Hills winemaker. He has his own label, Seven Directions Wine, making only rosé.

MY PICKS

The portfolio includes two well-crafted Gewürztraminers, a delicious unoaked Pinot Gris, a fruity rosé and a charming Pinot Noir. The non-mainstream varieties in the vineyard go into interesting blended wines such as Magma (50 percent Maréchal Foch, 20 percent Michurinetz and 15 percent each Zweigelt and Gamay).

OPENED 2009

2845 Boucherie Road
West Kelowna, BC V1Z 2G6

T   778.755.5550

W www.volcanichillswinery.com

WHEN TO VISIT
Open daily 10 am – 6 pm May to October; 11 am – 5:30 pm November to April.

RESTAURANT
Blue Saffron Bistro at Volcanic Hills Estate Winery.

WILD GOOSE VINEYARDS & WINERY

The bell tower above the new wine shop that Wild Goose opened in 2012 telegraphs an unintentional whiff of "I told you so." When the winery first opened in 1990, a government official suggested that founder Adolf Kruger would be lucky to sell 2,000 bottles of wine a year. Adolf proved him very wrong. Now, Wild Goose is producing 11,000 cases of award-winning wine each year.

Adolf, an engineer born in Germany in 1931, built a family legacy on this four-hectare (10-acre) Okanagan Falls property that he bought as raw land in 1983. With sons Hagen and Roland, he planted Riesling and Gewürztraminer, now the signature varieties for Wild Goose. Hagen, born in 1960, became the winemaker and viticulturist. In turn, one of his sons, Nikolas (born in 1985) also became a winemaker, studying at Okanagan College and gaining practical experience at Tinhorn Creek, Hester Creek and at Bremerton Wines, a family-owned Australian winery. Hagen's other son, Alexander, has taken up viticulture.

Roland Kruger, who handles marketing at Wild Goose, lives on the winery's two-hectare (five-acre) Mystic River Vineyard near Oliver. Purchased in 1999 to support the growing demand for Wild Goose wines, it grows Pinot Blanc, Pinot Gris and, of course, Gewürztraminer. In 2008, the Krugers planted more Riesling and Gewürztraminer but just small blocks of Merlot and Petit Verdot on their newest property, the 3.8-hectare (9½-acre) Secrest Vineyard, just north of Oliver. "We decided to stick with what we do best," Roland explained.

The winery has been highly acclaimed for white wines with, among many awards, seven Lieutenant Governor's Awards for Excellence in BC Wines. In recent vintages, well-crafted red wines have joined the portfolio. "Hagen has been working the red program pretty hard the last couple of years here," Roland says. "We have some good growers giving us good fruit. Hagen has been working with a couple of consultants

HAGEN, ADOLF AND ROLAND KRUGER

and the results are beginning to show."

The spacious new wine shop replacing notoriously cozy quarters gives visitors room to move about, or space to relax on a deck overlooking the vineyards. However, Wild Goose retains its warm family welcome because the tasting room is managed either by a Kruger or by staff imbued with the Kruger culture.

The bell in the tower formerly was in a German merchant ship called Simon von Utrecht. It was presented to the Krugers by a family friend who thought the tower deserved a bell.

OPENED 1990

2145 Sun Valley Way
Okanagan Falls, BC V0H 1R2

T 250.497.8919

W www.wildgoosewinery.com

WHEN TO VISIT
Open daily 10 am – 5 pm mid-April to mid-October; and by appointment November to March.

FOOD SERVICES
Licensed picnic area; dining room available for private functions.

MY PICKS

The white wines—Gewürztraminer, Riesling, Pinot Gris and Pinot Blanc and a blend called Autumn Gold—are simply outstanding. The reds—Cabernet Sauvignon, Merlot and Pinot Noir—are also well-made. Black Brant is the winery's delicious port-style red.

WILLOW HILL VINEYARDS

The focus here is on the rarest wine that Lanny Swanky and Patricia Venables, his wife, can produce from the Merlot in their two-hectare (five-acre) vineyard: icewine. But don't look for Willow Hill icewine in any wine shop. After they discovered how difficult it is to sell icewine, they came up with a more effective business model. Lanny makes icewine for other wineries with more developed sales channels. "I'm always looking for an edge," he confides. "I've been self-employed most of my life, so I haven't accumulated any pension to amount to anything. This vineyard and icewine operation will fund my retirement."

A big-framed man who speaks with a slow rumble, Lanny was born in Prince George in 1947, the son of a sawmill owner. He began studying engineering on a scholarship but dropped out to work as a logger, ultimately running his own contract logging business for about 18 years. He closed that to take over what he remembers as the "roughest hotel in Prince George" before selling that business to move to the Okanagan.

Lanny and Patricia took over the dome-shaped Willow Hill property in 1997. Then raw land, it is well-located beside the road to the Gehringer Brothers and Hester Creek wineries. In the first vintage, 2001, Willow Hill produced a mere 600 half bottles of icewine. In 2002, Lanny and Patricia made only a late-harvest Merlot because it had not become cold enough for icewine by the end of January 2003, when they had scheduled a vacation in Mexico. They have had good conditions for icewine in every vintage since then. The target has been to produce about 5,000 half bottles a year while selling the rest of the vineyard's grapes to other wineries.

Lanny, now retired after managing a large Vincor vineyard near Oliver, was steered through his first two winemaking vintages by consultant Michael Bartier. In 2003 Lanny took the Okanagan College winemaking course and has since made wine independently.

If you want to taste Lanny's well-crafted icewine, buy offerings from two of his clients— Dirty Laundry Vineyard and Church & State Wines.

OPENED 2005

551 Road 8
Oliver, BC V0H 1T1
T 250.498.6198

WHEN TO VISIT
No retail sales.

LANNY SWANKY

WYNNWOOD CELLARS

When Michael Wigen became interested in wine, a friend gave him a copy of *The Heartbreak Grape*, the classic book by Marq de Villiers with the subtitle, *A Journey in Search of the Perfect Pinot Noir*. Michael, who was born in 1955 into a pioneering Creston-area lumbering family, had grown up drinking varietals, with a preference for heavy California Cabernet Sauvignons. He had also begun enjoying red wines from Beaune, unaware that those are made with Pinot Noir. The book stirred his interest. When he planted his own 4.5-hectare (11-acre) vineyard on ideal limestone soil, beginning in 2007, he committed the majority to four clones of Pinot Noir. "We are hanging our hat on the traditional varieties because we are trying to mimic Burgundy where we are," Michael says.

The idea for a winery was born that spring when Dave Basaraba, an American-born school counsellor in Creston, approached Michael about growing grapes on an excellent site, an abandoned farm above Duck Lake that Michael owned. A decisive man and a lifelong risk taker (Michael spent a decade flying a souped-up Beaver in air shows), Michael soon had bulldozers clearing the limestone slope. In a few years, when there were enough grapes to make eight barrels of delicious Pinot Noir, Michael and Dave decided to go ahead with a winery on a nearby site owned by Dave and planted in 2013 to an additional hectare of grapes.

Dave, who grew up near Walla Walla in Washington, had worked in agriculture there and in Alberta before settling in the Creston area in 1987, where he became interested in grapes. In 2000, he planted an experimental vineyard of about 400 vines on his farm. That gave him a feel for the terroir and led him to approach Michael to partner in a winery.

Michael's great-grandfather, O. J. Wigen, came to the Creston area in 1892, opened the first hotel two years later and manufactured

MICHAEL WIGEN AND DAVE BASARABA

railroad ties. In 1913, he organized what is still called Wynndel Box & Lumber Company. After making boxes for the area's fruit growers, the company eventually moved to quality speciality lumber products. Michael, who studied business administration at Okanagan College, has been involved in the family business since 1977.

The winery partners—Dave is the winemaker—placed the winery and tasting room strategically on the popular and scenic Highway 3A beside Kootenay Lake. It is a short drive north of Creston, on what Michael likes to call the Creston Wine Route.

OPENED 2012

5566 HWY 3A
Wynndel. BC V0B 2N2

T   250.866.5155

W www.wynnwoodcellars.com

WHEN TO VISIT
Open daily 11 am – 6 pm mid-May to mid-October.

MY PICKS

The winery succeeds with Pinot Noir, Pinot Gris, Chardonnay and Sauvignon Blanc.

YOUNG & WYSE COLLECTION WINES

Stephen Wyse and Michelle Young, his wife, planned to call this the Black Sheep Winery until discovering that a British brewer had once registered the name for a cider while a Canadian distiller wanted to use it for a rum. So they came up with a bulletproof name—their own names.

"I kind of always have been the black sheep of the family," Stephen explains. He is referring to the family that started Burrowing Owl Winery, one of the Okanagan's leading producers: his parents Jim and Midge Wyse, and his older brother, Chris, who now manages Burrowing Owl, and his sister, Kerri. Stephen, who was born in 1967, set out to be an airline pilot but earned his commercial licence just as layoffs were sweeping through the Canadian airlines. He tried real estate sales before moving to Whistler with Michelle. She managed a major restaurant and they both worked as mountain guides.

The Okanagan caught Stephen's attention when his parents began planting the Burrowing Owl Vineyard in the mid-1990s, inspiring Stephen and Michelle to move to the region. He began working with vineyard manager Richard Cleave until construction started on the Burrowing Owl Winery. Stephen became a project manager and then began mentoring with consulting winemaker Bill Dyer. When Bill left in 2004, Stephen, who had also taken Brock University winemaking courses, became Burrowing Owl's winemaker. After three vintages there, Stephen helped Burrowing Owl recruit a winemaker from outside the family, having decided that "it was time for me to spread my wings and find my own identity."

In the summer of 2008, Stephen and Michelle purchased a highwayside farm south of Osoyoos, almost at the United States border, and quickly converted a former fruit cold storage building into a winery. Their first vintage, totalling 110 barrels, was made with purchased Syrah and Merlot grapes (they started the project too late in the season

STEVE WYSE

to get good quality white grapes). The fruit trees on the property were replaced in the spring of 2009 with four hectares (ten acres) of vines (mostly Malbec, Zinfandel and Viognier). Stephen also has contracted for grapes from other growers.

It is hardly a surprise that the wines echo the styles that succeeded so well at Burrowing Owl. Stephen has learned all of Bill Dyer's tricks and has added a few of his own.

OPENED 2009

9503 12th Avenue
Osoyoos, BC V0H 1V1

T   250.495.3245
    250.485.8699 (for appointments)

W www.youngandwysewine.com

WHEN TO VISIT
Open daily 11 am – 5 pm May to
mid-October (10 am – 6 pm July
and August); and by appointment.

MY PICKS

Everything, including the Merlot, the Cabernet Sauvignon, the Syrah, the Zinfandel and a complex Meritage blend called Black Label 33-30-24-13. The winery's whites, in addition to Viognier and Pinot Gris, include a blend called Amber, named after their daughter.

USEFUL BC
WINE FACTS

IN THE SUMMER OF 2011, WITH SPONSORSHIP OF the British Columbia Wine Institute, consultants Lynn and John Bremmer, who operate Mount Kobau Wine Services in Oliver, published their fifth periodic vineyard census since 1999. It is reproduced here as a snapshot of vineyards and grape varieties in British Columbia. An updated census is planned for 2014.

The Bremmers tallied 3,964 hectares (9,866.52 acres) in 2011. That compares with 3,626 hectares (9,066.32 acres) in 2008; and 2,653 hectares (6,632 acres) in grapes in 2006. They projected that another 376.37 hectares (930 acres) could be planted in 2012 and 2013. The 2014 census may show those intentions were tempered by the surplus of wine grapes that has developed. The area under vines in British Columbia has experienced eight-fold growth in the past two decades.

British Columbia's vineyard area is still small compared with other regions. Ontario has about 6,070.5 hectares (15,000 acres) of vineyard; Washington State has 16,166 hectares (40,000 acres) and California has 261,514.5 hectares (535,000 acres).

WHERE THE GRAPES GROW

REGION	HECTARES	ACRES
Oliver	1,433.92	3,543.18
Osoyoos	610.94	1,509.62
Kelowna/West Kelowna	377.07	904.46
Penticton/Naramata	363.31	897.74
Similkameen Valley	279.82	691.44
Okanagan Falls	218.05	538.81
Vancouver Island	174.77	431.87
Peachland/Summerland	143.53	354.67
Fraser Valley/Lower Mainland	106.62	263.45
Lake Country/Vernon	74.49	196.43
Gulf Islands	46.80	115.64
Kaleden	46.65	115.29
Spallumcheen/Shuswap	39.25	97.00
Kamloops	26.81	66.25
Lillooet/Lytton	21.93	54.20
Kootenays	27.84	68.82
Other BC regions	7.13	17.65

SOURCE: BRITISH COLUMBIA WINE INSTITUTE

TOP WINE GRAPE VARIETALS IN BC IN 2012 HARVEST

VARIETY	TONS (IMPERIAL)	AVERAGE PRICE PER TON $
Merlot	5,636.91	2,378.06
Chardonnay	2,979.63	1,991.17
Pinot Gris	2,787.56	2,063.43
Pinot Noir	1,980.85	2,406.70
Cabernet Sauvignon	1,964.37	2,556.93
Gewürztraminer	1,512.59	1,979.38
Sauvignon Blanc	1,434.53	1,804.55
Cabernet Franc	1,370.85	2,434.07
Syrah	1,327.74	2,555.12
Riesling	1,309.39	1,978.02
Pinot Blanc	1,187.60	1,609.92
Gamay Noir	461.58	1,911.90
Viognier	435.78	2,283.77
Malbec	203.88	2,790.71
Ehrenfelser	203.62	1,825.70
Sémillon	176.56	1,822.21
Petit Verdot	162.79	2,435.93
Maréchal Foch	153.71	1,702.48
Auxerrois	152.05	1,807.15
Bacchus	151.47	2,013.80
Cabernet Libre	130.43	2,037.74
Chenin Blanc	109.80	1,580.75
Muscat	87.36	2,289.28
Kerner	73.29	1,917.01
Remaining 57 varietals	1,260.87	

SOURCE: BRITISH COLUMBIA WINE INSTITUTE AND BDO CANADA LLP

BC GRAPE HARVESTS AND WINE PRODUCTION

VARIETY	TONS (IMPERIAL)	ESTIMATED PRODUCTION (LITRES)
2012	27,257	17,717,200
2011	22,722	14,769,300
2010	17,778	11,555,700
2009	19,979	12,921,350
2008	22,275	15,046,763
2007	19,177	13,394,757
2006	20,369	13,802,563
2005	14,084	8,450,400
2004	16,642	9,985,200
2003	16,897	10,138,200
2002	15,523	9,313,800
2001	14,137	8,482,200
2000	10,022	6,013,200

SOURCE: BRITISH COLUMBIA WINE INSTITUTE

HOW MUCH BC WINE ARE WE BUYING?

The Vintners Quality Alliance (VQA) program began in 1990 to identify those wines made entirely with British Columbia grapes. Because the program is voluntary, some producers do not submit wines to the VQA tasting panel. VQA wine accounts for the majority of wine grown in British Columbia. This table from the British Columbia Wine Institute reveals the steady growth in sales. In recent years, the average price has levelled off.

YEAR TO MARCH 31	SALES	PERCENTAGE INCREASE	SALES IN LITRES	AVERAGE PRICE / 750 ML BOTTLE
1991/92	$ 6,846,183		748,196	$6.86
1992/93	10,559,586	54	977,030	8.11
1993/94	15,306,430	45	1,289,672	8.90
1994/95	23,666,799	57	1,775,580	10.00
1995/96	31,321,592	22	2,035,877	11.54
1996/97	32,397,296	3	2,093,324	11.61
1997/98	39,758,907	22	2,324,068	12.83
1998/99	42,143,199	6	2,420,599	13.05
1999/00	48,740,017	16	2,585,217	14.16
2000/01	57,638,465	18	2,999,807	14.41
2001/02	70,418,708	22	3,717,452	14.21
2002/03	83,051,239	18	4,233,458	14.72
2003/04	91,998,327	11	4,728,612	14.60
2004/05	114,891,745	25	5,571,100	15.47
2005/06	141,390,804	23	6,472,816	16.38
2006/07	151,220,894	7	6,783,234	16.72
2007/08	156,730,109	4	6,594,213	17.83
2008/09	163,331,858	4	6,733,048	18.19
2009/10	183,754,152	13	7,846,642	17.56
2010/11	194,733,472	6	8,351,947	17.49
2011/12	198,520,410	1.9	8,266,209	18.01
2012/13	203,895,991	3.1	8,573,988	17.90
2013/14	225,928,405	10.4	9,548,592	17.75

SOURCE: BRITISH COLUMBIA WINE INSTITUTE

NOTES

NOTES